AGENTS
FOR
ESCAPE

AGENTS
FOR
ESCAPE

INSIDE THE
FRENCH RESISTANCE
1939–1945

ANDRÉ ROUGEYRON

TRANSLATED BY
MARIE-ANTOINETTE MCCONNELL

LOUISIANA STATE UNIVERSITY PRESS
Baton Rouge and London

Copyright © 1947 by Imprimerie Alençonnaise and André Rougeyron
Originally published in 1947 by Imprimerie Alençonnaise
Translation copyright © 1996 by Louisiana State University Press
All rights reserved
Manufactured in the United States of America
First printing
05 04 03 02 01 00 99 98 97 96   5 4 3 2 1

Designer: Amanda McDonald Key
Typeface: Bembo
Typesetter: Impressions, a division of Edwards Brothers, Inc.
Printer and binder: Thomson-Shore, Inc.

Library of Congress Cataloging-in-Publication Data
Rougeyron, André.
    [Agents d'evasion. English]
    Agents for escape : inside the French Resistance, 1939–1945 /
André Rougeyron ; translated by Marie A. McConnell.
        p. cm.
    Originally published: Imprimerie Alençonnaise, 1947.
    ISBN 0-8071-2019-7 (alk. paper)
    1. Rougeyron, André. 2. World War, 1939–1945—Underground
movements—France. 3. World War, 1939–1945—Personal narratives,
French. 4. Guerrillas—France—Biography. 5. Escapes—Europe—
History—20th century. I. Title.
D802.F8R6213   1996
940.53'44—dc20   95-23387
                                                                                        CIP

The paper in this book meets the guidelines for permanence and durability of the Committee on
Production Guidelines for Book Longevity of the Council on Library Resources. ∞

CONTENTS

190 600

ILLUSTRATIONS

FOREWORD

On every Fourth of July, which is the anniversary of the day I was shot down in France in 1943, I recall most intensely the remarkable French people who sheltered me from the German military and who helped make possible my escape.

When I was shot down over his hometown of Domfront, André Rougeyron took charge of my survival for the two months preceding my transfer to a larger Resistance network in Paris. I was the first airman that André had the opportunity to rescue. It was an opportunity to help that he welcomed. André hated the German occupation of France, and he greatly appreciated the efforts of the Americans and the British to liberate his country. He saw it as his duty to protect downed Allied airmen from the enemy.

André lived in what he called the "Châlet," on a mountain overlooking the town of Domfront. During the fifty-eight days I spent sheltered by André, either at the Châlet or at his aunt's house, I got to know him and the other French people who were willing to risk their lives to aid downed American and British airmen. André was an educated and cultured man, and had trained as a mechanical engineer. I gathered he had led an indulged childhood. He had learned to drive an automobile at age ten, and by age fifteen he could pilot airplanes. At sixteen he was too young to fly fighter planes in World War I, so instead he instructed Canadian soldiers how to fly. André was a very smart, courageous, tough man. He also had a wonderful sense of humor and enjoyed life to the fullest. He was willing to put himself and all he had at risk to help me and other Allied airmen. Even though at the time he saved me he was not yet connected with any organized Resistance network, he planned ways to provide me with shelter, food, and ultimately means to begin my journey of escape from occupied France. He accomplished these generous and courageous acts with the aid of other citizens of Domfront.

One of these was his aunt, a kind, elderly lady. The days I spent at her house were a lonely time, for she did not speak English and I spoke no French. She tried her best to break the monotony of my seclusion; she used to bring me medical encyclopedias to distract me as she thought the pictures would entertain me. André's father was an elderly gentleman who had been a professor of English. His house was next door to the aunt's, and his visits were welcome because we could converse in English.

Among others who helped André was Pépin, the local blacksmith. Pépin was known as a bit of an eccentric. He would pretend to do favors for the Germans but would actually sabotage or steal their equipment and supplies. He was often reckless in these pursuits, but to my knowledge he was never caught.

Paul Alasseur was a local businessman and a close friend of André's. He created and perfected the manufacture of authentic-looking identification cards for the airmen rescued by André. His involvement in Resistance activities led to his arrest and internment in Buchenwald.

The Bourgoins, who sheltered me when I was first downed, exemplify the ordinary people who bravely did their part in resisting the Germans. Caretakers of a local château, l'Ermitage, they were ready to risk their lives to protect and shelter Allied aviators.

Those I have mentioned were the resistants with whom I had most contact, but there were many more involved in our rescue, all unsung heroes. It was the support of these people that enabled me to survive. In their company I began to speak French, act French, eat French food, and wear French clothing, not only for my protection but also in appreciation of their culture.

My time in Domfront was a strange time, for while I was grateful to be alive and to have found people willing to shelter me, I could not help but be eager to escape occupied territory and get back to my duties in the war. André understood my position and contacted a wider Resistance network in Paris. Through careful maneuvering and hard work, he arranged for identification papers for me and my tail gunner, William Howell, rail tickets to Paris, and a guide who would meet us at the train station in Alençon. The guide was to connect us with other members of the Resistance in Paris. Thus, after two months in Domfront, I was on my way to Paris. After this time I had no further contact with

André. I had to stay in Paris five months and was finally able to escape into Spain in January of 1944.

I know that without the efforts of André and the other resistants in Domfront I would not have survived. For many of these courageous people, their activities led to imprisonment and torture. I will never forget them.

—Paul H. McConnell

TRANSLATOR'S ACKNOWLEDGMENTS

Grateful acknowledgment is made for the permission granted by the late Madeleine Rougeyron to publish the English translation of her husband's book *Agents d'Evasion,* thereby fulfilling the author's wish, some forty-eight years after the book was first published in France.

I am grateful to André Rougeyron's children, Dr. Jean-Louis Rougeyron and Anne-Marie Vizot, for their cooperation—and especially to Anne-Marie for providing me with many of the photographs originally used in the French edition.

In addition, I would like to thank the following persons: Gordon W. Bartow, Jr., for his help and encouragement in pursuing this project and for his introduction to Stephen E. Ambrose, director of the Eisenhower Center at the University of New Orleans; Professor Ambrose for his advice on the manuscript; Margaret Dalrymple, editor-in-chief of the Louisiana State University Press, for her assistance and advice; and Mariette J. Perkins, for her help in proofreading and editing the manuscript.

PREFACE

I had promised myself that I would never write about my activities in the Resistance. Why, then, publish this book? I was hostile for a long time—still a resistant—so I postponed as long as possible carrying out a project that presented many difficulties and went way beyond the means and time that I had. But I finally accepted this heavy task, first of all so that our American and British friends, by reading the English translation of these memoirs, might fully understand that the French were not all an unfortunate propaganda made them out to be. They must be made aware that some of us gave of ourselves and took risks for them because of sympathy, attraction, and belief in the same ideals— without hope of any gain. . . . It was also important that my fellow citizens of Domfront, who took refuge in the surrounding countryside as soon as the first Allied bombs fell, should hear from a witness (among about thirty who stayed in the town) what happened in their city during those crucial weeks that followed the landing of the Allied forces. Finally, I wanted to pay homage to all those who, between 1942 and the time of my arrest, and also during the days that followed, answered my call and gave me moral and material support, scorning the risks and dangers of which they were so well aware.

My thanks to all those who participated in this book, revised so many times, and who pointed out its imperfections.

Thanks also to Yvette Dubocq, who assembled her recollections for this volume.

Quite simply, this book represents the elaboration of notes hastily taken and fortunately recovered. Unfortunately, for compelling reasons, certain operations cannot be disclosed.

Perhaps you will notice in the pages that follow some errors in the dates or some facts missing. Very excusable, considering the cruelty of the Gestapo and my ten months of imprisonment. The only merit of this book—and I insist on it—is that it is true, true from beginning to end. And this, you see, is definitely something!

AGENTS
FOR
ESCAPE

1

SEPTEMBER, 1939

When war was declared, I expected to receive a mobilization order from the air force, my old branch in the military. But after the alarm of 1938, I received, in October, my assignment to an ordnance unit (perhaps this was due to my age—I was forty) with an order to join an equipment factory in Colombes. I was disappointed, yet glad at the same time because it gave me the opportunity to renew acquaintances with my old friend Goëtt. I knew Goëtt when he was an engineer at an automobile plant near Paris for which I used to race until 1930.

I took my post around the middle of the month. Being in charge of outside services, I was in constant contact with the military headquarters occupying the large hotels in Paris, near l'Étoile: the Claridge, the Kléber, the Majestic, and the Iéna. I'm not going to relate here all the mistakes and incoherences I witnessed during the months preceding the debacle. I could tell how, in April of 1940, while manufacturers were seeking workers with special skills, the plant of the Société des Wagons-Lits (sleeping-cars) in Saint-Denis had not even received their orders for the war. I could also relate the difficulties encountered, as early as February, in obtaining even small quantities of special steel. And who doesn't remember the comedy of errors of the special services? All those who, like me, had to argue with this service were familiar with the offices of the "Quarter 2" at the École Militaire and knew the good captain, who was completely submerged and bewildered by a flood of thousands of files, each in five or six copies. As a general rule, when a skilled worker was requested by a manufacturer, he would be sent by the special services six months later, when he was no longer needed.

My job at the factory also included inspecting the steel mills in the eastern region and scheduling deliveries. I traveled frequently to Charleville and Nouzonville, steel centers of the East. I also traveled to Gailly, Thomé-Cromback, Thomé-Génot, and Brisville, where we had warehouses. I also made frequent trips to mills in Maître, Colombiers-Fontaine, and in central France.

On May 8, 1940, during an inspection at the Thomé-Cromback plant in Nouzonville, I witnessed an air battle over Hauts-de-Meuse. When I mentioned the skirmish to Rousseau, chief of stamping, he asserted that everything was quiet; except for the presence of troops, one would not have thought this was wartime. Yet eight days later the Germans occupied Nouzonville, and the bridges had to be blown up in a matter of hours.

After the loss of the Meuse, we were in short supply of casting molds and steel. The administrator decided to place a number of orders with the Établissements Stacoffe and Gauliard in Friville-Escarbotin, a few kilometers from Abbeville. We sent these mills some molds that had been hastily manufactured. Alas, the Germans threatened and then took Friville. Come what might, it was essential to retrieve the molds, which were absolutely indispensable. We obtained an authorization from the ministry, thanks to the help of Captain B. of the rue de Presbourg services. With a formal order in hand, one evening in May I went to the park of Porte de Versailles to pick up the Citroën truck necessary for this mission. André D., a comrade on special assignment at the plant, accompanied me. We were supposed to pick up a few weapons at a barracks (I have forgotten the name), but we felt this was unnecessary and, time being of the essence, we decided against it. We departed at night by way of Pontoise.

The P45 truck, which we took turns driving, was splendid. In the forest of Neufchâtel, we were stopped several times by English sentinels. Shortly before dawn we passed through Eu, which was in ruins. Someone warned us that the area wasn't safe; the German troops weren't far away. But we had to get to Friville. We drove through the deserted countryside; all the electrical and telephone wires had been destroyed and were dangling pitifully. We were in the danger zone, and D. and I were sorry we hadn't brought weapons. At dawn we reached Friville, a little village whose only industry was probably the foundry we were heading for. In the middle of the town square we brushed past a wrecked German sidecar with two dead men inside—what next? At the sound of our truck, the shutters of a house opened and a woman appeared, very surprised at the sight of the tricolored cockade we had not bothered to remove. The foundry was about one hundred meters away; we swiftly made the truck disappear between two buildings and hid it at the rear of the courtyard.

Everything was abandoned. The only one left was the concierge, and she told us that the management had left about a week before, at the same time as the town authorities. The 150 workers had hidden in the countryside because the village had been taken over alternately by the Germans and the English. She was astonished to see two Frenchmen, and not having received any news for two weeks, she avidly read a newspaper we had brought. We also learned from her that the Germans had invaded the factory, killing a worker who resisted.

A French artillery battery posted a few hundred meters away, behind the kilns, was shooting at a château that housed the enemy headquarters. In the meantime, English armor was pursuing German cars through the streets.

I explained to the concierge the purpose of our visit: to retrieve our molds and take with us the pieces that were almost finished. She agreed to try to find the foreman and some workers. While waiting for her return, we went to the basement of a nearby café, where we shared a bottle of Pernod with the natives. The host was also very interested in our newspaper. He had received many visits from the Germans, who took all the tobacco and also the gasoline left in the cars' tanks.

The plant accountant and the foreman joined us while the workers opened the kilns to retrieve the pieces we were to take. This took almost all day, and because the truck was close by we agreed to take along some material destined for the Société Fibracier and other Paris manufacturers. On everyone's advice, we decided to wait for nightfall before we left; so late at night we took off at full speed, a bit worried— it was our first escapade—and reached Eu and Neufchâtel, where we finally ate a decent meal.

The next day we visited rue de Presbourg to give an account of our mission to Captain B. He was somewhat surprised to learn of the Boches' presence in Friville and of our safe return. A few days later he requested permission from the administrator to send us on a second trip to Friville, for the benefit of an important firm. That was too much; we flatly refused. One narrow escape was enough for us.

After the first bombardment of Paris, which I saw from Porte Maillot, difficulties increased very rapidly. It was no longer possible to stock supplies: the mills were not supplying, Ordnance was in utter disorder, and it seemed that the end was near. While in Domfront for Pentecost, I predicted for some good friends what was going to happen and they called me a defeatist.

On the morning of June 8, 1940, I received a phone call from Captain R. He informed me that the plant in Ezy (Eure) to which we were to retreat appeared to be threatened. It was necessary for us to find immediately another factory "south of the Loire and west of the Rhône"—as if it were as easy to find a factory as a loaf of bread at the bakery.

Upon his return I informed the administrator of this development. At first he went into a rage; then he left, accompanied by his manufacturing manager. The latter believed there were some vacant premises in Grand-Pont, in the Poitiers region. I was put in charge of the offices and factory, with orders to evacuate as best we could if the situation worsened. When they left, little did the plant manager and foreman know that they would not see me again for six months.

After they left, everything ran normally until the next Saturday evening. Goëtt had asked me to go on Sunday, June 9, to his Tourny property, where I was to pick up various items: accounting files, linens, silverware, a radio, and other objects. I left Paris in the early afternoon, but it was already impossible to cross the Seine. After several unsuccessful attempts, I decided to turn around because a truck driver who had come from Tourny told me German troops were approaching the banks of the Eure. That evening I ate at the Sanglier Bleu on the outskirts of the city with my old racing friend Gabriel Dugat and his wife. The news was bad, the diners dismayed, and the evening very sad.

When the factory opened the next morning, I was surprised to see Henri Rallier, a skilled worker at the Persan-Beaumont steel mills. He told me the Germans were very near Persan; the town had been severely bombed. Electric power was cut off, and the bridges on the Oise were to be blown up at any moment. A note from the plant manager con-

firmed Henri's story. We were sixty kilometers from Persan, and undoubtedly the situation was serious.

After instructing the workers to prepare to dismantle the machinery,
I went to the armament headquarters, rue de Presbourg, where I ran
across Captain B. and asked his permission to evacuate. He agreed and
gave me a note for Commandant B., who was at the Kléber Hotel. It
was lunchtime, and I had to wait two long hours before I could go to
the proper department.

The hotel was in a complete state of panic. The hallways were
crowded with manufacturers, suppliers, and officers: everyone had a
long face. The offices were in the process of being moved. Files, typewriters, and even luggage were taken out by the orderlies. I finally got
to see the commandant. His office was empty except for a table, two
chairs, and a telephone. I explained the purpose of my visit and showed
him Captain B.'s note. I requested a transport order for five 20-ton
wagons, ten 10-ton wagons, plus the trucks necessary to transport the
equipment to the Puteaux train station. The officer dryly told me he
didn't have a single wagon left, and furthermore, why didn't we stay
where we were? Suddenly anger overwhelmed me, and I asked if he
intended for us to leave a complete factory, including tools, parts, raw
materials, etcetera, at the hands of the Germans while he, Commandant
B., was concerned with moving his offices, including his secretaries'
typewriters. A nasty argument followed, and an old officer who was
present told me, "Young man, my son is on the front; it is you who
are right!"

In a rage the commandant opened his briefcase and ripped off ten
transport slips. He stamped them, filled out the first, gave me the rest,
blank, and said, "I forbid you to tell anyone in the hallways that I gave
you even one wagon." That wasn't necessary: The halls were loud and
crowded. I hastily returned to Puteaux, where the workers had already
set several machines on planks, ready to be shipped.

At the train station there was another setback. The stationmaster told
me he needed two hundred wagons, but was expecting only thirty.
Perplexed, I returned to the plant.

2

THE DEBACLE

There was complete panic throughout the Paris region—the evacuation had begun. In Puteaux the rue de la République was being vacated. The most unusual convoys were seen; anything was used to move, from wheelbarrows to baby carriages.

At the factory, I asked the personnel to keep dismantling equipment throughout the night. Then I went back to the Colombes offices, expecting the administrator's and plant manager's return at any moment. It was a sinister night: the whole area was covered by a very dense, black smoke resulting from the destruction of the fuel reservoirs; there was almost no light. From Pontoise, thousands of fleeing soldiers arrived by the boulevard du Havre. They abandoned arms and equipment on the sidewalks. A continuous stream of refugees arrived in T.C.R.P. (Paris public transport) buses. Tirelessly I went back and forth between Colombes and Puteaux. The situation worsened by the hour, and on Tuesday, June 11, we planned our departure for 9 A.M. I sent our draftsman to the Citroën plant—boulevard des Capucines—to collect almost a half-million checks. Then I took an inventory of the vehicles available: we had two front-wheel-drive cars (one was the plant manager's, the other his nephew's); Pierre Baratte's 402 (he was posted at the factory); someone's Renault; the draftsman's Ariès; the Delahaye service truck; a Derby sedan being picked up at a garage in Colombes; and last, my own Juva.

We had to pile some of the personnel and numerous pieces of luggage into these few cars. Fortunately a large number of workers decided to stay in the Paris area or to evacuate by bicycle.

We were divided into two groups: one convoy took the road for Grand-Pont, where the plant manager had property; the other followed me to Normandy. I will not elaborate on this exodus; so many French people went through it. Our convoy consisted of four cars: Baratte's 402, the Derby driven by Champ, de Perthuis' Ariès, and my Juva loaded with documents, typewriters, adding machines, and many other items. Henri Rallier rode with me. There was such a mob that we lost each other before we got to Fosse-Repose. First we lost track of the draftsman, whose Ariès could not follow; I was rather worried because he was carrying the office files and the foundry molds.

Before Versailles we had to take a detour by the Vallée de Chevreuse and make numerous stops because of machine-gun fire from German planes. We were moving very slowly; we left Paris at noon and would not be in St. Rémy until nightfall. We were also very hungry. I bought a loaf of bread from a soldier while Champ and Rallier searched the stores and found some canned goods. It was sheer luck, considering the crowd of famished people begging everywhere. After our hunger was appeased, and having waited a long time for de Perthuis' return, we headed toward Chartres. This time Champ got lost. A violent storm developed, and I noticed that my right rear tire was flat. Completely exhausted, I had to stop. I parked the car on the side of the road.

Henri had been sleeping for an hour or two when we were awakened by a bombing raid nearby. Unknowingly we had parked just across from the Chartres airport, which was under the Boches' attack.

Changing the flat in the mud was arduous; I was so tired that Henri did the job practically by himself; all the while cars and trucks were passing by. At dawn I found out that the fuel gauge read empty. No wonder—since leaving Paris, we had been driving in first or second gear. We drove a few kilometers toward Chartres, and we were lucky enough to meet a military truck fleeing the bombardment. An old sergeant major was willing to let me have some fuel. The transfer of his fifty-liter can into my tank was no easy task, especially when the arrival of a third party, who also wanted a share of the fuel, provoked a violent argument.

At last we were ready to go. The road was not as crowded by then, and we were able to drive a little faster. We arrived at Alençon on the morning of June 15 after being thirty hours on the road to travel two hundred kilometers. We stopped at some friends', then headed for Domfront.

At home the whole city was in a state of agitation. We expected the worst, and right away I made plans to evacuate farther west. Champ and some others decided to follow me. We also had to take with us the plant secretary and her mother, whom Pierre Baratte had brought from Paris shortly before my arrival in Domfront. The draftsman, whose Ariès broke down in Alençon, joined us by truck.

On June 18, while we listened to the news of the marshal's capitulation on the radio, an English soldier committed suicide in the street. We left late that evening, and at the last minute it was necessary for me to take Mademoiselle Vautier, a postal employee, and several bags of valuables for which no one wanted to be responsible. After a night spent in a courtyard in Ernée, we continued in the direction of Vannes. Because my car was overloaded, we had to interrupt our trip twice to replace a flat tire. We stopped in Sixte-sur-Aft, where we spent the night at the boys' school, which had been converted into a dormitory for refugees. The next day when it was time for us to leave, it was too late: we could not pass through. The school was located along the road down which the German troops were coming, and we were worried about our cars. After a long search, and with the help of a disabled soldier from the other war, we found lodgings in an old château. We hid the car just below our window, buried our fuel, and prepared for the night. The farmer had cleared a large storage room.

My plan was to get to England, but this was not possible: I had with me the documents from the factory in Paris, along with securities and other valuables, and I could not abandon the colleagues who had followed me. On the twenty-fifth or twenty-sixth we saw the first Boches: two motorcyclists as drunk as Poles. On June 28 we returned to Domfront. I was very worried about my family and wondered what had happened in the city. Well, I found out something had happened: Domfront was occupied . . .

A German observation post had been set up in the old castle, and I had to argue for a long time before I was allowed to go through and enter my house. Fortunately the draftsman recognized a German officer who used to work with him in Lyon as an engineer.

3

THE OCCUPATION

The administrator had taken refuge in Grand-Pont, and having received no news from him for several months, everyone stayed put. It was during that time that I had my first contacts with the Germans. There was an army base in Domfront, and it was occupied by a motorized unit.

The best houses in town had been commandeered by German officers. We received orders to bring all weapons, ammunition, and explosives to city hall. I carefully gathered all I had: a Colt .12 (my uncle's revolver), six or seven automatic pistols, some ammunition, and some cordite I was using to dig a well. I thoroughly oiled everything and buried my cache in the garden at the Châlet. This took most of the day.

We began to "cheat" the Germans. They had an installation in Notre-Dame district where batteries were repaired and charged. Thanks to Cl., the batteries had a way of disappearing in the direction of the Châlet.

Like many people in Domfront, my aunt had an undesirable boarder, Hauptmann Paul Emmel. He was, he said, a sewing machine parts manufacturer in Berlin and thought himself a very important person. There were some amusing scenes between him and me. Hauptmann Emmel, attended by his aide-de-camp, took his meals in our dining room. He tried very hard to make conversation with me. One day he asked for something to read. I made him "absorb" the Campaign of Russia, in three volumes, by Colonel de Marbeau (Emmel left for Russia a few months later, and I bet he often thought about his reading). We frequently argued about the course of the war: "Monsieur André, in two

months we'll be in England, and the war will be over"; "I don't think
so, Commandant, it looks more like two years, if then!" One evening
he came up with a bizarre idea: "I'm a German officer, and it's my
duty to do some propaganda every day. I'm going to give you one hour
of propaganda." Immediately I found some excuse to leave.

I also played dirty tricks on him. One day he told my aunt he was
expecting a visitor and would need a second bedroom. Sure enough,
that afternoon a "Madame Djinn" arrived. She said she resided in Di-
nard. That evening, while waiting for the commandant, she took a stroll
in town, and I ran into her with some of my friends. The opportunity
was too good to pass up; I invited her to join us for an aperitif. With
some encouragement from my buddies, she soaked up half a dozen
drinks before going back to the house. Her return was magnificent;
"Madame Djinn" could hardly stand up, and the commandant had been
waiting for over two hours. Drunk as a skunk, she insulted the stupefied
Hauptmann and absolutely insisted on kissing my aunt.

Around January of 1941, the idea came to me to obtain some information. It was easy to go into the commandant's room when he was
absent. It was just as easy to gain the confidence of his young aide-de-
camp. Unfortunately, I did not know yet of any channels through which
I could transmit the results of my investigations. Anyway, Emmel left
for the East at the end of February. He was succeeded by two lieutenants
with whom I had no contact.

Having resumed my profession as an expert in mechanics, I traveled
by motorbike through the Orne, Mayenne, and Manche regions. My
professional activity was severely curtailed, and so was automobile traffic. I vainly tried to get in touch either with Resistance groups or with
agents in London. During 1941 we saw only transitory German troops
in our area, except for those manning the fuel and munitions depots.
Other than automobile repair shops (such as Kraffarh-Park), there were
no important installations or fixed antiaircraft batteries: at any rate, not
much of a "pasture" for an intelligence agent.

4

The Camouflage

Soon the Germans began to enlist manpower for their factories. They also sought out those French people who were hostile to them. The infamous Gestapo had not yet penetrated the small provincial towns, but certain field police posts (such as in Flers), assisted by contemptible individuals, were already active. It was necessary for us to hide men sought by the Germans and also to provide them with new identification. This marked the appearance of false identity cards in our region. There was a Resistance group in Domfront whose leader was Herlemont (it took me a while to find this out). Paul Alasseur, Gilard, Guesdon, and some others belonged to the group. Ernoult, manager of the Standard des Pétroles, met regularly with a member of the Resistance in Alençon and brought back underground newspapers as well as instructions from the leader of the Orne region.

Paul Alasseur had made a rudimentary seal to stamp on identity cards made from prints bought in bookstores. These prints were grossly inadequate. At the beginning of 1943 we decided to improve on our system. On the advice of my friend Havas, I contacted Henri Robbes (mayor of Flers at that time), whose son was an engraver. By means of an aluminum block melted at Gilard's house, he produced a very official-looking seal; it was identical to the one used at city hall. Since I was frequently absent, Paul Alasseur became the expert at producing the "new and improved" false identity cards. Now it was necessary for us to obtain blank cards. After many unsuccessful inquiries, and against Alasseur's and Gilard's advice, I decided to go directly to the manager of the Domfront printing firm. He agreed to print some cards—about forty at first—but refused to print on the back the words "Alençon Printing Company." I felt this presented a danger and could lead to serious trouble if the papers were inspected by an observant policeman. Fortunately for us, the foreman at the shop agreed to print the necessary mention on a number of cards. Later we had a larger quantity printed, and the traffic intensified.

The cards were then perfect in every way, and G.'s dexterous wife had become quite adept at imitating the signature of the city hall chief of service. I cannot remember now how many false identity papers were distributed, but I do remember that none was ever discovered by either the French or German police, and we were never suspected.

It was also necessary for us to find refuge for those resisting compulsory labor. Thanks to the help of Lieutenant Séchet of the Mayenne department, we were able to send a great number of resisters into hiding at the Bellière coal mine, near Carrouges. I also hid a few men in Briouze (Cloteau), La Sauvagère (Rallier), at the Étoile lumberyard (the two Connard brothers), and in many other places.

5

FALSE ALERT

It was then, at the beginning of 1943, that things took a turn for the worse. My name appeared on a mysteriously established list of eleven "unemployed" Frenchmen who had to leave for Germany, for compulsory labor. On the morning of February 2, I was called to the German labor office in Flers for a physical. Quite intent on not going to Germany, I took with me a significant sum of money and decided—in case I passed the physical—to take off for Paris, where Claude Monod, of whom I will speak later, had offered me a position as an automatic weapon instructor at the Poissy quarries.

I reached the German labor office, rue de la Gare, before it opened. An older woman arrived (her name was Damery, I believe), and I helped her start a fire, not out of kindness but because I was very cold. Then came a young German who went into a nearby office. I asked the interpreter to have someone inspect my papers, but my request was denied. Since these "gentlemen" refused to look at my papers, I absolutely refused to undress for the physical. I stood firm in spite of the threats and did not take off my clothes. I do not think these "gentlemen" ever saw anyone so stubborn. About 11 A.M. I began to worry about being judged fit by reason of my refusal. So I left the labor office and went to the German gendarmerie to explain my case. Beller, the interpreter, was there; I told him the purpose of my visit. He took a look at my file, but when the German officer wanted to read it also, Beller told me abruptly, "Take the physical first, then take your claim to Alençon." I was annoyed about this wasted trip to Flers, but what could I do? Perplexed, I stopped in front of the recruiting office. Should

I tell them about my visit to the gendarmerie? It was almost noon. Dr. Martin, who was acquainted with my father, had just come in; he was in charge of the physicals. A German warrant officer was standing next to him. Hoping that the doctor would recognize my name, I decided to take the physical. He examined me in the room next to the front office, asked if I had any infirmity, and said in a low voice, "What do they intend to do with you in Germany?" I told him about the papers these "gentlemen" refused to look at. He wrote on my form "Unfit for Germany." Of course, no words ever pleased me more. I was a little nervous, and the doctor told me to take my time getting dressed. As I was leaving the labor office, that bitch, Damery, handed me a filled-out form: "Monsieur is not taking his contract for Germany?" But the good doctor opened the door and declared, "Monsieur is free; he is unfit!"

Back in Domfront I learned that many friends whose names were on the same list were also exempt, but we had great difficulties saving Maurice Macé from being sent to Sweden. All this made me wonder whether the Germans had informers who drew up those lists. I began to seek out and watch those who were suspected of collaboration: P.P.F. (Parti Populaire Français), Francists, and others capable of divulging our involvement with the Resistance or our aversion for the new order they liked so much. This was how Paul Alasseur drew up a list that was, we later realized, pretty accurate and complete: most of the Domfront people on that list behaved ignobly.

We were entering a bad period. Because automobile traffic was practically nil, there was not much demand for my expertise, and my earnings were reduced accordingly. At the time we were not receiving—nor did we receive later—anything from the Resistance groups (except that my accountant received three thousand francs after my arrest). German surveillance was tightening. Travel was permitted only for specific purposes, and special authorization had to be obtained. But luck was on my side: one day I received a letter from G. Berthier, manager of the Automobile Club of the West. He had known me for some twenty years, having followed my efforts during the A.C.W. automobile races. He asked if I would accept a position teaching technical classes organized by the Industrial Production Ministry under the direction of the club. Of course I agreed immediately. My authorization to travel by motorbike was therefore extended, and I also obtained from the Germans a permit to travel into the forbidden zone. I organized classes at the Cherbourg arsenal, then at Honfleur, etcetera. I covered a very wide area, all the way to Poitiers. It was really unexpected; at once I had all the mobility I wanted and the funds I needed.

Enrolled in my classes were privates and students and civil servants. This gave me the opportunity to collect, wherever I went, valuable pieces of information, which I transmitted immediately.

In June I learned that my very good friend Henri Rallier was in trouble: he had been sent to Germany for compulsory labor, and after having obtained a pass to return to France for the birth of his child, he did not want to go back. I decided to take him into my home. Henri became one of us for a year at La Sauvagère and at l'Ermitage, and he was a good assistant who shared our vicissitudes.

6

THE FIRST CAMPAIGN

It was the summer of 1943. July 4 marked my first action as agent for escape. As an old French saying goes, "Opportunity makes the thief." What I am about to tell will prove how true it is.

That Sunday, July 4, 1943, anniversary of American independence, I left Champsecret about noon in the company of Mademoiselle Vautier, a post office employee. We took the forest road connecting Champsecret to Étoile d'Andaines (five kilometers) by way of Petite-Étoile. We were on our way to the Château de l'Ermitage to help some good friends store hay, and we were looking forward to spending a nice, relaxing day. The weather was beautiful: clear blue sky, very little wind. The walk through the forest looked very pleasant.

All of a sudden we could hear, without seeing them, a sizable formation of planes flying at high altitude, coming from the north and going southeast. This was not unusual during the summer of 1943, as the Allied air forces were by then in command of the skies. We were continuing on our way without paying any more attention when suddenly we became aware of an air battle. We heard the characteristic crepitation of machine-gun fire. We could see, coming from the south and going north at an altitude of about fifteen hundred meters, a B-17 pursued by German fighters. The aircraft appeared to be in trouble; thick black smoke was spurting out of one of its engines, and it was losing altitude rapidly. From our position, our view somewhat obscured by the dense woods, we observed the bomber passing over Bagnoles and flying dangerously low over the Château. Seconds later we saw, coming out of the aircraft in two groups of three, six big, white balls floating in the sky. The plane, in distress, was still losing altitude. It made a curve, seemed to right itself again, then crashed into a pasture about eight kilometers to the north. I learned later that a seventh man, the pilot, after righting his plane, had jumped out at three hundred meters. The bomber crashed less than ten seconds later, at the very moment the pilot touched the ground.

The wind was almost nil, and the six parachutists descended very slowly, drifting slightly northeast. In great haste now, we resumed our trek toward l'Ermitage. While in the air force during the 1914–1918 war, I often worked with a team of Americans, among whom was my old friend Major Carl H. Clark of Tulsa, Oklahoma. I always felt great sympathy toward them, and I had only one thought in mind: to pick up those boys falling from the sky and help them escape capture.

L'Ermitage was a huge château surrounded by outbuildings and nestled in the middle of the woods. When we arrived there, we found the haymakers in a great state of excitement. The final part of the battle had taken place just above them. Everyone gave his own version of what happened. Among the assembled group were the Bourgoins, a trusty couple, the Château's caretakers; Grand Pépin, the blacksmith, strong, crafty, and daring; and also my friend Henri Rallier, who was hiding there at the time.

We decided at once to look for the parachutists. Apparently the plane had crashed in a pasture somewhere between the Noë and Le Val-de-Vée, about four kilometers north of l'Ermitage. The Germans had a lookout post set up on the ridge above the Château, between the grounds and the crash site; they would get there before we did. In addition, the enemy unit stationed in Bagnoles had been alerted, and within minutes a large number of trucks were unloading hundreds of soldiers into the forest. We did not go near the crash site for fear of being noticed.

We scoured the surroundings of the Château all afternoon, but to no avail. Around 5 P.M. we had a visit from a couple of gendarmes from a nearby station. They had been given orders to take part in the search for the parachutists, but they were not at all anxious to help the Germans. They stayed with us for the rest of the evening, and I had a feeling that, had they found an American, they would have hidden him very carefully.

At nightfall I had to return to Domfront. I asked my friends to notify me at once should they hear anything about the airmen.

7

PAUL MCCONNELL

On Monday, July 5, late in the morning, I received two successive phone calls asking me to go to the Château. When I arrived, the look on my friends' faces told me something was going on. Madame Bourgoin opened the door of the caretakers' house. There, in the guest bedroom, a tall, young, blond man slept soundly. He was so exhausted that our presence did not even wake him.

I found out that he had walked to the crossroads of Petite-Étoile, where he asked a coalman for something to drink. The man showed him a nearby pump, then led him into a coal shed. Pépin and Madame Bourgoin, informed immediately, brought the American a change of clothes and took him to the caretakers' lodge. They gave him something to eat, and he went to sleep.

When he awoke, I questioned him. He was a second lieutenant navigator named McConnell. He had parachuted into the courtyard of a farm. One of the farmers had led him to the forest, where he spent a rather bad night hiding at the foot of a tree in the company of mice, spiders, and mosquitoes, all the while listening to the barking of German dogs hunting for him.

I took an inventory of his clothing and equipment. In his possession were a waterproof pouch containing maps of France, Germany, Belgium, Holland, and Spain, a rubber bottle for water and various tablets, a small saw to be used in an escape, a razor, two photographs, and a tiny compass. He also had three thousand francs in hundred-franc notes dated 1939. We wrapped all these articles to take to my home later, except the French notes: he would need them if I was arrested.

I had a long talk with my friends about what should be done. Undoubtedly the Germans were going to organize a thorough search of the forest, especially if they did not find any airmen in the next two or three days. It was necessary to transfer the lieutenant to my home in Domfront (fourteen kilometers west) before surveillance of the road was increased. We had two choices: one was to hide the airman in a cartload of hay driven by Bourgoin, but the trip would take at least three hours; the other would be for Pépin to take him on the back of his motorcycle. (Pépin had "borrowed" a big, brand-new British B.S.A. motorcycle from the Germans.) Finally we opted for the motorcycle, while I returned immediately by bicycle. Just as I reached the Châlet, my home, built on the cliffs, I saw Pépin and his passenger arriving and going down the steps. Our airman, dressed in blue pants and a black canvas jacket, was pale and shaking. The trip had gone smoothly except for an encounter with two field policemen near La Croix-des-Landes, one kilometer from town. The frightened passenger nervously squeezed his driver's waist, but Pépin—who had lived through worse things than that—did not flinch and, trusting his B.S.A., accelerated and disappeared in a cloud of dust before the two representatives of the new order could even make a move.

At the time a Parisian, the wife of an old friend of mine, happened to be visiting. I had not warned her, and her bewilderment was great at the sight of the young American I entrusted to her care. Pépin and I went back to the gate to check if everything was OK. When we returned, Paul (McConnell's first name) and my visitor were in the midst of what appeared to be a lively conversation. Already one button from the American's jacket had been taken as a souvenir. In fact we had several such personal effects because Madame Bourgoin had sent along his clothes in a grain sack. Everything was there: overalls, boots, leather jacket, flight clothes, and so on. All these were hidden and later transported to the house of a mechanic friend of mine.

To celebrate our good fortune, that evening there was a gala dinner at the Châlet, and the Grand Pépin, very proud of himself, did not leave until the next morning. Upon his return to his home in La Sauvagère, the whole village was abuzz: two field policemen from Flers accompanied by that old scoundrel Beller, their interpreter, were going from house to house inquiring about the disappearance of the parachutists. They had already stopped at the forge, where Pépin's brother, my friend Rallier, and the young clerk gave them some rather surprising answers and resisted all their threats. All the while, our always imperturbable "motorcyclist escort," Pépin—later known to the Americans as "Mr. Umbrella"—put up spiritedly, under the watchful eyes of the Boches, the posters that in those days adorned the walls of even the smallest villages; one could not have been more docile. Another poster appeared a few days later. It offered a twenty-thousand-franc reward for information leading to the whereabouts of the airmen.

NOTICE

The people are again notified of the following regulations:

It is forbidden to hide, lodge, or help in any manner any member of the enemy armed forces (specifically air crew members, enemy parachutists, or enemy agents).

It is also forbidden to keep, transfer, destroy, or even touch planes that have landed or crashed, parts of planes on the ground, material from planes, or any object thrown by the airmen. On the contrary, any findings should be immediately reported to the nearest army post, or to the German police, or to the nearest French administrative service or police station.

ANYONE FOUND IN VIOLATION OF THE ABOVE REGULATIONS WILL BE TRIED BY A GERMAN TRIBUNAL OF WAR AND PUNISHED WITH THE MOST SEVERE PENALTIES, INCLUDING, IF SUCH SHOULD BE CALLED FOR, THE DEATH PENALTY.

Der Militärbefehlshaber in Frankreich

McConnell's presence at the Châlet forced me to change my routine. I usually ate my meals at the restaurant, but this had to change without arousing suspicion. At the time I had a bookkeeper, Marie-Louise Corbesier (she was about twenty years old). I felt I could trust her, and after some serious thinking I decided to tell her about Paul and to ask for her assistance. Very frankly I explained to her the risks involved and left it entirely up to her whether she wanted to help or stay out of it. She accepted without hesitation, and for nearly a year she was involved in our activities. She was a good Samaritan to all those who "landed" in my home. Good-natured, she put up with their demands and their jokes, not to mention the epic arguments that often broke out. During this difficult period she never said an imprudent word to her friends or anyone else. This by itself deserved our gratitude.

I had to take some precautions. I installed my boarder in the large bedroom upstairs and put a folding bed in the small drawing room where I could be ready for any emergency. I fastened a long rope along the rocks beneath the turret to facilitate a possible escape. I informed my good friends Gilard and Guesdon, who did their best to help me. Thanks to them, we didn't lack anything.

The first thing we had to do was dress our American "normally." He was slimmer and taller than I. Not wanting to arouse suspicion, I spoke to Gilard, who promptly obtained the necessary garments from Délépault, the clothier. McConnell was a quiet young man, rather taciturn. All the same, he soon became more trusting, and we engaged in long conversations. The lieutenant had great affection for Edna, his fiancée, of whom he spoke often. He told me in great detail about the American war effort with regard to aviation, about the pilots' training on the huge Florida airfields. I learned that all the "flying fortresses" came from America by air, via Newfoundland and Iceland, complete with crews and normal loads: the bombs were replaced by auxiliary fuel tanks. The flight took eleven or twelve hours, and as far as McConnell knew, only one crew was lost. He described the life of the airmen in England, scattered on small fields and living strictly on American goods.

He also gave me an account of his last mission:

Report by Paul McConnell
Second Lieutenant A.C.-A.O. 796562
Concerning the Crash of a B-17 F Shot Down in France,
July 4, 1943, Between 12:30 and 12:45 P.M.

On our way to our target, Le Mans, we were intercepted by a significant number of German fighters. Thick smoke escaped from our number four engine, which had been hit. Right after, our elevator was hit. The formation swerved to Laval toward the target while we continued south despite the opposition of enemy planes. Unable to rejoin the formation, we headed toward England at 12:35, losing altitude at a rate of twenty-five hundred feet per minute.

THE ANDAINE FOREST

German lookout posts:

A) Dieufit

B) Rocks of l'Ermitage

C) Sainte-Geneviève

D) Château de l'Ermitage

E) German fuel depot

1. Chêne du Val: Crash site of the "flying fortress," July 4, 1943. The six parachutists touched ground at La Lande, Sombreval, and Le Mont de Mousse.

2. Near the fish farm (Buisson River). Crash site of the "Mustang," July 16, 1944. The pilot, Lieutenant Thomas Watkins Cannon, made his way to Lafontaine's home in L'Être-Guérin.

3. Forester's house at Sept-Frères, where Sergeant Le Moal sheltered Copilot John Carah on July 4, 1943.

+ + + Route taken by Lieutenant Paul McConnell on July 4 and 5, 1943, between his landing site and l'Ermitage.

– – – Route taken July 4 and 5, 1943, by Sergeant William Howell, heading to the forest of La Motte.

x x x Route taken by the Englishmen Green, Potten, and Pask during their transfers between l'Ermitage and Domfront, May through July, 1944.

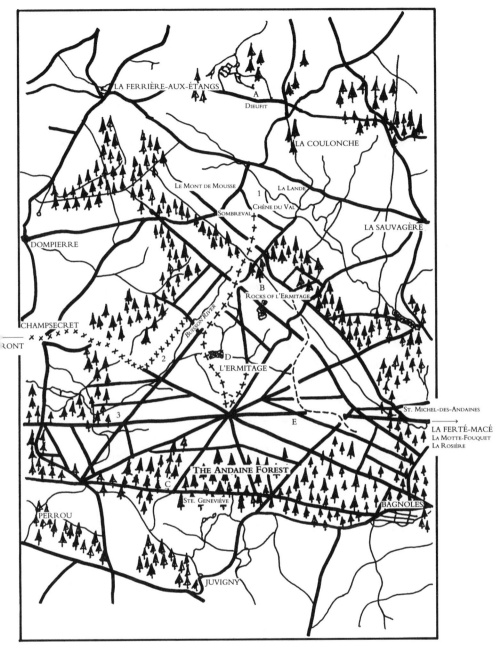

Map 1. Crash sites and escape routes in the Andaine forest area.

The fighters—I don't remember how many—continued their attack on our plane. At 12:37 P.M. and at about eight thousand feet, we encountered heavy and light antiaircraft artillery fire coming from a point not on our maps, north or northwest of Laval. We turned sharply west, then north. When we got out of range, the fighters were still pursuing us, and at that moment, from my navigator compartment, I fired at the cockpit of a Messerschmitt 109, which fell into a tailspin. Then I fired at the trailing aircraft, and it turned back. Then the order was given to abandon the plane.

I jumped, followed by the others. The plane crashed in a pasture, and some of the bombs exploded. Before the crash, the horizontal right stabilizer folded up. I landed near a farm, about three hundred meters from the forest. A French farmer took my flight boots, helmet, and parachute, then led me into the forest and left. I walked for a while until I found a place to hide, underneath a fir tree surrounded by bushes (it was full of mice). The Germans came to the forest and fired gunshots that sounded like our .30-30's; they also had dogs. Crawling and walking, I went about a mile, until I thought I couldn't be seen anymore. I went south through the forest. I was very thirsty; I had been without water or food for about thirty hours. I walked toward a lake, but a forester saw me, and I walked away without stopping to drink. Then I walked along a road, and again I was seen, this time by a man working in a sawmill. I was very tired, and I had to have some water. I walked away, then came back and asked him for water in the Indian manner. He led me to a well in a clearing about 150 yards away. I drank some water, then a coalman asked me to go into a building that looked like a railroad office. There an English-speaking man gave me food and wine. Quickly he had someone bring me clothes. I was still wearing my leather jacket and overalls. Then a woman and a man came by bicycle and told me to follow them. We went to a castle in the woods called l'Ermitage; this is where André Rougeyron found me. He was also searching for my crew.

This is what we thought happened: Pilot Olaf Ballinger, escaped. Copilot John Carah, escaped. Bombardier George Wil-

liams, killed. Mechanic Cronstall, wounded. Radio operator John
Lane, wounded. Gunner Wackerman, killed during the attack.
Gunner Bouchée, killed during the attack. Machine gunner
Owens, escaped. Tail gunner William C. Howell, escaped.

We went through some tense moments because indiscretions occurred. The Germans were conducting an exhaustive search of the region, and the repulsive interpreter for the field police post offered a
twenty-thousand-franc reward for information. Hostages were taken in
Dompierre, Champsecret, and La Sauvagère, and reward posters, both
enticing and threatening, appeared everywhere.

I feared that the spouses or relatives of the hostages might turn us
in, if they knew anything, in order to obtain the release of their loved
ones. I kept myself ready for any emergency, and I was prepared, in
order to save my skin, to kill any Germans, gendarmes, or interpreter
who might come to my door.

My American was now wearing a pair of gray striped trousers, a
corduroy jacket, and a Basque beret—he was looking very presentable.
His flight clothes and personal belongings were carefully wrapped and
hidden away. Accompanied either by me or Marie-Louise, he went to
my aunt's house, where he stayed a day or two at a time. Every morning
I went on my bicycle to the northern part of the forest and searched
for the crew members McConnell told me about.

Pépin and Bourgoin were also looking for the parachutists. They
went all over the countryside searching without respite and innocently
questioning the farmers and foresters. We searched vainly for a long
time, and I was fuming at the thought that at least four airmen were
yet to be found. Pépin came in triumphantly one evening. He had
traced a second American who was at La Ferté-Macé and had to be
evacuated. I decided to take him in immediately.

8

WILLIAM HOWELL

On the evening of July 19, according to schedule, Madame Bourgoin arrived at the Châlet in a horse-drawn carriage. She was accompanied by a twenty-one-year-old lad, the tail gunner of the aircraft: his name was William Howell. He was from Goldsboro, North Carolina, the son of a tobacco grower. He looked like a kid, a boy scout on a hike. Very judiciously, Madame Bourgoin had him dressed in a pair of shorts, a sweater, a Basque beret, and carrying a basket full of vegetables. He was a cheerful boy who called me "Mr. Red" because, despite his best efforts, he never could remember my full name.

He came to us exhausted. Despite a prior visit to a doctor in La Ferté-Macé, pieces of shrapnel remained in his back that could be felt under the skin. I will never forget the operations that followed: Billy stood near the dining room door, and with a Gillette razor blade, Pépin removed a splinter. Then I cleaned the wound with calvados and our patient had a small drink. We had to repeat this procedure eight or nine times.

At dinner that evening, the "kid" so enjoyed the French wines and the calvados that he became sick. We didn't have time to prepare a bedroom, so he spent his first night on a camp bed in the small drawing room. A little later McConnell woke me up because Howell was calling. When I entered his room, our young boarder had fallen off his bed and had thrown up all the liquids he had imbibed in the course of the evening. He was very sorry about what had happened, and he apologized. I was really the one at fault and told him so. We cleaned up his bed, and finally he fell asleep.

The next morning at breakfast he narrated his adventures since landing. I found that in the course of our search we had come very close to where he was, and we should have found him much earlier.

Since July 5, Billy had not been very happy. He occupied the position of tail gunner in the aircraft; during the final attack, a Messerschmitt 109 had machine-gunned the steering control of the B-17. Howell, at his post underneath the elevator, had been hit by a dozen pieces of shrapnel on his right side, on his head, shoulder, torso, arm, and hand. Having bailed out through the rear door as soon as the order to evacuate was given, he must have been among the first three men to jump out of the plane. Like his comrades, he landed between La Lande and Sombreval. Quickly he hid his parachute and flight gear in the brush near a brook; then he ran to the nearby forest (he was unable to find his equipment when the two of us returned to the crash site on August 22). The Germans had already organized a search. Weakened by loss of blood, he had to hide in a ditch for six hours in order to evade the trained dogs that were after him.

In the evening he met a poor coalman who took him to his cottage and comforted him with the only bottle of wine he had, then put him to bed next to his son. The next day the man guided Billy through the forest. Howell would always speak of these kind people with the deepest gratitude, but unfortunately he could not remember their names. Alone, he continued through the woods and arrived at Carrefour-Ferrière, near St. Michel-des-Andaines. He wanted to cross the road to Domfront at La Ferté-Macé, but he noticed that German soldiers were almost everywhere. The poor kid thought he was being pursued; actually he was near the Andaines petrol station, swarming with Germans. Panic-stricken, Howell dove into the woods, then followed a forest path from which he finally crossed the road. After three or four kilometers he reached Le Gué-aux-Biches, where he could see from afar the villas of Bagnoles spread along the edge of the forest. Frightened, he decided to bypass the village at the north, crossed the road from Couterne to La Ferté-Macé, and went into the forest of La Ferté, via La Vallée-de-la-Cour. Though he was exhausted, he kept walking until he could go no longer. He was found in the woods of La Motte-Fouquet by a farmer who worked for Monsieur Challemel des Roziers, owner of the Château du Petit-Jard. Despite his wounds he had walked about forty kilometers. Monsieur Challemel had a branch-covered shelter built in the woods for him. Howell stayed there, on an inflatable mattress, for five to six days. His host also gave him some clothes: a sweater, short pants, a gray striped jacket, and heavy winter shoes. Everything for a seventeen-year-old boy scout on a field trip.

But his wounds needed treatment. Although Monsieur Challemel and his people had managed, with great difficulty, to remove some of the shrapnel, the intervention of a doctor was necessary, so Billy was taken to La Ferté-Macé. For several days Viel (a Resistance group leader), his daughter, and my old friend Jojo Ruest took him in and had a doctor treat his wounds. Then they brought him to me. . . .

Lieutenant McConnell was very happy to be reunited with a crew-mate; they stayed in their room for days at a time and had lengthy conversations centering on the fate of the other crew members. I took them back and forth from the Châlet to my aunt's house. Each time, we had to cross the public park, then go down to the train station and up again in order to avoid the field of vision of the Germans posted on the watchtower. Fortunately my aunt's house had several exits. I especially feared one local resident well known for his Germanophile tendencies, and I was forced to act with extreme caution. At first my protégés feared these outings: when they passed a German soldier, they instinctively walked closer to me and looked at me with great distress. When we met people from Domfront, I would always start a conversation in French in such a manner that my interlocutors would only have to answer "oui."

We had to be constantly on the alert, and no detail could be over-looked. A few trusted friends kept me informed on the doings of the Germans. As I mentioned earlier, my bed had been moved downstairs to the ground floor of the Châlet, and I did not sleep much. Each morning the alarm clock rang at 5 A.M. I knew very well how the "Polizei" operated when they seized someone: a surprise at dawn, the house surrounded in force. That was the way it happened in Alençon, Avranches, and elsewhere. In addition to other weapons, I always kept a Colt within reach.

All this did not keep me from noticing the fear, and also the bore-dom, of my protégés. I did my best to divert them. Sometimes we had guests, mostly the longtime friends mentioned earlier, Guesdon and

Havas. I made a point of serving my protégés the specialties of the region, including crayfish, buckwheat pancakes, and stuffed tomatoes. Many of these dishes were unknown to them, and their expression and embarrassment when they tasted the new foods was always a source of laughter.

One very hot afternoon at the end of July, worn out by the restlessness of my two young fellows, I took them down the Cents-Marches path through the countryside to take a swim at Truble, about three kilometers from Domfront. It was a picturesque spot, very popular. On that day there were lots of Parisian and Domfrontais bathers, and also a group of children from a summer camp. We installed ourselves in a secluded spot, and my two Americans, who were good swimmers, joined the other bathers. We stayed until evening. The locals would have been very surprised had they known they were in the company of two overseas airmen.

On the way back I did an imprudent thing that could have been disastrous. My two charges were very thirsty, and I decided to buy them a beer at the Rendez-vous des Pêcheurs, at Pont de Caen. We were sitting at a round table at the rear of the café when, through the wide-open door, I noticed that a gasogene-run sedan had stopped on the other side of the road. The driver was Arlet, a car rental man in Flers. It was a car requisitioned by the Flers field police post.

Two German gendarmes got out of the car, accompanied by the sinister Beller. The car had broken down, and the driver was checking the gasogene while the gendarmes rested on the side of the road. Beller, sleeves rolled up, panting and sweating, admonished the driver to hurry up.

What I feared happened; the vehicle wouldn't start. Beller crossed the road, followed by the two "cow collars" (the nickname we gave them because of the metal plates hanging around their necks), and went into the café. My two Americans turned pale; the smallest mistake could have been fatal. I started talking volubly, and McConnell answered "oui" from time to time.

Beller ordered drinks and sat at a nearby table with the two representatives of the new order. I paid the check and left calmly, my two protégés ahead of me. Flashing my most engaging smile, I gave them a "Bonjour, Messieurs," which they answered pleasantly. Oh, what a relief! We took the road briskly without looking back. Fortunately we were not accompanied by Ballinger and Owens (I will tell about them later)—six feet and six feet three inches tall, recognizable as "Yankees" a kilometer away . . . that would have been something. We got back to the Châlet at a leisurely pace. My protégés were proud of this escapade, but I was determined never to try it again—it was too close a call for me.

Back at the beginning of July, right after McConnell's arrival, I investigated ways of getting in direct contact with the Intelligence Service or with an organization that could assure the return of the Americans via Switzerland, Spain, or even by plane. I made several requests to some trusted friends, without disclosing the fact that I was hiding downed aviators in my house. The results were very discouraging.

I then received an unexpected visit from Edouard Paysant of Sées. His name in the Underground was Dominique Tinchebraye.[1] He operated the regional B.O.A. (air operations bureau). Paysant asked me many questions about the aviators—the men's names, their ranks, the site where they had crashed—in order to prepare for their escape. Unfortunately, being already suspected of hiding aviators who bailed out over Belfonds, also on July 4, he had to leave Alençon for the northern region. This turn of events turned out to be very costly for the Resistance, and many executions and deportations followed.

Two attempts made by friends in Paris were equally fruitless. The American organization appeared to be less effective than its British counterpart because the members of American crews were given no instructions on whom to contact in France. Any information, McConnell explained, could endanger the French, because the airmen, some of whom could be killed or imprisoned—even tortured—would have to carry with them a great number of names: these lists could fall into the Boches' hands.

In the meantime I learned that two other crewmen, the pilot and the mechanic, were staying at a farm a few kilometers from Sainte-Opportune, also waiting for a chance to escape. One morning I received a visit from Ernest Guesdon. He was very happy; he had found in his pasture a carrier pigeon that had been parachuted. This was one of many pigeons discovered with call signs:

333 NURP/40
135 NURP/40
NURP W 4093
43 37 582 N.R.S.

(Guesdon also discovered two others whose call signs he did not note. They would all be returned under the call name "Trois Bas-Normands.") This British method of conveying information worked remarkably well: the birds were dropped at night in a cage attached to a small parachute; they were found the next morning by the user of the pasture or orchard. The equipment to accomplish the communication was meticulously put together: a packet of food for the bird, a parchment envelope containing the necessary instructions, and two molded tubes to hold messages. The tubes were attached to the ring encircling the pigeon's leg. There was also some very thin special paper, a pencil, instructions on how to feed and return the bird, and a questionnaire about the occupying troops, their moves, and their morale, as well as the defensive works, aviation, and the civilian circulation.

The pigeons were much stronger and quicker than the ones we were used to seeing; it was difficult to tend to them without inflicting harm until it was time to send them back. When the bird left, he was carrying some military information and the following note: "Eagle Club London: Owens, Howell, McConnell, Ballinger 381, are safe." We did not want to say anything else, fearing the pigeon might be shot down on its way.

Time passed very slowly for my protégés, and it became more and more important to amuse them and keep them from becoming depressed. This is a problem only those who have kept foreigners for a lengthy period of time would understand. One day McConnell was more somber than usual, and I decided to take him on a tour of the town. We were there at high noon and made several stops. First we drank an aperitif at Studer's, where the proprietor showed quite a bit of concern at the sight of a foreigner; he quickly shoved us upstairs. Then we walked along the main street and made a second stop at the Café des Fleurs. This two-hour outing was enough to cheer my young lieutenant.

On Sunday, August 22, I took Howell, still dressed as a boy scout,

to lunch at Mademoiselle Vautier's, in Champsecret. After lunch we
planned to visit the wreckage of the "flying fortress." We leisurely
crossed Domfront on our bicycles and reached the countryside. After
lunch we left Champsecret and headed for Val-de-Vée. Billy was anxious to see the wreckage and to recover his flight clothes and parachute.
The large quadrimotor, after crushing some enormous trees, had
crashed in the middle of a field at the edge of the forest. The debris
was scattered over several hundred meters. We found different articles,
among which were shreds of McConnell's headband and map case. Of
course Billy was saddened at the sight of what was left of his plane, and
especially at the thought of his dead comrades, but still I think he was
pleased to have seen the crash site. Before leaving, we searched the
nearby fields in the hope of finding the exact spot where the "kid" had
touched ground. Alas, each time he was mistaken, and we did not find
his equipment. Later I would learn from the pilot, Ballinger, that Howell had parachuted much farther north than he thought.

Back in Champsecret we had a champagne dinner; then we returned
to Domfront. Billy related to McConnell the details of the afternoon,
the condition of the plane, and how it had crashed. The conversation
was animated, and I suspected Paul was a little jealous of this escapade
in which he had not participated. From time to time I took my boarders
to spend some time at my father's house. They spoke English for hours
and returned cheerful from these visits.

Soon Billy found a diversion. He noticed a whole multitude of rabbits among the rocks surrounding the Châlet. He asked me for some
boards, nails, and tools to make a trap. This craze led to the destruction
of all the wooden crates I had, but not to the destruction of the rabbits.
One day I confided to the frustrated trapper that French rabbits are
much slyer than American rabbits, but this didn't stop him from building
more and more traps. I still have some samples today.

Of course, my protégés eagerly awaited the British or American
news on the radio. A Resistance comrade, usually Gilard, would relate
to me the news coming from London or New York. I had to give my
two Americans a detailed report that, depending on the situation, would
make them happy or unhappy.

Around August 15 we had a visit from Givette Monod (Madame
Fontaine), Claude's sister. She went into my aunt's dining room, where

Paul McConnell was resting on a couch. Surprised and delighted, she talked with him for a long time. Claude arrived a few days later; his sister had told him about my "side job." He took great interest in the American and spent all his time with him. I pointed out to Claude the antiaircraft batteries set up in Bernières. It was an extremely deadly German post, located at an important air corridor. Despite several reports sent to London via different methods, nothing would ever be done to destroy this flak, which until the end would continue to cause great damage to Allied aircraft.

9

CLAUDE MONOD AND HIS ESCAPE NETWORK

Claude belonged to the Resistance group Defense of France. He knew of my desire to take an active part in any action against the Germans. I asked him to let me join his group, and after explaining certain rules and what would be expected of me, he readily agreed. In the following months my friend would return to Domfront on numerous occasions. At the time of the debacle, Claude was finishing his medical studies in Laennec. As early as June, 1940, he tried to go to London, but he did not succeed. At the end of 1941 he became a member of Defense of France. With the help of his sister Givette, he worked for the group until the end.[2]

Claude left by train the same evening; I asked him to find a channel through which I could evacuate my protégés. Life went on without other difficulties. The presence of Marie-Louise at the Châlet was a source of diversion for the airmen. They made countless demands on her and took unfair advantage of her good nature. She had to go up and down the stairs time and time again for nothing, and she fought with Billy but never gave in. Despite all the hassles, she was always pleasant and devoted.

Billy, by the way, had become quite bold and had made himself at home. One day I arrived unexpectedly to find him standing by the fence near the public park. He was whistling madly to attract the attention of some young ladies walking by. I reacted very strongly; I was willing to risk being shot, but certainly not because of some kid's foolishness.

I frequently brought home pamphlets from the B.B.C. that were avidly read by the airmen. Once in a while Ernest Guesdon stopped by with extra food, and on those days we splurged a little. Occasionally I went fishing for crayfish and took Billy with me. He knew nothing about them, and he regarded my preparations with perplexity, but when I asked him to pick up the menacing-looking crustaceans, he became a bit worried. Going up and down the riverbank to spot a full net, he ran back to me yelling "Monsieur Rouge, Monsieur Rouge" until I came to retrieve the catch. Billy Howell could never call me anything but "Mr. Red," but his tone would change depending on the circumstances. At the beginning of his stay at the Châlet, when he saw, from the balcony, a German passing below, he would call in a frightened, soft voice, "Mr. Red, Mr. Red," pointing to the enemy. I had to reassure him often. Like Kid Billy, Paul had never eaten crayfish before; the first time it was served at dinner, they just watched me curiously, waiting for me to start, then tried to imitate me. This was a source of great laughter.

The Châlet du Brouillard ("Châlet of the Fog"), home of my protégés, was nestled high up in the rocks, away from the town. Power was provided by a generator, which required quite a lot of fuel. Gilard, who was in charge of supplies, used the most various and unorthodox means to obtain fuel: Hauptmann's car was parked in Gilard's garage, and one time he gave the chauffeur some cheese in exchange for gasoline; German gasoline provided lighting for our American aviators. Later, when we needed gasoline to transport our boys, it was Gilard who, once again, "borrowed" it from the German police Chevrolet entrusted to his care.

As I mentioned earlier, McConnell stayed at my aunt's house, which was contiguous to my father's; the Americans visited my father frequently. My father's house was occupied by the *Kommandantur* (commander's office) and its Oberst (colonel), a loudmouth imbecile. Every night an armed sentinel kept watch in the street. I chuckled at the thought that this idiot was conscientiously, though unwittingly, keeping watch over an American lieutenant who often would spy on him from behind the curtains.

Pleased to have saved my young protégés from German jails, I followed up on the fate of the other crew members: three of them, Wackerman, Williams, and Bouchée, had been killed before the crash; the

Canadian, John Lane, seriously wounded in the side, had probably been taken prisoner; Cronstall, wounded in the face and taken to the Clairmont Hospital in Bagnoles (at the time a German hospital), had managed to escape in a rather unusual and comical manner, with the help of the French. I was told the approximate whereabouts of Ballinger, the pilot, and of Owens, his gunner. The second in command, John Carah, after wandering for many hours in the forest, found refuge with my friend Le Moal, a forest ranger at Sept-Frères and an experienced member of the Resistance. Le Moal fed and clothed him, then sent him to La Chapelle-Moche, where he became the charge of Gautier, the mechanic; then he was transferred to the Lassay gendarmerie, which took care of his repatriation. Had I known about this earlier, it is probable that John Carah would have been joined by McConnell and Billy.

Time went by, and I was beginning to have serious doubts about the evacuation of my protégés. We were unsuccessful in finding a means of escape. I had no news from Dominique, who had been forced to flee; no news, either, from Claude Monod since his return to Paris. One day, during a short stay in Flers, I mentioned the problem to my friend Havas, who was in contact with the Associated Press representative in Paris.

Havas' search took him first to Caen, then to Rouen. Finally, on August 24, he advised me of the results: he would arrive the next day after 3 P.M., accompanied by some men who would take charge of the Americans. I told my protégés about the good news, but their reaction was not particularly joyful. Perhaps they had become accustomed to their seclusion, but more likely they feared the trip to come. Gilard and I agreed to use extreme caution; the plan was not without dangers. The most serious would be that Havas had been duped and that we would find ourselves in the presence of Gestapo agents. We had to consider this possibility seriously, and we took numerous precautions to dispose of these "gentlemen" if it became necessary.

On August 25, no one showed up. We feared that this channel was, as many others before, just an illusion. I called Havas the next morning; he, too, had waited all day but had not heard anything. I felt desperate and had resigned myself to the idea of being a permanent baby-sitter when, between 4 and 5 P.M. on August 26, Havas arrived in a Simca 5, accompanied by two men and a woman.

The leader of the group, Fiquet (his Resistance pseudonym), was from Nantes and was an officer in the Intelligence Service. I would never learn his true identity. He had been condemned to death several times by German tribunals. Posters offering a fifty-thousand-franc reward for his capture had been put up in the Loire-Inférieure region. In January, 1941, his wife had been caught by the Gestapo (while he watched, helpless) and then incarcerated in the fortress of Romainville. Consequently, he hated the Germans with a passion. He was always armed and ready to strike at a moment's notice, and because he would leave an area immediately after his work was accomplished, he had no reason to hide. This scared us somewhat. He was accompanied by a couple, Louis Maury and his wife. (Louis Maury was a history professor at Evreux University and a delegate to the 1940 Armistice Conference.) Their mission was to effect the transfer of Allied airmen shot down in France. Because I didn't want them to know about the Châlet, I had taken Billy the night before to my aunt's house, where he was reunited with McConnell. I took them to the study and introduced them to Fiquet, who questioned them at length and verified their identity. Satisfied that he was in the presence of authentic Americans, he examined their attire. I had taken care of getting them ready for the trip; Billy was now wearing long pants and a sports coat over his sweater, and like McConnell, he was very presentable. With the help of Marie-Louise, they had given each other a haircut and had shaved very carefully. Fiquet and his group approved of their clothing and decided not to change anything. Immediately it was decided that we would drive the two Americans to Flers, where they would take the night train, Granville-Paris, at 11:30 P.M. In the meantime we had a light meal at Studer's. I had contacted Gilard once more, asking him to drive us to Flers around 9:00 P.M. He had clandestinely, I suspect, borrowed the grain dealer's sedan, and he picked us up at my office. Havas' Simca was ahead of us with Fiquet and his group. After tearful good-byes to my father and my aunt, the young Americans left Domfront with heavy hearts.

We had planned to wait out the evening at Havas' house, and when we got there our Yankees had quite a scare. The *Kommandantur* was just across from my friend's house, and a guard was standing in front of a sentry box beautifully decorated with the colors of the Grand Reich. The sight of the guard and sentry box had a peculiar effect on Billy, who would have liked to leave. The Boche very placidly watched us get out of the car and enter Havas' home.

The dinner prepared by Madame Havas was very much appreciated by everyone—including the Americans, who felt more at ease now that they were acquainted with Fiquet and his people. At the given time, our travelers left for the station to catch the train to Paris. After a short stay they were to be taken to Spain. I learned later through the American headquarters that Billy was repatriated very quickly but that McConnell, after a failed attempt to reach the Pyrenees, had to return to Paris, after which he went to Brittany. After a prolonged stay in France, he finally made it back to England.

Lieutenant McConnell had spent fifty-three days in Domfront; Sergeant Howell, thirty-nine days. I want to take this opportunity to thank all those who helped me so willingly and faithfully: Guesdon, Gilard, my aunt, my father, Havas, Mademoiselle Vautier, the Bourgoins, and last but not least, Marie-Louise, who all along looked after and took care of my protégés.

10

SEARCHING FOR THE PILOT

Our work was not over yet. Fiquet and I had an agreement: I would find and regroup the rest of the air crew, and he would organize their escape. Although I had been given some information about the other airmen, I did not know exactly where they had found refuge. My search began on the morning of August 27. Lady Luck was with me: through Viel, the "Maxime" of the Resistance, I learned of the presence of two airmen at a farm in Sainte-Opportune. Viel said I could pick them up on the condition that I would be accompanied by a guide he would send the next day. Very pleased, I was back in Domfront that same evening and asked Gilard if he would be willing to take part in the expedition (it would be an opportunity for him once again to pump the gas he needed from one of the German police cars). On August 28 we left for La Ferté-Macé to meet our guide; she turned out to be Simone Viel, who a few weeks before had nursed William Howell for four days. This brave young woman, who accomplished so many dangerous missions for the Resistance, would later be arrested and sent to Ravensbrück following the Lignières-la-Doucelle affair.

We left from Briouze, passed through Sainte-Opportune, and arrived at a farm owned by Geslin, a former sailor and escaped prisoner. André Mazeline, who would later become the commander of the Forces Françaises de l'Intérieur, had been hiding two survivors at the farm: the pilot, First Lieutenant Olaf Ballinger, a tall, twenty-four-year-old Canadian living in Ohio; and Sergeant Francis Owens, from Pittsburgh. The latter was even taller than Ballinger.

Those two had been living in an outbuilding of the farm without ever venturing any farther than the surrounding fields. Very well organized, they had transformed their barn into a gymnasium; exercise was their main occupation every day. Their outfits consisted of mismatched civilian clothes obtained with much difficulty, considering that Ballinger was six feet tall and Owens six feet three inches. The two Americans had won the sympathy of the farmer and his wife, who tried to hide their presence as much as possible from the younger members of the family; the airmen were very touched by the hospitality of their hosts, who treated them like their own. No sooner had I arrived than Ballinger narrated his odyssey, his life as a recluse, and the kindness of his hosts; he questioned me about the fate of his crew. Lively and long conversation followed during which the Canadian, just as if he were at home, served us drinks.

Finally we left the farm. Our intention was to drop off our passengers at the Châteu de l'Ermitage in the Andaine forest, where they would stay until the day of departure for Paris, then England. On the way I realized that we would have to travel again through the forest swarming with Germans guarding the munitions depot. We risked being stopped at a control checkpoint, or worse. Also, the escape route would be more difficult from l'Ermitage. After pondering all the options, we decided to go directly to the postmistress of Champsecret and to leave the Americans in her care.

We reached our destination around 5 P.M. and got out of the car under the neighbor's watchful eyes. Followed by my two "guests" and Simone Viel, I rushed inside through the private entrance while Gilard walked over to the blacksmith's shop next door and distracted the nosy neighbor. Naturally, the postmistress was dumbfounded by this invasion, yet she did not show much worry or hesitation. She was a good woman, a calm and quiet civil servant who was certainly not ready for the unexpected and eventful life that had befallen her. She readily accepted our scheme that the Americans would be her guests from August 28 to August 31.

I am sure they never forgot the hospitality of the postmistress. It had been weeks since they had slept in real beds, and the spacious and comfortable bedroom was for them a most pleasant sight. Their delight and gratitude were expressed with many "Oh, Madame"s and "merci beaucoup"s. I bet our two friends had not eaten with such an appetite since they left Ohio and Pennsylvania. Great lovers of champagne, they drank it at every meal with remarkable enthusiasm.

The following day (Sunday afternoon) the Bourgoins, Lieutenant Ballinger, and I rode our bicycles to the crash site at Val-de-Vée to look at the wreckage of the plane. The pilot was so thrilled that I did not have the heart to refuse him this pleasure, even at the risk of committing an indiscretion. So the four of us took the La Pesnière road for a leisurely fifteen-kilometer drive through this region where we were well known, encountering many friends along the way.

Ballinger spotted the wreckage long before we reached the crash site; he looked intensely all around him, and I understood that at the time of the crash no details had escaped him. We got off the road to go across fields. As I said earlier, the aircraft had been totally destroyed; what was left of its engines was half-buried in the ground.

For a long time Ballinger wandered among the debris, picking up or discarding pieces here and there. He told us many details about what had happened. After ordering his crew to abandon the plane, he saw each of his men follow McConnell and bail out, one after another. Certain that all had jumped (with the exception, of course, of the three men killed during the air attack), he attempted to right the aircraft so that he could jump himself. Finally he bailed out at a very low altitude, about three hundred meters. He noticed that the plane crashed less than ten seconds later. Ballinger pointed toward the orchard into which he parachuted (next to Idy's house at the crossroads of Val-de-Vée and La Coulonche). I knew the orchard's owner very well; he and I used to have some wild times together in the good old days. Some French people came running toward him, and a few minutes later they found Owens, who had landed nearby.

Being last to jump, Ballinger had been able to see all his men touch ground. He showed me, with surprising accuracy, the spot where each had touched down. His story corresponded exactly to what McConnell and Howell had told me. Ballinger also remembered that one of his men appeared to be seriously wounded on the left side, and that two hundred meters away, he saw the Germans capture Cronstall, who had been wounded in the face.

At nightfall we returned to Champsecret, where an excellent dinner awaited us. Ballinger, who was usually laconic, became very talkative during dinner. He told Owens all the details of the afternoon, the location and condition of the plane, and the spots where each of their friends touched ground.

We planned to transfer the two airmen to Paris on Tuesday. Monday was spent finding clothes for them and making identification papers. They each needed a haircut, and Bourgoin performed the operation with surprising talent. For two hours the post office was transformed into a barber shop *ne plus ultra*. Then the final inspection, but Ballinger was hopeless; he looked American no matter what. Cap, beret, or hat, nothing seemed to help; it was frustrating, but we had to take the chance. About 5 A.M. on Tuesday, Bourgoin arrived by bicycle. A little before 6 A.M., the four of us (Bourgoin, Ballinger, Owens, and I) left on foot for the Saint-Bômer train station, five kilometers away. The Americans said good-bye to their hostess with emotion. Owens had somber forebodings, and in a low voice he said that he would never see America again. These apprehensions were, alas, to be justified: in May, 1945, I learned that Owens disappeared during the crossing of the Pyrenees. Among all our protégés, he was the only one who did not make it.

We had to be very careful (the taking of hostages, the Germans' investigations, the general upheaval—all these were still very recent). But everything went smoothly; we encountered no one except a farmer on his way to the fields. A short distance from the train station, Bourgoin went ahead, very slowly and carefully, to buy tickets. In order not to attract attention, we waited until the train entered the station to get to the platform. The stationmaster had an inquisitive look at the sight of our two tall friends, obviously noticing that they were strangers to the area. With my two protégés on my heels, I walked to the front of the train. As I opened the door to one of the cars, a young girl from the area, who knew me very well, rushed to climb in with us. I had no intention of traveling in her company, and giving her a big smile, I politely shut the door. We got into the next car. Only two seats were occupied; I signaled to Ballinger and Owens, and they sat down facing each other, opening the German newspapers I had taken the precaution to give them with instructions to read attentively, even though they did not understand a word. In the meantime, standing in the aisle, I chatted nonstop with a hog breeder I knew from Champsecret. He did not appear to suspect anything.

A comical incident occurred just after passing through Le Châtellier (an iron mining region). While my two companions continued to be absorbed in their "reading," a huge suitcase slid off the rack and fell on Ballinger's head. Stoic, he picked it up and gallantly replaced it securely on the rack. The owner of the suitcase, apologizing and thanking him profusely, carried on and on. Ballinger, who did not understand a word and could not answer, turned red as a lobster and pretended to be oblivious to everything but the content of his newspaper. A little nervous, I wondered how this little scene was going to end, but the lady, not getting any response, finally gave up.

The Domfront train was scheduled to arrive in Flers at 9:00 A.M., and the train to Paris was not due to leave until 11:20 P.M. Therefore Havas and I had agreed to "store" our two Americans at the Institute of Notre-Dame. Havas made the necessary arrangements with Madame Boschet, the headmistress (who deserves our deepest gratitude). Here are the instructions we had given our protégés: they were to follow me at a distance, and when I was approached by a man (Havas) with a bicycle and wearing glasses, they were to leave me and follow this man instead.

Coming out of the train station, I didn't see my friend, so I was proceeding toward the Notre-Dame Institute via the Domfront Bridge and rue de Belfort when—unluckily—just before reaching the intersection, I met an old friend from Lonlay-l'Abbaye on his way to visit his mother at the hospital. I could not avoid him, and we walked together for a while; then he turned right while I went left. I looked back a moment later, and what did I see but my two Yankees innocently following my friend to the hospital. It was a disaster. I whistled like a madman to call them back. I think the good man never figured out what came over me. That's when Havas appeared, and I explained what was going on. We looked back; our Americans had realized their mistake and were now following fifty meters behind us, one on each side of the street. It did not look like we were being followed.

Getting inside the Notre-Dame Institute was equally difficult: because part of the school was occupied by the Germans, both civilians and Boches had to use the same entrance. When we arrived, a group of students were leaving on a field trip. I bent over, pretending to tie my shoelace, indicating to the Americans, who were following a few feet behind, that they should slow down. At last the four of us passed through the gate. Quickly we climbed to the second floor, where we were greeted by the headmistress. After granting us the title of "repair-men of the chimney system on an inspection tour," she led us very calmly through corridors and classrooms, all unoccupied except for one where two students were practicing the piano. Finally, she "locked up" our protégés in a small classroom after having provided them with a bucket (which was indispensable), some crackers, and a bottle of white wine. In addition they had the victuals provided by the farmer from Sainte-Opportune, so they were all set to wait it out until the evening.

Pétrel (alias Schoegel), the guide sent by Fiquet, arrived at noon on the Paris train. He went to Havas' home and introduced himself. Accompanied by this tall fellow (much calmer than his superior), we returned to Notre-Dame around 8:00 P.M. to reclaim our Americans. They told us they were beginning to get very bored at the Institute. They followed us to rue Richard-Lenoir, where Madame Havas had prepared a substantial meal for our little group. Just like their predecessors, Ballinger and Owens left Flers by the 11:20 P.M. train to Paris.

So goes the story of my first escapees. I am very proud of all those who were able to help and who did so without hesitation. In spite of strict searches and monetary rewards offered by the Germans, no information was ever given.

As soon as our "boys" left, I received a visit from Georges Guillemin (whose name in the Resistance was Gilles). He belonged to the Burgundy Resistance network and had been sent by his chief, Broussine, to carry out the escape of the Americans. He identified himself by showing me half of a torn picture I had given Claude Monod. What we had been looking for so long arrived too late; the poor fellow returned home very disappointed.

It was obvious that an efficient and well-organized escape network was becoming more and more necessary. I was planning the formation of a group capable of providing a wide range of services. So far the housing of the escapees had worked well, but it was crucially important to have people on the lookout for aviators in distress. In addition we needed a safe and regular method of transfer to Paris or any other destination. Of course, the greatest problem was locating the crash sites and finding the aviators. It was necessary to have more informers in various locations. We already had informers east of Domfront, including Viel in La Ferté-Macé, Pépin in La Sauvagère, Bourgoin at l'Ermitage, and Mademoiselle Vautier in Champsecret. To the north were Havas and Fautrel in Flers and Geslin in Sainte-Opportune, to the south Ernest Guesdon (already in touch with the Resistance of the Mayenne region) in La Baroche. I had also contacted Anne, a mechanic in Ambrières, and asked him to bring me in as an expert every time a British or American plane was shot down. But the most important region, the west, remained to be covered. I deemed it the most important because of the extremely dangerous German antiaircraft battery of Bernières-le-Patry. The Germans had extensively developed their antiaircraft capabilities in the region during the last few months, with equipment such as casemates, concrete shelters, radar, and an electric power station with numerous batteries: in short, this area had to be thoroughly covered. I got in touch with Jéhan, an old friend from Paris who was then a mechanic in Tinchebray. He was a resourceful and funny character. I explained briefly that I knew some people who occasionally could "take care" of aviators in distress. If a plane was shot down in his area, he was to call me on pretense of needing my expertise.

As far as lodging was concerned, I had at my disposal—besides the Châlet, which was extremely convenient because of its isolated location and multiple exits—the large house of my aunt, the Château de l'Ermitage (where the Bourgoins were always ready to help), and finally the Champsecret post office. In addition I could hide some airmen in the bungalow of La Masseronnière, my father's farm, less than two kilometers away. The problems of transportation and food supplies were solved thanks to Gilard and Ernest Guesdon. Care of the airmen was entrusted to Marie-Louise Corbesier, who was quite thrilled at the idea. We had to think of all the details, including communications. I was aware that the Germans conducted frequent searches of post offices. When a member of our group communicated with me, the message was dutifully destroyed by one of our people in Flers or Domfront.

For a while we ran into some bad luck. In the fall of 1943 a large aircraft of the "Liberator" type crashed at high noon in Pas, near Ambrières. The plane was barely damaged, and of its twelve occupants only

one was hurt, with a broken leg. I was notified in Domfront and immediately left by bicycle to search the area, but to no avail. The aviators
had already been taken care of. During the days that followed, this event
brought about terrible repression from the Gestapo of Angers: Count
Paulet was arrested, as well as Duchesne and several other patriots; Col-
lin, chief of the Resistance, had to flee the region.

Also in the fall of 1943, an American fighter plane shot down by
the antiaircraft battery of Bernières crashed near Tinchebray. I was immediately notified and left, accompanied by Marie-Louise. Not wanting
the Germans to see me at the crash site, I sent the young woman to
reconnoiter. Upon her return she explained that the plane had crashed
on a hill; the pilot, a very young officer, had been thrown out of the
plane, still tied to his seat by his harness. He had been killed instantly,
his arm folded over his face as if to protect it. The Germans, who
arrived on the scene at the same time as Marie-Louise, administered
the last rites to the dead man. There was nothing we could do, so we
returned to Domfront.

About that time an Israelite, Etienne Milhaud, a judge whose son
had been deported to Germany, was persecuted and threatened with
imprisonment—as was his entire family. I obtained a new set of identity
cards for him. Emile Goupil, Guibet, and Christiany arranged the transfer of the "Martin" family to the Mayenne, where they were safe.

The seriousness of the situation did not prevent us from having some
good times and playing dirty tricks on the occupiers. My Parisian
friends visited us once a month; they would never forget that memorable haymaking to which they had been invited at Edward's farm. After
the harvesting was over, we did some horseback riding under the August sun. Following a hearty meal accompanied by abundant libations,
we carried on our partying and singing under the moonlight until
3 A.M., right under the watchtower of our "lords and masters." I must
admit that the Germans showed unusual tolerance that night.

Another evening, on our way back to the Châlet around 10 P.M., a
friend of mine, having had a few drinks too many, started shouting at
some German officers and enlisted men gathered at the Hôtel du Don-
jon, "What the hell are you doing here? Why don't you go to Russia!"
The whole thing degenerated into a scuffle that, fortunately, ended well.
We were quite pleased with ourselves.

Another night we were lingering around a table at a neighborhood café after curfew when the Feldwebel from the field police post entered. Despite our explanations, he ordered us to go to the room upstairs, where we had to spend the night pell-mell on children's mattresses, laughing at the Boche sentinel who conscientiously walked back and forth in front of the café all night long. The next morning at six we left this hospitable place, marched out the door in single file, carrying the jugs we had filled during the night. Then there was the time when a young German soldier got stuck climbing the rocks above the carp pond and had to be pulled up with a rope. His clothes torn and dirty, face and hands bloodied, he ran off, followed by the mocking remarks of the Parisian ladies. I must skip many other such stories.

— 11 —

INTELLIGENCE

One morning Claude Monod arrived by train, without advance notice as usual, under the false pretext of having to pick up supplies. He informed me that he had been put in charge of the group Defense of France. His role in the Resistance grew steadily, as well as the scope of his activities. He asked me to supply the weapons he needed to carry out some cleanup operations in the Paris region, and also to equip the group Action. A few days earlier, Gilard and Herlemont had driven back from Assé-le-Boisne with a truckload of weapons: I knew our group had them in hand, and I requested, through Paul Alasseur, a meeting with Herlemont. Following this meeting, Claude got what he came for. He returned to my house very happy and left two days later. I took this opportunity to search the countryside with him for parachute landing sites, and to gather information. It was agreed that I would provide him detailed plans of the fuel and munitions depots the Germans had set up in Andaines and Bagnoles, as well as a plan of the furnace in La-Ferrière-aux-Étangs, underneath which were hidden the liquid fuel tanks of the Luftwaffe. It was agreed that Claude would pick up these plans in a few weeks. Once again I brought to his attention the existence of the antiaircraft battery of Bernières, which had caused so much damage to British and American planes, and I pointed out the exact location on the map. He assured me that he would relay the information to London as soon as he returned to Paris. Last but not least, I denounced the activities of the interpreter for the Flers field police post, which had been extremely damaging to the patriots. The interpreter's residence—27, rue des Archives—would be placed under surveillance, and the necessary measures would be taken to put a stop to his activity altogether, if needed.

In the morning Ernest Guesdon and I drove Claude to the Briouze train station. He was carrying a huge suitcase loaded with arms and ammunition. This tall man, calm and impassive, almost nonchalant, had no apprehension whatsoever about the final outcome of his expedition and his "landing" in Paris. After his departure I made several trips to the forest to locate the munitions depot. It was situated between Bagnoles and La Ferté-Macé, to the right of the road to Couterne, in the vicinity of La Vallée-de-la-Cour. This depot extended almost one kilometer in length, and its depth into the forest was difficult to determine. Moroccan prisoners stationed on the other side of the road transferred the munitions from the Bagnoles station to the depot, named "Martha" by the Germans. The Boches always used very tender names—Maria, Bertha, Dora—to designate their most deadly war machines.

Once the exact site of the depot was located and marked on the map, it was necessary to find out the quantity of munitions stocked there, and just as important, the manner in which they were stored, whether above or below ground, in separate piles or all together. We would have to infiltrate the camp long enough to obtain detailed and accurate information. The idea came to me to call on my friend Henri Le Moal, a guard-forester at Sept-Frères and a dedicated patriot. I arrived at an opportune time; the Germans had just requested delivery of a large load of wood for mines. This gave Le Moal the opportunity to get inside the camp and to obtain valuable information, which I was able to elaborate on during a three-day search.

I learned that the unit—numbered 26-9-26—controlled both the munitions depot of l'Epinette and the fuel depot of Andaines. Its commander, Major Lucas, had taken residency at the Hôtel de l'Ermitage in Bagnoles. The munitions were stored on the right and on the left of the route de Cossé, along a stretch of 2,200 meters, between the crossroads of l'Epinette and Antoigny. The storage was handled by some twenty Moroccan prisoners between 8:00 A.M. and 5:30 P.M.; therefore, the munitions would have to be blown up after 5:30 P.M. The depot was connected via telephone to the antiaircraft battery of Saint-Michel-des-Andaines and to the command post of Bagnoles-de-l'Orne. I drew a detailed map that included the exact location of the camp, its distance from Bagnoles and La Ferté-Macé, the quantity of munitions stored (approximately 150 railroad cars), and the location of the antiaircraft batteries. The Germans had also set up an important antiaircraft battery on the ridge between La Ferté-Macé and Saint-Michel-des-Andaines; a watchtower had been installed on Sainte-Geneviève hill. The purpose of these posts was to protect the munitions and fuel depots in Andaines.

Claude returned a few days later. I gave him several copies of the map, and once again we searched the Champsecret area for possible parachute landing sites. It became evident that the area was hardly suitable for parachute landings: besides the famous Flak of Bernières (thirty-five kilometers away), a number of small observation stations and antiaircraft batteries had been set up throughout the region. There was a radar near Oisseau in the Mayenne, an antiaircraft battery in Ceaucé (at Bordage), another near La Ferté-Macé (in 1943), an observation station at Sainte-Geneviève chapel, one in the rocky hills of l'Ermitage (in 1942), and one in Beaumont, near the château (1943). A plane descending for parachuting or landing would be spotted immediately. Furthermore, the area was too densely wooded, with enormous electric cables.

A copy of the map was attached to the leg of a carrier pigeon that landed at Guesdon's place. Handling pigeons was his specialty, and in 1943 and 1944 he received and returned eight such birds. The code for pigeons carrying information about munitions depots was W.P.G. 333-LURP 40, plus the usual signature "Trois Bas-Normands" ("Three from Lower Normandy").

Before he left, Claude decided to send me a Moroccan sharpshooter lieutenant who was to contact the prisoners working at the depot. When the lieutenant arrived, I set him up at Tessé-la-Madeleine. About the same time, Fiquet's assistant, Pétrel, arrived to locate parachute-landing sites. Gilard, Guesdon, and I accompanied him throughout the region, but without much success. There were too many hedgerows and too many high-voltage cables, not to mention the German stations.

12

FIRST TROUBLES

In mid-January, 1944, an incident occurred that upset our plans: a German soldier was seriously wounded near the Domfront gendarmerie. The attacker was not found, and on January 22 the Germans took a large number of hostages, some at random, some deliberately. Among these hostages were Alasseur, Studer, Vénara, Fourmond, Jules Levée, and Amiard. That evening around 7 P.M. the infamous interpreter Beller went to Delatouche restaurant, accompanied by field policemen, looking for me. Later I was told that they came back during the night, and that they rang the doorbell at my aunt's house early on the morning of January 23. Fortunately I was out of town at the time, having left for Poitiers two days earlier to teach a technical class on the use of gasogene to a group of drivers for the postal service. My father immediately informed me of what had happened, and instead of going home once the class was over, I headed for Paris with a work order from Berthier, director of the Automobile Club of the West. My intention was to stay away from Domfront for a while, but a note I received in Paris informed me that Viel, from La Ferté-Macé, needed to see me urgently. I had the feeling it had something to do with a plane crash, and I had to leave Paris. No sooner had I boarded the train at Montparnasse than I noticed Beller pacing up and down the platform. What a trip that was, with this pest on my trail until I reached Flers. Havas arrived a few minutes after me; he would be of great help. The next day I arrived at La Ferté-Macé, where Viel informed me that, indeed, a British pilot had crash-landed and was waiting for me at Geslin's house, in Sainte-Opportune.

13

CECIL ECKEL

Without wasting any time, I jumped on my bicycle, accompanied by Mademoiselle Vautier on hers. Geslin took us to a small building adjacent to his house where he was hiding a tall twenty-three-year-old. Immediately I started to question him in English. He was originally from Trinidad, in the Antilles; his father was a building contractor in Port of Spain. Cecil Eckel was the pilot of a "Typhoon," a light fighter-bomber that was much faster than the "Mustang." On February 4, 1944, around noon, his plane caught fire about two thousand meters above Messei; he jumped out, and while coming down, he saw his plane crash to the ground. Eckel hid in a haystack and remained there from Tuesday until Thursday. The Germans and their dogs searched the area, several times piercing the haystack he was hiding in with their bayonets, terrifying our escapee. At last, on Thursday night, two men from the Flers Resistance (I learned later that it was Max Legrand and Bob) found him, stiff and aching all over, and took him to Geslin's house. I examined Cecil carefully; he was wearing a gray suit provided by the men who found him, and he looked inconspicuous enough, but he needed an overcoat. Finding one that fit him was difficult because of his frame. Fortunately I had at home a beautiful black coat left by my friend Cazault, an orchestra conductor; the overcoat fitted Cecil perfectly. I hoped my friend would forgive me—he would never see his coat again.

I had to do some serious thinking before deciding the next step to be taken. I was now a suspect and risked being brought to the attention of Beller, so I decided to take Eckel not to Domfront but directly to Paris. Time was of the essence, and because the pilot was alone, I felt it wasn't necessary to notify the escape network; I would figure out what to do once we were in Paris. We would depart from Briouze. I would pick up Eckel one hour before the train's departure the next Monday, March 6. I got home late that evening, and the following day I notified Guesdon to prepare the transfer. Havas would accompany us and would get our tickets at Flers station. He would send them to me, and it was agreed that he would meet us at the train in Briouze.

Monday at 7 A.M., Marie-Louise left for Flers, where she was to meet Havas and save us seats on the train we would be boarding in Briouze. At the agreed time, Guesdon picked me up in the Citroën. We took back roads and arrived very early in Sainte-Opportune. Cecil Eckel was ready to go, but a minor dispute arose between him and his host: Cecil insisted on taking with him, as a souvenir, the brand-new wooden shoes Geslin had given him. We settled the matter by promising that we would save the shoes for him until his next visit. Saying good-bye was hard; like his predecessors, Cecil had already won everyone's sympathy. Geslin decided to accompany us to the station. On the way I gave Cecil his ticket and reminded him again that he should watch my every move and follow my signals. During the trip he would have to pretend that he did not know me and busy himself reading some newspapers I had brought along. At the Montparnasse station and in the metro, he was to follow me a few meters behind.

At the station Guesdon and Geslin bought platform tickets, and the four of us reached the train at the last minute. Cecil, who was seeing German soldiers at close range for the first time, was not looking well. Pale and worried, he walked very close to us. As the train pulled into the station I spotted Havas, who was signaling us from a doorway. We climbed into the compartment where Marie-Louise had saved two seats. Without a word, Cecil took a corner seat next to Havas; Marie-Louise and I took the seats opposite. It was an uneventful trip, except for a friendly woman who insisted, while I was in the aisle, on starting a conversation with Eckel—to no avail, of course. At the Montparnasse station we were met by our guide, Henri Robbes, whom Havas had telephoned. Henri went first, thus indicating that everything was OK, and I followed him, with Cecil Eckel on my heels.

In the metro, I bought our tickets and slipped one furtively to Cecil, who stood aside with Marie-Louise. Havas and Robbes left in different directions. Then an incident occurred that could have been funny under different circumstances. I do not know if there is a metro in Trinidad, but if there is one, surely the doors do not open and close automatically. A bewildered Eckel saw the door shut right on his suitcase. Our friend had to pull very hard on his luggage to pry it loose. The other passengers watched his struggle, and he turned beet-red. I must say, I got a little worried. On top of that, Havas had given Cecil a cigarette, and I realized suddenly that, despite my desperate signals, he was about to light up in the metro, not understanding the "no smoking" signs. At the Concorde station, where we had to change trains for Pont-de-Neuilly, it was agreed that Marie-Louise should stay behind with Cecil in the subway while I did some checking; we had to be alert to the possibility of a police block or raid. Fortunately all went well, and we arrived without further incident at the Neuilly station.

I left the subway and walked toward the bridge with Marie-Louise while Eckel followed a few meters behind. As I was about to cross the bridge, I noticed a group of policemen and Germans checking the identity papers of the passersby. (I learned later that we could not have come at a worse time: the Resistance had led an expedition against the Bronzavia factory in Courbevoie, and all the bridges were under surveillance.) I had to "store" Cecil at a friend's house on boulevard Bourdon. It wasn't until several hours later that we were finally able to reach Puteaux, where I planned to ask my friend Michelin (plant manager at the factory where I had been mobilized) to harbor us. He was not surprised at our arrival; some time before, he had offered his help. He had two guest rooms at our disposal. Cecil would be taking his meals at the home of Michelin's niece, where we were invited to dinner that evening.

I had a meeting with Havas the following morning. It was imperative to find an escape network as soon as possible. For one long week we ran into difficulties we had never encountered before. First it was impossible to locate Pétrel (André Schoegel). Apparently he was doing a circuit in the Evreux region, and no one knew how to get in touch with him. There was another network organized by inspectors and agents of the Bordeaux police, but I soon learned that many of its members had been arrested; the chief of police himself had had to seek refuge in Paris. At the time I felt I was not familiar enough with another network located on rue Assas to go there by myself. I was also not familiar with groups like Comète, Pat O'Leary, and Bourgogne, though I was aware that my own group was incorporated into this network. There remained only two possible alternatives, and Havas and I parted, having agreed beforehand that each of us would seek a solution separately.

As a last resort, Havas contacted his friend Pécune, a correspondent for the Associated Press in Paris. Although under surveillance himself, Pécune agreed to try to locate an escape network, or at least to find a temporary shelter for our pilot. He planned to hide Eckel in a convent, but he nearly got arrested in the process. In fact, when Pécune arrived at the residence of Reverend Huet, chaplain at the Fresne jail, around 5 P.M. one day, he was not aware that only an hour earlier the priest had been arrested by the Gestapo. Pécune was forced to go inside the house, where he was confronted by the German Lutetia staff and had to undergo interrogation that lasted several hours. He insisted, without ever losing his composure, that he was only a very old friend of the priest and that he was absolutely unaware of his activities. Unable to get anything out of him, the Germans let him go.

The following day Michelin, very embarrassed, told me that he had not slept all night. He feared that Cecil might be found in his home, and he did not want to risk the safety of his nephews and nieces; he asked me to take Eckel back as soon as possible. The poor fellow was concerned about my being upset, but I understood his fears very well. This unexpected turn of events was so much the more unfortunate because I now had nowhere to hide my protégé. In desperation I called on a friend from Courbevoie, Madame Andrée C. She agreed immediately to take Cecil into her home. He had already become good friends with Michelin's nieces and nephews, and they were sad to see him leave.

In the afternoon I paid a visit to a colleague from Vincennes, a former prisoner, who had previously offered to help me. I explained my dilemma. He was very anxious to assist and tried to get in touch with a friend. He said he would call me later, when I reached Puteaux, and let me know the results of his efforts. In the meantime I met with Havas that evening. Havas had had another talk with his friend from the Associated Press, but the results were very discouraging. Pécune was

closely watched by the Germans, and he could not make a move because of his position as a representative of the American press in Europe.
Furthermore, the escape network he knew of had been exposed, and
he had to find some other solution. Yet he promised to do his best and
arranged a meeting with Havas two days later. Rather disheartened, I
went to visit Eckel at Madame Andrée C.'s home. He seemed to be
doing very well and was having a good time in company of the ladies.
Yet he noticed that I was preoccupied, and he asked many questions. I
assured him that everything was going well and that I would soon be
able to finalize his escape. The truth of the matter was that I had only
one hope left: my Vincennes colleague, from whom I was anxiously
awaiting a telephone call. The next day I still heard nothing. That evening I agreed to take Cecil and the ladies out for a cocktail at the
Voltigeur café, our headquarters. The Antillean was dressed very correctly, and in our company he did not risk attracting attention. We spent
a couple of hours in Puteaux, and Cecil returned to Courbevoie in very
good spirits. Still, during the night I pondered the situation, and I was
very concerned: Madame Andrée C.'s husband, a former conscript of
the S.T.O. (compulsory labor), had refused to return to Germany. He
was a defaulter, and as such was wanted by the German police. A search
at his wife's residence could expose Eckel and be catastrophic. The next
morning I arrived at Courbevoie at 7 A.M. and told Eckel we must leave
and to get dressed immediately. Everyone thought I had gone crazy. We
found ourselves in the street with nowhere to go. Suddenly I remembered a good woman who lived in a furnished hotel room a couple of
blocks away; she was willing to take in my pilot. She even wanted to
ask the concierge for another mattress. This was taking a grave risk,
because searches in this type of residential hotel were quite frequent,
but I had no choice.

Once my man was taken care of, I visited my friends the Pinders
(of the famous circus family). They lived in Pré-Saint-Gervais. Alas,
despite their numerous and varied connections, they were unable to
help me. I also met with Claude Monod. Unfortunately his group was
not involved in escape activity—he promised to find help, but he told
me it would take some time. I was beginning to think the situation was
hopeless when I finally received a phone call from my friend G., an
accountant. We set a meeting for the next day at an attorney's office

on rue Assas. The three of us—G., Havas, and I—met at the appointed time. The attorney was going to contact a friend who was an expert on escape. He was, if my memory serves me correctly, one of the chiefs of police in Paris, and was hostile to the Germans and to Vichy. It was becoming more and more urgent to find a solution promptly; I had to return to Carentan to teach my course on gasogene, and I was reluctant to leave Cecil in Paris, uncertain of his fate. The poor boy clung to me and was constantly asking for me. There was also the financial situation to worry about: Havas and I had already spent over ten thousand francs each. Fortunately, Guesdon came to Paris and met Cecil and me at the Voltigeur. He gave me a large sum to go to the woman who was taking care of Eckel. I had one last meeting with the friend of the escape expert, who told me he was still searching. I told him to call Michelin at his factory; then I had to leave Paris. I asked Marie-Louise to look after my protégé and to keep track of the various contacts I had made in the past week. It was then March 14, and I had spent eight days in Paris.

Once my teaching in Carentan was over, I returned to Domfront. I learned from Marie-Louise that Cecil had been transferred to Villedieu-les Poëles, where he was waiting for a chance to escape via Switzerland. I would not have further news about him until my return from deportation. I then learned that he ran into a lot of difficulties: he had to stay in Villedieu for a long time, then went back to Paris and was still there on Liberation Day. I was told he celebrated this unforgettable occasion in his own way and had to be carried, dead drunk, into an elevator. He was living it up in the capital. Then, in Paris, Havas one day was surprised to see the name of our protégé written on the slate wall of a little kiosk in the Saint-Lazare train station. Our "Typhoon" pilot had become a captain, had married, and was now living in England.

14

THE "STIRLING" OF MAY 8

During the next few weeks I had no "boarders" to take care of, and I spent all my time teaching classes on the use of gasogene: I taught in Honfleur, Carentan, Saint-Lo. I took advantage of these trips to gather information on the Boches, their organization, their coastal defenses, their air forces, etcetera. I transmitted all my findings to Claude Monod. We were then in the spring of 1944; Allied raids were more and more frequent. On the morning of May 10 I received a communication from Jéhan (my informer in Tinchebray) urgently requesting my "expertise." I immediately understood the true reason for his call: an air crew was in distress. I left at once for a meeting with Jéhan. He explained that during the night of the eighth a British bomber was shot down at Saint-Jean-des-Bois by the antiaircraft battery in Bernières. Three of the aviators were hiding in the forest of Ger; Henri Durand, a farmer well known to Jéhan, had been supplying them with food. No one knew what had happened to the other crewmen. I asked Jéhan to take me to the aviators. We had to proceed with caution because the Germans were still looking for the crew and were conducting searches; we heard that there had been several arrests. We headed for the forest accompanied by Achard, the lumber merchant, who was also one of us. A few kilometers from Ger, on the road to the valley, we met the farmer, who confirmed the presence of his "clients" in the area. I started to whistle the tune "It's a long way to Tipperary," but without results. Then I called out in English. Finally, from behind the embankment, one head appeared, then two. Our three men, dressed in bizarre garb, approached fearfully. After looking them over carefully, there was no doubt in my mind that I had in front of me three genuine Englishmen. Under the surprised eyes of Jéhan, the farmer, and the lumberman, I started a thorough interrogation, as was customary. Under the circumstances, this safety measure was a must.

The boldest of the three, Sergeant Philip Ernest Green, serial number 1.480.251, the navigator, explained that he belonged to the third group of bombers of the R.A.F. (commanding officer, Captain Morris). His aircraft, a heavy "Stirling" bomber, crashed during the night of May 8 on the way to a parachute drop in the Bordeaux region. Like so many others, they had been victims of the antiaircraft battery of Bernières-le-Patry. I was sure the Boches were now celebrating this victory with a feast and champagne, as usual. It was such a shame that the Intelligence Service had not acted upon the numerous warnings about the battery.

The bomber crashed on a hillside, its fuselage ripped open by an artillery shell. None of the seven-man crew had been seriously wounded, though the pilot bled profusely from a deep cut on his face. The airmen had parted at the foot of the hill; before heading in a different direction with two of his men, the pilot had shaken hands with Green, saying: "Good-bye. See you again in London."

Upon my request, Green stated his civil status and gave his address as 11 Grove Road, Harrogate, Yorkshire; he reported that he was born in 1921. His father, now retired, was an inspector for the National Society for Children's Assistance. Green had two brothers: one was with the R.A.F. in Italy, and the other was stationed in Hampshire. After listening to Green, I pulled aside his crewmate, Sergeant Royston John Edward Pask, the radio operator. He confirmed Green's statement.

Pask was twenty-one. He lived in Walthamstow (London) and worked for a tailor. His father was a manufacturer of briar pipes. Finally I approached the third survivor, Sergeant Charles Potten, the mechanic. Potten was twenty and worked with his father as a butcher at 29 Ailsa Street Poplar in London. He had six sisters and brothers. He explained to me how the plane crashed, mentioning that it was his thirty-third raid.

It was urgent to evacuate the three men, but it was impossible to do anything that day. The Germans were searching the woods and watching the surrounding roadways. I had a difficult time making the men understand that they would have to return to their hiding place in the forest and wait forty-eight hours. I assured them that the farmer would supply them with blankets and food and that I would pick them up the day after next around 7:00 A.M. They looked like the picture of misery at the thought of spending two more nights in the woods, but there didn't seem to be any alternative.

My two guides, Jéhan and Durand, returned to Tinchebray while I headed back to Domfront via Ger and Lonlay-l'Abbaye. My first concern was to alert Ernest Guesdon in La Baroche. I apprised him of the situation and requested his help to drive the men to the Châlet in his 15 CV. As usual, he accepted without hesitation. We decided that he would pick me up in Domfront about 6:30 A.M. the day after next. The following morning, while I was getting the house ready for my "guests," I received a call from Guesdon: he would rather carry out the operation that evening at 7:00 P.M. Somewhat reluctantly, I agreed. I then called Jéhan in Tinchebray to inform him of the change of plans.

Guesdon arrived in Domfront at the scheduled time. He explained that, to avoid the risk of a possible leak or trap, he preferred to advance the evacuation of the Englishmen by twelve hours. His decision was wise, and immediately we left for Ger. I remembered exactly where the aviators were hiding, and I went into the woods while Guesdon turned the car around. The farmer was also there, right on time, but we had to call and whistle for quite some time before the first Englishman came out of the woods. Finally the three of them showed up, one after the other. One of them kissed the little boy accompanying the farmer; then they followed me to the car. I instructed them to lie on the floorboard, and we were on our way. The car sped through the village of Ger, down the hill, through Lonlay-l'Abbaye. Soon we passed the Domfront train station, and finally, following a circuitous route, we arrived at the gate of the old dungeon; our car stopped across from the bathhouse. We immediately got out of the car, and I led our three men through the alley of the Cent-Marches while Guesdon took the road back home. We entered the Châlet without having to pass through the Promenades. Marie-Louise had been expecting us and was preparing a meal. It was only then that I had a really good look at the garb of my protégés. All three were wearing worn-out clothes discarded long ago by the farmer. They looked pitiful, to say the least.

The conversation during the meal was animated. We talked about the events of the previous days. Around midnight the three Englishmen went up to the large bedroom on the second floor where they would spend a much more relaxing night than in the woods. The next morning Jéhan informed me that the Germans were intensifying their investigation. Dr. Ledos had been arrested, and three young electricians from Paris had been interrogated; furthermore, the Germans were searching all the farms in the area. For safety's sake I felt it would be wise to evacuate my protégés for a few days. I hopped on my bicycle and rode over to Bourgoin's; I asked him to hide them at l'Ermitage. It was agreed that Bourgoin would pick up two of the men, and I would take the third to the Champsecret post office. Late the next afternoon I got the necessary bicycles ready. Bourgoin took charge of the navigator and the mechanic; shortly thereafter, Pask and I took the road for Champsecret. We bypassed the town and took the long way via Frileuse. It was nightfall, May 13, when we arrived at Champsecret. Our Londoner quickly got acquainted with his hostess, and we all stayed up late. In the morning I left Pask in the care of the postmistress and took the forest road back to l'Ermitage, where Bourgoin had already arrived with Green and Potten without incident. The airmen had been put up in the large bedroom, and they were still sleeping when I got there. Madame Bourgoin had already remedied their lack of proper clothing; more important, she had hidden any personal belongings that could give them away. When they woke up, I took pictures to be used for their identity cards.

Then Green told us his story:

It was my thirty-first raid. Our mission was to drop arms and supplies to the Resistance. This type of operation is usually carried out on a clear, moonlit night, and requires flying at low altitude and precise navigation. We were to fly as far as southern France. In summertime it is imperative to adhere to the strictest timing: to reach the coast immediately after sundown, and on the way back to be out of France before dawn. Everything went according to schedule. We flew over the coast near Caen without noticeable reaction from the German defenses. We were flying at low altitude sixty miles inland, in an area we believed free from antiaircraft batteries. As navigator, I was double-checking my calculations when our heavily loaded aircraft oscillated and vibrated violently. From the corner of my eye, I could see tracer bullets grazing the nose of the plane. The pilot tried to fly out of range of the firing, but while making a turn, the aircraft was hit by a well-aimed volley from a second gun. Instantaneously, the starboard engine caught fire, the port engine failed, and several shells penetrated the fuselage, fortunately without causing injury to any of us. The aircraft was losing altitude rapidly (we were already flying low). It was impossible to jump; we were too low for our parachutes to open before we hit the ground. There was no choice; we had to crash-land our plane. Our pilot, courageous as well as skilled, continued to struggle, with the help of the bombardier, to keep a semblance of control. Meanwhile the rest of the crew gathered in the rear of the craft, the least dangerous place in a crash. We had already taken our crash positions when the plane came in contact with French soil. We felt like we were in the belly of an enormous metal fish struggling for its life at the end of a fisherman's line. The impact was accompanied by violent shocks and terrifying sounds. It seemed impossible for us to survive. Suddenly everything was quiet, as if someone had shut a safety door. There was an instant of complete silence and total darkness; then the flames of the starboard engine shot up again.

While looking for a way out, we were thinking about the hundreds of gallons of fuel stored in the wing tanks. Above us we could see a large patch of starlit sky. The upper turret in the middle of the aircraft, as well as a large part of the fuselage, had been destroyed. One after the other, we got out, jumping into the tall, thick grass on the good and firm French soil. The pilot and bombardier had also survived, having suffered only cuts and bruises. After calling everyone's name, we walked away from our burning aircraft in small groups, each group taking a different direction.

At times like these one's thoughts are drawn to small things; while I was running, I thought about my chocolate bar melting and dripping all over my map.

In the afternoon I left for Flers to see Havas; I asked him to notify the escape network about the three Englishmen. Without hesitation, he offered his help. But after two unsuccessful trips, Havas informed me that the repatriations had been stopped several weeks before. He returned with me to the Châlet, where we had lunch. While there he took the measurements of my protégés and later supplied them with three superb, brand-new blue overalls, quite adequate for the season.

During the following days, I read local newspapers to find out whether the Germans had made reprisals in the Tinchebray area or whether they had caught the other crewmen. Also, every two or three days I visited Champsecret and l'Ermitage; never in my life had I done so much bicycling. I always brought food with me, and each of my visits was an occasion for a pleasant lunch or dinner with everyone. A week later I decided to transfer Pask to the Château, where he was reunited with his two companions. While in Champsecret, Pask found himself bored and isolated; he spoke only English, and despite mutual efforts it was impossible for him to converse with his hostess. Also, because the house was in the center of town and had no yard, he could not step outside for fresh air. To pass the time, he wrote for me the following report:

May 9, 1944

Our plane had been hit by antiaircraft shells. I escaped about 11:45 P.M. The front engines had been damaged and probably the controls as well. We were flying too low to jump, and we had been given the order to take the crash position. In case of trouble, if parachuting is not possible, the crew members are ordered by their commander to assume the crash position, which is to stand against a highly resistant crash-landing partition. I put my foot through a hole in the floor; oil from a damaged pipe was spraying us. The pilot managed a very good landing, though I was thrown backwards. The cockpit was damaged in two or three places, and it was impossible to open the escape door.

I followed my navigator outside by passing through the torn roof, jumped two or three feet into the grass, and ran down the steep hillside. The mechanic was running behind me, and we joined the rest of the crew at the bottom of the hill. The pilot asked if everyone was accounted for and was safe and sound; he had a large cut on his temple and was covered with blood. I removed my parachute, my straps, and my overalls and threw them into a bush. As I was leaving with the navigator and the mechanic, I heard Dave, the pilot, saying, "I'll see you in England, good luck!" Then we left in another direction. It had been approximately four minutes since we had crashed. We walked about four to five hundred meters away from the aircraft, which was then engulfed in flames. The navigator checked his compass, and we headed south. The moon was bright, so we went through the fields in the shadow of the hedgerows. We heard dogs barking, but we figured they were farm dogs: we had crossed several rivers, the ground was wet, and the German dogs would not have been able to track our scent. We saw several sweeping searchlights in the sky, always coming from behind us, probably German signals. We heard shots and explosions, most likely coming from our burning aircraft. Suddenly we heard a car. We lay down in a ditch; the car stopped, and some people got out and went away. It was almost 4:00 A.M. We looked for a haystack or a barn where we could stop and get some sleep. By chance we found a barn with a loft, and we climbed up and lit a cigarette. A dog barked but, luckily, went away. We slept a little, until 7:00. About 7:30 we saw a little boy (around six years old) out in the farm courtyard, and we called out to him. He saw us and went to fetch his mother, who approached with her husband. We explained that we were with the R.A.F. The farmer took us into his house and gave us food. We were cold and very tired. He put our shoes and socks to dry in front of the fire and gave us civilian clothes to put over our uniforms. We stayed in this house for an hour or two while our clothes were drying. The farmer explained where we were. Several people came to see us; then a man came who took us to another farm, where we were given a bedroom and told we could stay four or five days if we wanted. We lay on the bed and slept three or four hours. When we woke up, we were feeling much better, and we were given something to eat. Then we decided to continue south until we reached the Spanish border. We slept here for one night, and the next day we were taken to another farm, spending the day hidden in the bushes because we had been told the Germans were still looking for us. We were very well taken care of in our various hiding places. On the afternoon of May 12, the farmer led us through the fields and woods for about 1.5 kilometers until we reached a road where we got into a waiting car.

Sergeant Pask Roe (No. 1-320-7780)

Late on the afternoon of May 22, Pask and I left Champsecret and crossed the woods to get to l'Ermitage, where he was put up in a small bedroom next to the room occupied by his two companions. During these beautiful spring days, the escapees spent most of their time lying on their beds writing their "memoirs" or conversing for hours on end. Madame Bourgoin was the only one to break their boredom by charging them with washing the dishes or cleaning the house. Accompanied by Bourgoin, they went out at nightfall to take a stroll along the two large ponds. Conversation with their hosts was most difficult because none of the airmen spoke French and the Bourgoins did not know a word of English. On May 21 I spent all day with them. I brought cigarettes and tobacco, along with a few bottles of wine for Madame Bourgoin, who could not get any. We spent most of the day at the dinner table.

Monday began very inauspiciously: I left the Château de l'Ermitage on my bicycle as usual, and I was about to enter Domfront around 9 A.M. when I spotted old Louise running toward me. From as far away as I could hear her, she shouted, "Please, please, do not go into town; Herlemont has just been arrested, the German police are here!" I asked her for details, but that was all she knew. She had simply come at my aunt's request to warn me. Immediately I decided what to do and left for La Baroche via Saint-Front. My intention was first to warn Guesdon and then to see what happened. Guesdon was not home; his wife pointed to a nearby pasture where I found Butaeye, a man from Ferté wanted by the Boches. He informed me that Viel's house had been searched Saturday. I was not really surprised; I knew that Viel was a suspect, and I had warned him. Evidently things were going badly. Yet I had to return to Domfront. Taking the railroad to Saint-Front, then the old prison road, I arrived at my aunt's house through the gardens.

She had not seen anything unusual. I walked to the train station, where I could get a good view of the Châlet and the surrounding rocks: I could see nothing suspicious going on. A few minutes later I scaled the rocks up to the Châlet and found, with certainty, that my home had not been visited.

1.   Paul McConnell in April, 1943, before the doomed flight over Domfront.
Courtesy Marie-Antoinette McConnell

2. Some of the crew members of the B-17 shot down over Domfront on July 4, 1943. From the left: Paul McConnell (navigator), Olaf Ballinger (pilot), George Williams (bombardier), and John Carah (copilot). This picture was taken at Ridgewell Airfield, England, about July 1, 1943.

Courtesy Marie-Antoinette McConnell

3. The Château de l'Ermitage, where Rougeyron hid some of the downed aviators.
    The Bourgoins were caretakers here.
    Courtesy Marie-Antoinette McConnell

4. The Châlet du Brouillard, Rougeyron's home, where he hid downed airmen.
    Courtesy Marie-Antoinette McConnell

5. William Howell, Marie-Louise Corbesier, and Paul McConnell in July, 1943. Corbesier, Rougeyron's bookkeeper, befriended and looked after the airmen.
Courtesy Marie-Antoinette McConnell

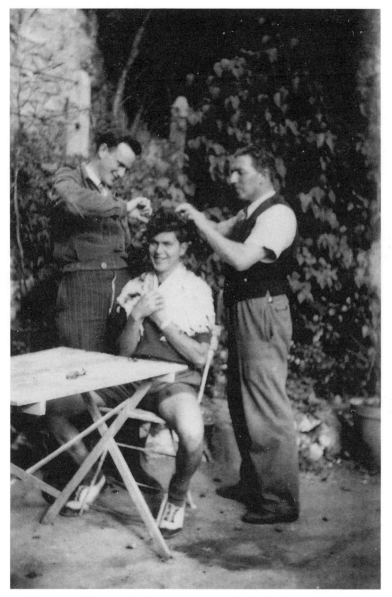

6.   William Howell getting his hair cut, July, 1943. Paul McConnell is on the left, Rougeyron on the right.

Courtesy Anne-Marie Vizot

7.   Relaxing after a swim in the Orne River, July, 1943. Sitting: Paul McConnell, Madame Cornu, Marie-Louise Corbesier with small child. Lying: Billy Howard. Kneeling: Rougeyron.

Courtesy Marie-Antoinette McConnell

8. House of Rougeyron's aunt, where Paul McConnell was hidden during most of his time in Domfront.
Courtesy Marie-Antoinette McConnell

9. Ruins of the old fortified castle in Domfront, where locals sought refuge during the bombardments.
Courtesy Marie-Antoinette McConnell

10. Kenneth Hagan, one of the airmen aided by Mademoiselle Dubocq.
Courtesy Anne-Marie Vizot

11.   Radar of Oisseau-le-Grand after destruction by the Allied forces.
Courtesy Anne-Marie Vizot

12.   American plane shot down by the deadly antiaircraft battery at Bernières.
Courtesy Anne-Marie Vizot

EINREISEERLAUBNIS FUR DIE KUESTENSPERRZONE NR. 367

Permis d'entrer dans la zone côtière interdite

Nicht gültig für die Departements Nord und Pas-de-Calais
Pas valable pour les Départements du Nord et du Pas-de-Calais

ROUGEYRON, André , Lehrer Gasgeneratorvor-

(Vorname, Familienname, Beruf) lesungen.
(Prénom, nom de famille, profession)

aus Domfront (Orne) I4 Rue Montgemmery.
de (ständiger Wohnort, Strasse, Hausnummer)
(domicile, n°, rue)

ist berechtigt, unter Vorlage des Passes — Passersatzes — amtlichen
est autorisé, en présentant le passeport — la carte d'identité —
Lichtbildausweises — der Kennkarte *) —

Nr. 87.426

ausgestellt von Präfektur der Orne in der Zeit
délivré par
vom 10.März 194 4 bis zum 30.März 194 4
à partir du jusqu'au

einmal *) und zurück *) — wiederholt *)
une fois aller et retour — plusieurs fois

von Domfront (Orne)
de

nach Honfleur (Calvados)
à

zu reisen.

Caen, den 27.Februar I944

(Stempel) Für den Feldkommandanten
Im Auftrage:

*) Nichtzutreffendes streichen.

25252 CARON et Cie Imp. - Caen

Militarverw. - Oberinspektor

13. German permit Rougeyron was carrying when arrested by the Gestapo. It was
found in the Buchenwald archives.

Photo by Studio Véronique, courtesy Anne-Marie Vizot

14.   Drawing of Rougeyron at Buchenwald. This sketch and the three sketches that
follow were apparently made by a fellow prisoner, whose identification number appears
in the lower right corner of the subsequent drawings.

Photo by Studio Véronique, courtesy Anne-Marie Vizot

15. Rougeyron as Kommando electrician with his aides.
Courtesy Anne-Marie Vizot

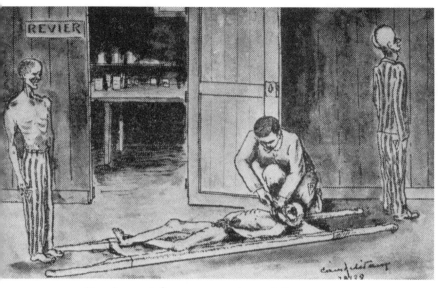

16.   A camp infirmary—extracting teeth from a corpse.
Photo by Studio Véronique, courtesy Anne-Marie Vizot

17. Transport of dead prisoners to the communal grave.
Photo by Studio Véronique, courtesy Anne-Marie Vizot

18. Rougeyron at about sixty years old.
Courtesy Anne-Marie Vizot

19.   August 14, 1994: Ceremony commemorating the fiftieth anniversary of the liberation of La Coulonche, near Domfront, where the B-17 crashed on July 4, 1943. A
monument was erected to honor the crew members who died.

Courtesy Marie-Antoinette McConnell

15

THE BOMBARDMENTS

The following Sunday, May 28, 1944, I left early in the morning for l'Ermitage, planning to be back in Domfront by lunchtime. At l'Ermitage, around 9 A.M., while we were all involved in a lively conversation in the main room of the guardhouse, we suddenly heard the sound of an engine above us. We looked up, and toward the west we could see about forty planes diving in formation; these planes went away, then came back and dove again. At the same time, violent explosions could be heard. The raid lasted about twenty minutes. This was quite unexpected, and the Englishmen and I speculated that Domfront was the target. I returned home in haste and learned of the first bombardment of the train station area. The bombs had hit the railroad tracks and adjacent buildings. The damage was severe, but fortunately no one had been hurt. Alas, this was only the beginning.

On Friday, June 2, about 6:45 P.M., while I was busy watering the rocky vineyards around the Châlet, I heard a formation coming from the north. Soon the planes appeared, flying at low altitude. They were P-47 "Thunderbolts," American fighter-bombers characterized by their short bodies and rotund fuselages. They bypassed the town to the south, and then one of them, flying west to east, suddenly roared above me. I distinctly saw the firing of its two guns. A second plane followed, then a third; in all I counted about twelve. Backed against the rocks, I could see the houses around the train station collapsing, one after another. Numerous fires were shooting up, and I thought of all the unfortunate Domfront people caught up in this devastation. The bombardment was extremely violent: I heard the rattle of machine guns; I saw the tracer bullets blazing on the hospital roof; shells were cracking against the rocks. When the attack was over, I ran to city hall, where the Passive Defense Forces were leaving for the train station area. The scene there was terrible. The whole area was destroyed, from the hospital to Pignon-Blanc: four hotels, the restaurant, a service station, several shops, the distillery, the fuel depot, and many private residences. I learned that eight people had been killed.

To fight the dozen fires, it was necessary to call on the firemen of the neighboring towns, in particular Lonlay-l'Abbaye. The disaster was too severe for our men to handle (as well as for the Passive Defense, whose chief, however dedicated during the drills, now showed a complete lack of efficiency). There was another alert an hour after the bombardment, but it was only reconnaissance aircraft taking photographs of the devastation.

Just before lunch the next day, I had a visit from Ernest Guesdon. He had been told to inform me of the landing that would take place on the Normandy coast during the night of June 5. That same day, a little after 3 P.M., some American fighter-bombers dropped two or three bombs southwest of Domfront on the distillery near Bazeille, on the Mortain road, and on the train station. A man from Domfront, Monsieur Coupel, who was unwisely driving his car, was killed.

The next day, Sunday, I left early for l'Ermitage and had lunch with my English friends and their hosts. I announced the good news: landing in forty-eight hours! No need to say how happy they all were. I got home late that evening. A sad ceremony took place the next day in Domfront: the funerals of those killed in the bombardment of June 2. Many people evacuated the town and took refuge in the country, mostly in Saint-Front, La Haute-Chapelle, or Saint-Mars.

For the first time since the occupation, I would have to be on guard duty June 6 at the German depot; another man from Domfront and his superior would be my companions. The guardhouse was located in the caretaker's lodge of the hospital.

The night of the fifth was eventful: there were numerous bombardments north of town; surveillance planes were constantly flying at low altitude above the area; and at dawn a bomb fell on the cemetery of Saint-Front, hitting a German convoy. The Notre-Dame area was all but evacuated. When I arrived at the guardhouse, no one was there.

Shortly afterwards, the train to Alençon was bombarded by surveillance planes, as well as the train to Laval. The machine-gun fire was so intense that I had to take refuge in a ditch near Notre-Dame, where I found a trucker, his employee, and a collaborator with her German boyfriend. All morning long, German vehicles—mostly ambulances—passed through the town in the direction of Mortain. No doubt: the debarkation had begun. I was still alone at my post around noon when one of the hospital nuns arrived with the gardener, old Déséchalliers; they were there to take care of a few animals still left on the grounds. Then my faithful Louise brought me lunch. I had hardly started to eat when the P-47 "Thunderbolts" reappeared. Almost grazing the roofs of the hospital each time they passed, they bombed the railroad tracks about one hundred meters away from us. Louise and I left the caretaker's lodge to seek shelter in a vaulted passage near the hospital kitchen. The nun and the gardener were there also. The bombardment continued for about twenty minutes; doors were shattered, glass and plaster fell from everywhere, and the vault shook. I was especially puzzled because I noticed that every two or three minutes a plane flew by without dropping any bombs, then was immediately followed by another that did. Since then I have surmised that the chief of the squadron was guiding his young pilots, but I have never understood the technique. When the alert was over, the nun offered us a drink in the kitchen, which was now in shambles. Then we went over to the railroad tracks to view the bombardment site and the gaping shell holes. The freight cars, loaded with flour, were burning, and Commandant L. attempted to order us to unload them for the Boches. Finally, back at my post and bent on staying there until evening, I was told that the train to Laval had been destroyed just a kilometer from Torchamp.

My guard duty over, I returned to town, where I heard that Flers had been bombed. Columns of smoke were rising from the city and could be seen from our city hall. By evening a dozen Domfront people had asked to spend the night in the basement of the town hall or in the casemates of the old fortified castle. Some brought chairs, some mattresses; all made do as well as they could. Again it was a very troubled night, and it would be, alas, followed by many others.

German convoys of all kinds—infantry, artillery, tanks—were passing through town to converge toward the coast. Numerous American patrol planes were surveying the area, and from time to time the whole countryside was lit by star shells. They were so bright that one could read a newspaper in the streets. Far away, we could see huge fires caused by bombardments lighting up the night sky. From time to time we could also hear a dull, distant sound, probably coming from navy cannons.

On June 7 people were still evacuating the town. Around 4 A.M. the American bombers appeared once more, bombing the train station as well as two of the hospital buildings (including the kitchen where we had taken shelter the day before), which were destroyed. Come to think of it, we were lucky that they hadn't missed their target the day before.

On the morning of June 8, a large group of workmen from the Todt (German) factory invaded the town. They were there to repair, or rather to attempt to repair, the railways. We soon experienced how unpleasant these undesirable visitors could be. They entered the Notre-Dame area, now deserted, and systematically looted hutches, hen houses, and wine cellars.

Very early in the morning on June 9, Bourgoin arrived on his bicycle. He told me about a catastrophe that had occurred the previous evening at l'Ermitage: a German detachment of about one hundred men had taken over the grounds, most notably the barn, in which, under a thin layer of hay, were stored nearly two tons of arms. The Boches slept in the hay during the night and apparently did not notice anything. The farmers had to flee into the forest, taking with them my three Englishmen. Bourgoin explained that it was no longer possible for him to keep the escapees; we had to move them immediately from their current hiding place near the forest road between l'Ermitage and Mont-en-Gérôme. This was not going to be an easy task because the Germans were everywhere. In addition, the lookout post set up on the rocks above l'Ermitage was more dangerous than ever. Hopping on my bicycle, I went to see Le Moal, the forester at Sept-Frères. I asked him to escort me and the airmen through the forest—he knew the woods like the back of his hand—to Champsecret.

Madame Bourgoin came to meet us as we reached the forest path. She had kept an eye on the three men all night. When she saw us, she went into the woods to tell them we were there. They had made a shelter out of branches and had slept there bundled in their coats. Although not looking very good, they seemed glad to see me, but they were startled at the sight of the ranger's uniform. Le Moal led the way, and we entered the forest. I followed about twenty meters behind him with the Englishmen. My thoughts were that we absolutely had to avoid going through the village of Champsecret in broad daylight. How could we bypass it? A Resistance friend of mine, Georges Dubois, should be able to help us. After a long walk through the forest, we reached the Petite-Étoile road and stopped at Gué-Vallier, hiding on the riverbank while Le Moal went to alert Dubois. It was about 2 P.M. After what seemed a long wait, my friend showed up; I explained the situation and left the three airmen in his care. He was to take them to the Pont-de-Pierre road, near the cheese farm. I would meet them there and take them in charge.

An hour later Green, Potten, Pask, and their guide showed up where I had been waiting. They had had a close call. While crossing La Coulonche road (the only one they had to cross) near the cemetery, they found themselves face to face (so to speak) with two German trucks and had to wait for quite a while, lying in a pasture. I told them to walk about fifty meters ahead of me, without looking back, and that they must not appear worried; then we left for Domfront. Bicycle in hand, I followed calmly behind my protégés. Everything went very well until halfway up the road to Pont-de-Pierre, about two kilometers from our destination. At this point, as I glanced behind me, I saw two gendarmes from the brigade of La Ferrière-aux-Étangs—Bourget and Vallienne—coming up on their bicycles. They caught up with me very quickly. They knew me and stopped. After the usual greetings, one of them remarked, "Here are three fellows in a hurry!" I answered casually, "So it seems." At this moment, alas, one of the Englishmen looked back, saw the gendarmes, and alerted his companions. Our three men lost their cool, started to run, and disappeared through a hole in the hedgerow into the pastures. The gendarmes' reaction was immediate; they hopped on their bicycles to pursue them. Taking a chance, I stopped them by saying, "Don't worry, I know them." This satisfied the lawmen. We walked together for a few minutes and said good-bye; then they went on their way without showing any more interest in my friends.

The gendarmes now gone, I had to retrieve my protégés. Finally I found them lying flat on their faces behind a hedgerow. I gave them a good scolding and told them to wait for me at the top of the hill on the right at the crossroads. We passed through the grounds of the château of Frileuse, then Le Val-Nicole and the Tanneries. At last we arrived at the Châlet via the Cent-Marches (after passing a few Germans on the way). Our Englishmen had walked approximately twenty kilometers, mostly through the woods. They were exhausted and shaken. Big Pask—drenched with sweat under his two sweaters, his tunic that he had refused to give up, and his blue overalls—looked like a beaten dog.

Life at the Châlet went on. From its heights we observed the endless deployment of troops, cannons, trucks, and ambulances going to or coming from the coast. The area was frequently the target of machine-gun fire, and one day around 4 A.M. American fighter planes set fire to a convoy of five tanker trucks on La Haute-Chapelle road. June 11 was marked by the arrival in Domfront of more German troops and by the beginning of systematic looting. Many automobiles were stolen. A bomb hit Les Princetières during the night. The next two days were relatively calm except for some machine-gun fire. But on the evening of the twelfth, a formation of thirty-six planes bombed the railroad station area; five buildings were destroyed (Poutrel, Maisonnier, Day, Lemonnier, and Lecrônier). There were no casualties because the area had been evacuated long before. There seemed to be no particular reason for the attack, except, perhaps, the presence of a fuel convoy in the yard of the Poutrel garage. Air patrol was flying all through the night, and at a distance we could hear, more and more distinctly, the roar of cannons.

The following day, June 14, was a bad day for Domfront. Early in the morning, intense gunfire was directed at the railroad station. In the opposite direction, in the vicinity of La Croix-des-Landres, two trucks were burning. Around 8:15 P.M., as Goupil and I were sitting down to dinner, we heard the sound of engines. Goupil ran toward the casemates and I toward city hall. The thunderous roar of the planes and the explosions were deafening. Our friend Huvé showed up, frantic; he told us that the center of town was completely annihilated. I ran to the Châlet to check on my Englishmen. They told me that they had seen about twelve planes coming from the direction of Mortain. They believed they were American "Mitchell" bombers (B-25s), equipped with seventy-five-millimeter cannons. A few seconds later they heard the bombardment. The Châlet shook, and many windows shattered. Because the sounds were muffled by the rocky hillside, they thought the attack was taking place in the forest. It lasted only twelve to fifteen minutes. After reassuring them, I ran to the center of town; the scene there was horrible. It seemed that the bombers had hit all the main north–south thoroughfares. The large hotels, the banks, and numerous stores were in ruins; a building next to the pharmacy was burning. Rescue operations were under way, and dead and wounded were being pulled from under the rubble. At Chêne-Vert, of the six members of the Pontoire family, only a young girl survived. The bodies were taken to a room at the old rectory, now a makeshift morgue. Rescue operations were difficult because no one knew how many people were buried under the rubble. As we were taking away the body of the Pontoire father, the bombers returned, and we had temporarily to abandon the body in the middle of the street. Under the peristyle of city hall, Dr. Lévesque tended to the wounded with the help of a nurse, Mademoiselle A. Goupil was in charge of transferring the wounded to the Château de la Guyardière, which had been converted into a hospital. He had some problems on the way—his car broke down, and the wounded had to be carried into another car. He finally returned at nightfall, exhausted. The whole city was like an inferno.

The upper part of town was also damaged. A house on place Saint-Julien had collapsed and was burning, and we fought the flames all night long. The only hydrant we could use did not have much pressure (sixty cubic meters). It was hooked up near the post office and operated by René Sonnet. Within hours the few people still in town had fled. The Passive Defense was failing; the only people left were sixteen firemen and a handful of civilians. Fires were raging, and new ones were starting up everywhere. Around midnight I ran to the Châlet to see how my protégés were doing. Taking a risk, I asked them to come and help us. That night, with the complicity of René Sonnet, three Englishmen operated the fire hoses, and no one even noticed. The night ended in complete chaos. People were evacuating their furniture through the windows. We tried to protect the roofs that were still untouched next to the ones already burning, but our work was frequently interrupted by air raids. From time to time the firemen had to stop to get some rest and to eat; fortunately, the owner of a delicatessen had kept his shop open. Alas, the number of volunteers diminished steadily. At the end, the only ones left were the pharmacist, Monsieur Lecrônier, my friend Yves Noire, the lawyer Goupil, and the fire crew.

Even in the midst of the most distressing circumstances, sometimes a comical incident can occur: in the morning I noticed a young man going back and forth with a wheelbarrow heavily loaded with papers. Each time he passed by, he ran over the fire hoses. Irritated by his maneuvers, I admonished him. He shouted back that he was a tax comptroller and he was going to report me to the civil service. An altercation followed (I was to regret my harsh words later on: the comptroller, Soureilhan, proved to be a good citizen, and I owe him an apology).

At dawn, after taking my three Englishmen back to the Châlet, I paid a hurried visit to my aunt and my father to see how they had withstood the bombardment. Their homes were damaged, with doors torn away and windows shattered. My father insisted that he was not going to leave and stated that from then on he would stay in the basement at night. His housekeeper would sleep there too. I decided to evacuate my aunt to Champsecret so she would not be exposed any longer to the increasing danger. She packed her bags hastily, and we loaded them into a baby carriage—the one she had used when I was an infant. The silver and other valuables were already stored in the cellar (I had made the mistake of storing my Zeiss Contax camera as well). Just before 9 A.M. Goupil and I accompanied my aunt along the Tertre-Frileuse footpath in order to avoid the main roads. We parted with her at Briouze, and I said good-bye with a heavy heart, hoping that the American "Mustangs" would not come that morning. I estimated it would take her at least two hours, pushing her carriage and pulling her dog, before she reached a friend's house. Despite the planes overhead, Goupil and I quickly returned to Domfront and reached the devastated town square. Behind the Ange-Gardien we retrieved the mutilated body of Madame Déséchalliers, wife of the hospital gardener.

The following days were trying. The few houses still standing in the bombed-out areas burned down one after another because of strong winds. Despite the firemen's efforts, the Hôtel de la Poste and Dr. Rémon's residence fell prey to the flames. In the upper part of town a fire that started at the bailiff's house spread to two adjoining buildings. Upon checking the cisterns, we found that the pump was not working and that the water supply would soon run out. René Sonnet immediately went down to the turbine: we had to have water until the cisterns filled up again. At our request, the firemen agreed to take the pump down to the drainage canal, which had enough water left to last two to three hours. It had been in use for fifteen hours, supplying not one pump but two, since the arrival of the firefighters from Lonlay at noon. At that time, in the upper part of town, the fight against the flames was somewhat effective.

Then around 6:30 P.M. on June 15, there was a new attack on the train station by heavy bombers: the hospital was hit, and Madame Lechippey's house was destroyed by the flames despite the firemen's efforts throughout the night. On June 16 the fairground fell prey to the fire. The firemen from Bagnoles arrived that day, and their chief, Lieutenant Brichard, was wounded. The following day, the number of Germans invading Domfront increased considerably. The infamous "Das Reich" division, renowned for its atrocities, was coming from Toulouse to Cherbourg, unfurling like a wave on our town. Pillage was widespread. The Boches were like rats; they showed up everywhere. The firemen, Goupil, and I multiplied our patrols through the town, chasing the Germans out of the public buildings and the houses. We found them in basements, attics, etcetera, and they were often reluctant to leave.

Although exhausted, we did not let up; but on the fifteenth I took some time out and invited Goupil to have lunch at the Châlet with my three protégés.

The restaurateurs had all left town, and we had to organize a canteen. We were fortunate to find a refugee, Mouzillat, who had been a chef in Paris. Like so many others, he and his wife had been spending nights in the basement of the city hall. During the next four months he would be in charge of the hastily set up canteen in the old rectory's kitchen. This canteen would always be remembered by those who did not fear coming to Domfront during these troubled times; it was the stage for so many incidents, both sad and funny, that it is not possible to remember them all. Organized haphazardly by just a few, it became a meeting place for all and a home for the firemen and the members of the Passive Defense. On Fridays and Saturdays, up to sixty meals were served. (It should be noted that our little business, far from running a deficit, gave the city about forty thousand francs when it closed its doors.)

Happily, our suppliers made regular deliveries: Madame Loisel supplied the meat, and Maurice Derouet not only supplied bread to all the refugees in the Saint-Front region, but also furnished daily the dozen or so large loaves we needed. I don't think he missed his deliveries even once. Vegetables were found in abandoned gardens . . . scenes of epic battles between our firemen and the pilfering Boches. Beverages, at first salvaged from destroyed homes, were later bought wherever we could get them. (I would like to mention Monsieur Marsollier, who despite the machine-gun fire and bombardments never left our side, except for a few weekends spent in Champsecret. He took care of the accounting at our canteen. I am very grateful to him.) The city had had no electrical power since June 15. At city hall, the canteen, the Châlet, my aunt's house (where I still managed to find a few hour's sleep), and my father's house, we had to light oil lamps. It was not so bad, really, and quaintly "old-fashioned."

In the rectory we installed a food store (managed by Monsieur Carré), a post office, and the salon of the hairdresser Ducreux, who had survived the June 14 bombardment. It was our trade building.

The gendarmes and their chief were rather fickle: they occupied the casemates of the old castle, migrated to Saint-Brice, then returned to Saint-Front. They were not always very happy: a leather coat was stolen at the gendarmerie; a motorcycle disappeared at the guardhouse. It was a run of bad luck.

Back to chronological order: on June 17, if I remember correctly, I ran across the keeper of the tobacco warehouse, Monsieur René. Miraculously, his store on rue Clemenceau had not been completely ransacked; he wondered how to salvage his remaining supplies. I proposed that they be stored in a large upstairs bedroom at the rectory. All day firemen moved the cartons of tobacco that would keep us supplied for a few weeks until the delivery of a shipment from Le Mans. Many times the S.S. stationed around Domfront tried to lay their hands on these hidden treasures. (I remember, for example, that little bastard noncommissioned officer who came one morning under the pretense of "inspecting" the warehouse.)

Faced with the ever increasing encroachment of the Boches, I was apprehensive that some day they would go into the Châlet and find my boarders. I decided to evacuate them to my father's little house at the farm of La Masseronnière, two kilometers from town. If they were a little farther from the formidable Das Reich division, we would breathe easier.

Just before leaving for the farm on the afternoon of June 17, I received a visit from Captain Lefèvre and Viel; they asked if I could give shelter to an American lieutenant whose plane had been shot down near Laval. Madame Gahéry had found him wandering in a field, and the airman was awaiting my answer at the home of Lécuyer, a farmer at La Baroche and a friend of Ernest Guesdon. I gladly accepted, and it was decided that the following day Lefèvre would take my new charge to La Masseronnière. They would walk along the railroad tracks. I took this opportunity to explain to the captain that the Passive Defense was in dire need of volunteers; he agreed to detach from the Lonlay Underground a few men capable of handling all kinds of situations, from fighting fires to transporting the dead, blowing up trucks, and executing Germans. A few days later he sent three strong and able men to help us.

At nightfall we left with my three Englishmen, who had prepared haversacks. We went down the Cents-Marches, passed Notre-Dame, crossed the woods of La Raterie, and finally arrived at La Masseronnière. It was a one-story house that had escaped bombardment, with a large wood-paneled room and two adjoining cellars. It had been deserted for years and was in a complete state of decrepitude, full of rats and spiders. In the evening we had to eat by candlelight, with a very small fire in the fireplace, in order not to attract attention. The place was sinister, and the three airmen were in a somber mood. It would get even worse during the night, lying on the cold cement huddled against each other, shivering for hours. At dawn I realized very quickly that the site was not as safe as I had expected: a group of Germans from the Todt factory had set up camp in Bazeille, about three kilometers away. They roved about in small groups, ransacking the area farms.

Around noon, the agreed-upon time, I caught sight of Captain Lefèvre bicycling along the railroad tracks; I whistled, and he joined me by a hedgerow. He told me that the American was following, on foot, a short distance behind. A dark-haired man soon arrived, stocky and of average height. He had the look characteristic of his compatriots. We took him inside the house and submitted him, like his predecessors, to the customary interrogation. He had a dry wit, and I must say I was somewhat puzzled when I asked what his profession was and he answered me, very seriously, "I arrange the faces of dead people so that they look good." I wondered for an instant if the Americans embalmed their dead. His name was Leonard James Schallehn, second lieutenant, born in 1923, a bank employee in Saratoga Springs, New York. He explained that he belonged to the 509th Squadron, Group 405, and piloted one of the "Thunderbolts," the American fighter-bombers I had nicknamed "pig snouts." He had been shot down June 15 near Laval after successfully bombing the viaduct, a feat of which he was very proud. Schallehn was to become a very good friend, boisterous and unbearable at times, yet so devoted and warm. All of us continued to talk until Lefèvre left. I remember an incident that occurred at the times, through my own fault: as I was checking a revolver, it went off inadvertently; the hole the bullet made in the wooden wall of the shelter is still visible.

Captain Lefèvre left to return to his maquis in La Baroche, and I decided to make a brief visit to Domfront. Apart from the sporadic machine-gun fire and the usual looting, nothing new was happening. The firemen were still fighting the blazes that were flaring up just about everywhere. The Châlet had not yet been visited by the S.S., and neither had my aunt's house. I quickly returned to La Masseronnière, where I found my protégés in a very worried frame of mind. During the few hours of my absence, they had seen some of the Todt groups prowling and pilfering. Furthermore, they had heard the sound of engines coming from a nearby park, from a German munitions convoy encamped under the trees; therefore, it was a most undesirable neighborhood for us, because the presence of the Germans could bring about an air raid, a house search, or both. I made the decision to return to Domfront early the next morning. My aunt's large house wasn't occupied, and I would install everyone there.

We left our shelter early on June 19. Via La Grésille, La Grange, and rue de la Gare, we arrived at my aunt's house. Two of the Englishmen would sleep in one bedroom, the American and the third Englishman in another. During the day everyone would stay out of sight.

It was not long before my boarders organized their own watch and stood guard in two-hour shifts so that surprise was impossible. Their main diversion consisted of watching, from behind the curtains, the endless stream of German convoys—and of listening to the German subofficers shouting to direct traffic. The airmen had also set up an ingenious warning system in case of emergency: every evening they placed an empty bottle atop a cracked-open door, so that if a German walked in they would be instantly wakened. I left the aviators for a while to go to city hall. Nothing new to report there, except that a serious fire had erupted at Pichon's house, on rue du Chêne-Vert.

I want to mention here one member of our group, the postmaster of Domfront, a brave man who since the bombardments started had been unable to get his employees to return. He did his best to replace his truant personnel and to expedite, sort, and deliver letters throughout the countryside. On June 19, around noon, the postmaster pulled me aside and asked me to accompany him to the post office. I was intrigued and went with him at once. Once inside, we found ourselves in the presence of an S.S. man, young, blond, well-built, who told me in perfect French that he was from Alsace. A prisoner since 1940, he had been taken from the detainment camp and forced to enlist in the German army as a driver for the Das Reich division. After many vicissitudes, he was trying, unsuccessfully so far, to reach Cherbourg. He had made up his mind to desert, and in return for our help he offered to give us his Renault truck loaded with four hundred liters of fuel, seventy-five kilos of butter, arms, ammunition, two bags of grenades, and two ewes. The truck was parked on a farm road near Torchamp.

I was perplexed. Obviously the offer was tempting, but there was a risk. What if the man was sent by the Germans? Yet he seemed sincere, and I asked for his papers. His soldier's book identified him as Joseph Marrer, a teacher in Oberen, on the lower Rhine. I had the distinct feeling that the Alsatian was not setting a trap. While he was removing his clothes, I rushed up the steps of the Chaventré house, cleaned out long ago, and found under the rubble a hunting outfit in English fabric and a pair of golf trousers. Our Joseph was clothed at once. After destroying his uniform and his compromising papers, we took him to the canteen, where he was hired immediately as a kitchen assistant. He would prove to be a reliable help, as we would see later. Just before

nightfall he led my men to his truck to retrieve the supplies; the arms
and the truck itself would be picked up later by the Lonlay maquis.
The whole operation went without a hitch, but leading the two ewes
through dirt roads and alleys was not easy.

That same day, June 19, around 10 A.M., two American "Mustang"
light fighter-bombers collided in a dense fog. One crashed near L'Epinay-le-Comte, the other near the road from Saint-Front to Lucé. One
of the pilots, Captain C. W. Blair, nineteen years old, must have tried
to jump, but too late; he was killed instantly. About thirty Germans
arrived by truck, paid their last respects, and buried him without a
casket. Two days later a Resistance team—Captain Lefèvre, Guesdon,
and Boisgontier, among others—gave him a proper burial.

During the period of the bombardments, we were isolated by a
complete lack of news. The electric power was cut off, so even if we
had had a radio, we could not have used it. Therefore it became urgent
to build a crystal receiving set. I remembered that young Mille had such
a set, and I sent Goupil to buy it from him. René Sonnet found a pair
of earphones in his home, and that very evening we tested our receiving
set; the results exceeded our hopes. I cannot express how invaluable this
set proved to be: it allowed us to follow in detail the battles of Caen
and Avranches and to inform our friends several times a day of the
Allied advance. For over a month either an Englishman or an American
was appointed each night to come over (at one in the morning) to
listen to the American broadcast and to inform his comrades. My boarders used to wait impatiently for this nightly outing. They made bets,
played games of cards and dice, and had contests, each wanting to be
the lucky one selected to listen to the radio.

On the evening of the twenty-first, at chowtime, I had a heated
altercation with a second-rate bureaucrat. It seemed to me that this was
not the best time for rigid enforcement of food control regulations.

On Thursday, June 22, we were advised that a prefectural decree
dated June 15 had named André Timothée mayor of Domfront, the
resignation of the previous mayor and his deputy having been accepted.
In another part of town, the clearing of the Chêne-Vert area was under
way. The badly mutilated bodies of Monsieur and Madame Truffault
and of Mademoiselle Duval were found. The excavations were frequently interrupted by the ceaseless passing of American planes. Robert,

the cooper, dug graves in Dr. Rémon-Beauvais' garden, and the victims were buried. In the evening we all met at Goupil's house to listen to the radio; Sonnet wore the headphones and gave us the news from London and New York. Afterwards we went to patrol the town and discovered that many garages had been broken into and automobiles stolen by the S.S. Everywhere doors had been forced open, houses ransacked, furniture smashed; we were helpless to stop such plunder.

On Friday morning, June 23, we could hear the rumble of bombardments coming from the direction of Saint-Bômer and Saint-Clair. We assumed that the forest of Halouze was the target. Around 11 A.M. an attack on the Caen bridge resulted in one casualty; the Guénerie father, who had refused to evacuate, was killed near his home. The bombs that fell on the surrounding pastures killed many head of cattle. On Saturday, June 24, around noon, the train station was again bombed, resulting in severe damage. We spent the evening moving Monsieur Timothée's furniture out of his house, which had not been ransacked yet. Throughout the night Goupil, Mazurier, and I patrolled the city. German armored convoys, supply trains, and ambulances were crossing the town in both directions, coming from or going to the coast. This intense traffic caused numerous collisions accompanied by screams and insults. The highway police billeted in Domfront under the command of an Austrian sergeant major were directing the convoys and mustering isolated soldiers to move them out by truck—without much success, I might add.

At the firehouse I had built about fifty tire-puncturing apparatuses, which we placed on the roads at night. We sawed wooden boards seven to eight centimeters long by five to six centimeters wide, then placed a sharp nail through each. We placed the boards, nails up, wherever the trucks were going. At dawn we checked the efficacy of our system: most of the boards had split in half under the weight of the vehicles, but the nails stayed in the tires. This procedure was almost infallible; we noted an average failure rate of just 15 percent. In order not to arouse the Boches' suspicion, we made a point of retrieving debris left on the roads before daylight. All this was relatively easy for us because, as members of the Passive Defense, we had various permits and wore helmets. These seemed to impress the occupying troops.

Sunday, June 25, was relatively calm. Despite our efforts, the systematic looting by German troops was increasing. Early that morning we learned that Monsieur Riandière's car had been stolen, and stores and homes were methodically stripped. Unfortunately, the Germans were not the only guilty ones; the doings of a local family, the Contés, attracted our attention, and we resolved to watch them closely. The news on the radio was good: Cherbourg had been taken by the Americans. We spent part of that day at the canteen; there we felt at home and could talk freely. In spite of all the sadness and difficulty of the times, we spent some unforgettable moments there. The canteen was rather picturesque. The front room was furnished with a large stove, a sideboard, two tables, and a sink; the walls were bare except for a large map. The "civilians" took their meals in this room. The second room, just as sparsely furnished (minus the stove), was the firemen's mess. All those who came during these troubled times would never forget the hearty meals that comforted us there.

On June 26 I received a visit from Gabriel Hubert. He was lamenting the loss of the country house he had so tastefully furnished and decorated. He had a valuable collection of paintings and an irreplaceable library. Now all his patient historical researches had come to nothing. I felt very bad for poor Gabriel, and I thought we should try to salvage what little was left of his possessions; I proposed that a few of my best men from the Passive Defense should help him. André Timothée furnished the cartons, and over several days, working nonstop amid the ruins of his house, we were able to salvage a number of precious things that would be stored in the town hall. The operation was not without risks; American squadrons were flying over us several times a day.

Tuesday, June 27, turned out to be a very bad day, with air raids, machine-gun fire, and bombardments throughout the region. The night was even worse: endless formations flew over the area; the rumbling of the cannons sounded closer and closer. From the rectory and from the old castle, we could see sprawling fires lighting up the horizon. Star shells flashing through the sky illuminated the countryside as if it were daylight.

It was imperative to evacuate the paintings and objects of value from the museum as soon as possible, and also to shelter what had been salvaged from Gabriel's house. I could think of only one safe place, the vaulted caves at the estate of my friend Alexandre Bignon, at L'Epinay-le-Comte. We loaded the pumper, and three of the firemen drove the precious cargo. (We figured that a fire truck, with its uniformed men, would be the least likely vehicle to attract the Boches' attention.)

On the afternoon of June 28, while I was quietly working at city hall on some paperwork for the Passive Defense, the door abruptly opened and two big S.S. devils walked in, tommy guns in their hands. They brusquely shoved me aside, searched everywhere, then left without a word. Before I recovered from the shock, I heard them go upstairs. I asked the good Hélène, concierge at city hall—a remarkable woman who never left her post—what was going on: she did not know either. After searching everywhere, the two brutes left. Very puzzled, I headed for the rectory, in search of news. If there was any trouble, it could only come from the rectory, where so many unexpected things were taking place daily. As a matter of fact, Mouzillat informed me, Joseph Marrer, the deserter, had been going out daily with the firemen. One day he found himself face to face with his former commandant from the Das Reich division. No need to dwell on his reaction: it was a disaster. Joseph panicked and ran, even though he might not have been recognized. The puzzled German called two S.S. men and sent them after him. Joseph escaped by the rectory steps and fled toward Flers. From then on it would have been impossible to keep him at the canteen. That evening I sent Mazurier to accompany him to the maquis in Lonlay-l'Abbaye, where he would be promoted from kitchen assistant to head cook.

Also on that day, my friend Goupil, after some laborious negotiations, was able to buy 12,800 francs' worth of tobacco from the warehouse keeper, to ours and the Englishmen's great satisfaction: God knows how much they smoked every day. . . . In the evening there was an argument at the canteen between Mouzillat and the firemen; our cook threatened to turn in his apron, and I went into a fit. Luckily Goupil remained calm and intervened; once more, all ended amicably.

On the twenty-ninth there was more looting. Monsieur Roger's warehouse was ransacked by a group of Germans apparently led by a collaborator; Mazurier and Locoq (the baker) warned the Passive Defense about him. A fire had erupted at rue du Champ-de-Foire, with Daniel's house and the police station in flames; the firemen managed to extinguish the blaze. In the evening we obtained from a German at the postal search service some information concerning the Conté family. A search of their residence, rue Saint-Julien, by Goupil and me revealed stacks of men's and women's clothing, shoes, and bottles of cognac—a stock of obviously stolen goods. The Conté woman and her friend were found in the casemates of the old castle and arrested, to the great relief of Dr. Lévesque, who had been taking shelter there also and was very pleased to be rid of his undesirable neighbors. We advised the public prosecutor in writing, and he arrived in Domfront the following day.

The need for food supplies increased every day, and it became imperative to organize some definitive system. During a meeting with Monsieur Marsollier, we drew up a plan with a board of directors composed of Goupil, Marsollier, and me. The aviators were then alone at my aunt's house; Marie-Louise had been evacuated a few days earlier. I did not have the time to keep them company. The town was still infested with troops, and I worried, with good reason, about them being alone in the large house. One day the S.S. broke into the basement and stole the silverware, the linens, and my Zeiss. While this was going on, my protégés were fearfully hiding in their rooms.

On the morning of June 30, I had a visit from Raymond Guesdon and Maître Erout, a lawyer. We had breakfast at the canteen, and they proposed to take my boarders to the maquis of Lonlay-l'Abbaye. We agreed that they should leave immediately. An hour later Green, Pask, Potten, and the American, Schallehn, left Domfront by bicycle (thanks to Goupil) accompanied by Raymond Guesdon. Around noon that same day a team of young first-aiders arrived from Alençon; we found them a cantonment near Saint-Front. All day long the looting got worse; the firemen and the few men of the Passive Defense were unable to stop it. We were faced not only with the S.S. from the routed Das Reich division, but also with the Todt factory workers, who were becoming bolder than ever and who penetrated everywhere.

At 10 P.M. there was a serious alarm while we were at the canteen: a house in the Notre-Dame district and an adjacent warehouse were burning. For the past few days these two buildings had been prey to marauding German troops (trucks were parked there from morning to evening). The Germans were helped, alas, by some unscrupulous Frenchmen. The Boches were drunk; they threw matches to the ground, and the alcohol—of which there was a great quantity—caught fire. The firemen left immediately, and I accompanied André Timothée to Notre-Dame. For hours we viewed the destruction of what used to be a beautiful warehouse. The firemen, helped by National Rescue crews, fought the flames all night long. Despite their efforts the flames, fueled by casks of alcohol, could not be controlled. Nevertheless, our brave and tenacious firemen managed to limit the fire to the two buildings. Their action saved the Notre-Dame district from certain devastation.

On Saturday, July 1, the buildings were still smoldering, and the firemen continued their efforts. During the day the public prosecutor gave orders to transfer the Conté family from the municipal lockup to the prison. As usual, in the evening we patrolled the town. As we were making our rounds, we deployed here and there our tire-puncturing devices. We were certain of their effectiveness, and this encouraged us to expand our little industry.

On Sunday, July 2, a mass was celebrated at the Church of the Miséricorde by the Reverend Bazin: one could have counted on his fingers the number of the faithful who attended. It should be mentioned here that the courageous nuns never left town and never ceased to provide devoted care to the sick. Goupil went to Lonlay to fetch his bicycle, which he had loaned to evacuate my English and American boarders. Upon his return he told me that the presence of the airmen in Lonlay had not gone unnoticed. I was beginning to feel that it would have been better not to have sent them there. Around 9 P.M. I was warned that the Germans wanted to take my Juva. Until then, I had been concerned with the fate of many cars . . . but not mine. My Renault was parked at the rear of my garage on rue des Fossés-Plissons. Accompanied by a couple of firemen, Goupil and I ran immediately to the garage; a German truck was waiting in front of the door, which had been staved in. Not inclined to acquiesce easily, we had a heated discussion with the S.S., who finally gave in, but not until we showed them all our papers. From the attitude of the occupiers, I foresaw that there would be much to fear in the future.

On Monday, July 3, Monsieur Barbier, a division chief, was our guest at the canteen. He was in charge of reorganizing the Passive Defense, whose leader had resigned. The day was rather calm. I received

a visit from Raymond Guesdon, who brought me news of the American
and the three Englishmen: they were still with the Underground of
Lonlay, but because they had been moving about the farms in the area
with the maquis fighters, their presence was beginning to be known.
The Châlet had not yet been visited, and I could count on the precious
help of men such as Raymond Fouré and Gondoin, so I decided, with
the approval of Goupil and Guesdon, to get my airmen back to Domfront as soon as possible. We planned their immediate return.

On Tuesday, July 4, Monsieur Barbier called a meeting at city hall
to ask André Timothée if he would accept the duties of mayor. Monsieur Timothée accepted, providing that Goupil and I assist him. Then
an order was drafted recalling all members of the Passive Defense to
Domfront. It would not have much effect, and neither would the in-
dividual summonses mailed a few days later. By prefectural decree, I
was appointed chief of the Passive Defense. On the fifth and sixth of
July, the bridges and highways department began tearing down those
walls damaged by the bombardments. They were short of personnel,
and I frequently sent some of my men to assist them.

Gabriel Hubert had been back in Domfront since July 4. After talking it over, we decided to transfer the contents of his library, the books
of Confessions, and the museum pieces to L'Épinay-le-Comte. Bazille,
from Ambloux, agreed to handle the transfer, which would take place
during the night of July 6. At dawn a large truck camouflaged with
branches pulled up to the city hall. The loading took just a few minutes.
Then, taking advantage of darkness, Bazille sneaked the truck into a
German convoy (he would part from the convoy at the Égrenne bridge
to reach Épinay, where the precious cargo would be stored in a vaulted
cave). This accomplished, we returned immediately to Ambloux, where
Bazille concealed his truck in a pasture. After a little rest at the local
mill, we left in the morning with a cart loaded with flour. We had just
started down the road when we heard the machine-gun fire of "Mustangs" over the countryside. Despite the distance (seventeen kilometers)
and my swollen legs, we returned on foot; we arrived in Domfront
about 11 A.M.

Early that afternoon Len and the three Englishmen arrived at the
Châlet after an epic trip through the fields of Sainte-Anne hill and the
Tanneries under the energetic lead of Raymond Fouré. They arrived

just in time to view a beautiful display of fireworks; the American bomber command had decided to blow up the rocky Sainte-Anne hill, probably attempting to destroy what was left of the railroad tracks and the road. For about an hour the "Lightnings" furiously bombarded the rocks, without great success. Splinters of bombs and fragments of rock were flying everywhere. The homes in the Tanneries district absorbed the brunt of the attack. I ran to the Châlet, where I found my boarders lying on their stomachs in the basement while firmly holding a rope tied to the door. They were a pitiful sight, and I could not help telling them what they were missing and that it was less interesting being underground than above. This attack gave us a wonderful opportunity: one of the firemen and a member of the Passive Defense told us that a partially disabled German truck had been abandoned at the foot of the hill. Four men (Lechevallier, Labrit, Fleury, and Tachet) went to inspect the truck. It was loaded with five 200-liter barrels of fuel, gasoline most likely. Four of the barrels were immediately rolled down in the tall grass, but the fifth had to be thrown into the river when our lookout warned us that two Boches were coming to retrieve their vehicle. These two idiots left without even checking the contents of their truck. Not wasting any time, our men opened a barrel. Alas, it was not gasoline, but white gas-oil. Still, it could be used for the canteen's oil lamps and for the fire pump. The contents of the opened barrel were carried across the rocky hill in ten-liter cans and stored at city hall. By evening the men were exhausted. René Sonnet used the fire truck to pick up the remaining three barrels. These would be stored in the transformer station behind city hall, out of the inquisitive Germans' sight.

Toward the end of the afternoon, as I was going back to Domfront from the Tanneries, I noticed ahead of me a small German truck heading downtown. At the same time, a formation of American patrol planes appeared in the sky. The two Germans immediately abandoned their truck and ran for cover. When I reached the vehicle, I took a look at its contents, which included German clothing, two or three crates of equipment—no arms as far as I could tell—and a jerry can full of gasoline. The opportunity was too good to pass up; I opened the can and toppled it, then lit a match. The truck burst into flames. Then, very calmly, I took the steps leading to city hall and returned to my office, just thirty meters away. The effect was immediate: soon I heard the firemen shouting from the terrace of the rectory while contemplating the column of black smoke rising from the nearby road. I pretended to be as surprised as they were. To our great delight, the truck kept burning for two hours. July 7 was truly a day well spent.

Saturday, July 8, was much quieter. The weather was miserable, and the low clouds prevented American patrol planes from flying over the region. We continued to do our best to pursue the looters. Nothing out of the ordinary was happening, so I was able for the first time to spend all afternoon with my boarders. I tried to teach them a few French military songs. Their goodwill was obvious, and Charlie's accent was indescribable when he sang: "Quand je vois que je n'ai plus / De poils sur le cuir chevelu . . ." ("When I see that I don't have any more hair on my scalp . . .").

Obtaining food was getting more difficult. We had to feed only four boarders, but having nothing else to do, they ate and smoked like ten. Thanks to favorable circumstances and Goupil's purchase, they were amply supplied with "Nicot's herb." The only butcher in town who had stayed at her shop must often have wondered how my father could have such an appetite, since I was pretending to be shopping for him. While on patrol in the evening, I ran across Medelkopf—the Austrian sergeant major I mentioned earlier who was in charge of the highway police—and we had a long talk. Incidentally, our relations with him had always been fine. He had a perilous job; regrouping the runaway S.S. troops and sending them back to the front was not without risks. He often had to ask for our assistance, and in return he frequently helped us. After a while Goupil and I took our leave and went to set out our tire-puncturing boards.

On Sunday, July 9, the good weather was favorable to air raids. During mass a plane flew very low over the center of town and, said Goupil, it gave you a chill. At noon the canteen was busier than ever because of the presence of the young first-aiders. Nevertheless, Mouzillat was equal to the task.

Monday morning, Goupil heard that Madame Pottier's van was in the hands of the Germans; he took at once the many necessary steps to have the vehicle returned to its owner. An unexpected diversion occurred after lunch. Around 2 P.M., I decided to go to the Châlet with Monsieur Barbier, Raymond Guesdon, and a couple of other friends.

My home was vacant, my boarders as usual being at my aunt's house. From the Promenades I noticed with great surprise that one of the shutters of the Châlet was open. I rushed inside, followed by my friends. Dashing into the large bedroom, I found myself face to face with three little Germans from the Das Reich division who had been awakened by my untimely visit. They became panicky at being surrounded by so many visitors. We ordered them to follow us; one, smarter than the others, escaped through the roof, but the other two sheepishly and reluctantly followed us to city hall, where I forced them to pay three hundred francs to Monsieur Marsollier, who had never before seen this species of taxpayer. Because they were tired and asked if they could sleep, we locked them up in the municipal jail after having searched them from head to toe. One of the little bastards had taken several things, including a set of keys to the Châlet. They were set free the following day, not too proud of their escapade. Lucky for them that I had ordered my men to let them go.

On July 11, the three men sent by Captain Lefèvre to help me with the Passive Defense arrived. They were led by René Leray, a tall man, built like Hercules. A specialist in policing the city, René would prove to be of great service to us. He had a unique way of "ejecting" Boches from homes, and I never saw him back away from anybody. One day in particular, he delivered some well-placed kicks to two S.S. men he found sleeping in a bed in Chaventré's house. We had a little problem when we met a German officer who became upset at the sight of the enormous wooden cudgel with a nail at the end that Leray carried. We explained that the stick was to go after French looters, but the German was no fool; he shouted, "You, French, not correct, you terrorists!"

Some of the Todt factory mercenaries had invaded the town and looted the Grand-Carrefour district. René Leray caught one of their leaders, gave him a good beating, then took him to city hall, where he was detained for two days without food. This had a salutary warning effect on the others. During his stay in Domfront, Leray and his men retrieved the loot taken by two pillagers by pelting them in the face with some well-aimed eggs. These same good men put a stop to the thefts at Monsieur Chevalier's house and at the Chassé store, where the Boches were stealing—of all things—bedside table lamps. They also put an end to a bonfire in a house near the gendarmerie and to an "organ recital" given in the church by German soldiers of the antiair-craft battery. Occasionally they "borrowed" a wheel from a German truck being repaired at Gilard's or "found" a jerry can of gasoline left on the sidewalk by a distracted S.S.

At lunchtime we had a visit at the canteen from two unsavory char-acters from the C.O.S.I. (Coopération pour Organisation Sécurité In-térieure); they said they were delegates from Paris. Our welcome was quite cool. They looked like they should not be trusted, and during the meal we exchanged some sharp words. They clearly realized that they were in unfriendly company, and they left without knowing how lucky they were. Ah, if only I could have foreseen my fate.

In the evening there was a commotion at Goupil's house. Our little wireless radio had been working beautifully and incessantly; it was really a godsend. But that night, while Goupil was listening to the radio and waiting for the American's nightly visit, his house was invaded by a dozen runaway S.S. men. It was almost midnight. Startled, Goupil had just enough time to pull the tablecloth over the radio. Despite his pro-tests, he had to put up the soldiers for the night in his attic. Even this did not stop our friend Schallehn from listening to the news from New York at one in the morning.

On Wednesday, July 12, I was out as usual until two or three in the morning. For weeks I had slept only a few hours at night, and I was very tired. My ankles were so swollen that it was impossible to put my shoes on, and my face was badly bruised from a fall at the Châlet. Goupil's undesirable boarders left for Flers early in the morning, and then we could breathe easier. Later we were informed that Mademoi-selle Esnault's house had been ransacked. I went there with Goupil and Mademoiselle Deverre. It was a total disaster; everything had been turned upside down. We could not even walk into the rooms without stepping on something. I asked two of my men to help Mademoiselle Deverre salvage whatever valuable articles were left and to store them at La Juvinière. That day the weather was beautiful, but we did not appreciate it because it meant a resumption of air raids all day long.

On July 13 the firemen and Passive Defense members were getting ready to celebrate our national holiday in style. The energetic Madame Goupil arrived in the evening to spend the holiday with her husband. She invited André Timothée, Captain Sarrazin (department chief of the

Passive Defense), and me to lunch. She had prepared an excellent meal, and we all had a good time despite the uncertainty of the future.

On the evening of July 14, there was a great celebration at the canteen for about forty of us. The two rooms had been cleaned and decorated, and it looked as if all the flags and garlands at city hall had been gathered here. The men were pretty excited, and the celebration went on all night long. Five or six times we sang the "Marseillaise" at the top of our lungs, all windows open. The night ended with more patriotic songs, and before we knew it, it was daybreak. Our celebration had been wonderful, marred only by the departure of two firemen who had to take to the asylum of Mayenne a poor fellow from Saint-Bômer who had suddenly gone mad.

On Saturday, July 15, Madame Goupil returned to the Mayenne with her husband. It looked like the day was going to be rather calm until around 4 P.M., when a deputy of the mayor of Lonlay-l'Abbaye informed me of the imminent arrival of 240 American soldiers taken prisoner in Saint-Lô and of their German escorts. We were given orders to prepare a meal and to provide sleeping quarters. I advised André Timothée at once (he was in Saint-Bômer) and hastily gathered my men. Mouzillat, the cook, would take care of the meals, and as far as lodging was concerned, there was only one place possible, the Sacré Coeur school. I called all the available personnel, and we got to work. We were short of manpower, and I asked Albert Hochet, the mechanic, and his son to pitch in. They cleaned the washing vats we used to boil potatoes, and they peeled the vegetables. Mouzillat lighted the ovens, and the Passive Defense men brought the fuel. The firemen drove to Saint-Front for the cold meats, the bread, and the cheeses. The dining hall was very large, and despite the numerous lootings we found enough dinnerware to accommodate the expected crowd in two seatings. About 7 P.M. the long line of troops arrived on foot: 240 soldiers of all colors from all the states of America, from Mexico to Canada, from California to Virginia. They were surrounded by about twenty Boches under the command of a brutish-looking sergeant major.

He wanted to demonstrate right away who was boss, so he ordered me to bring to the middle of the courtyard a washing vat full of soup, into which the men would plunge their mess tins. This was not exactly what I had planned; I explained that there was a large dining hall ready with all the necessary tableware, that two sentinels were enough to guard the exits, and that I had prepared a special table for twenty guards. Faced with my persistence, he began to soften, and finally he acceded to my wishes. I think the Americans could have kissed me. They were accompanied by just one officer, a young lieutenant, formerly a journalist in Trenton, New Jersey, whose name was Fontaine. We conversed in English. During the battle of Saint-Lô, his group had advanced too far and could not receive supplies—food, arms, and ammunition—and had to surrender. I also got acquainted with the noncommissioned officers, among them a French-Canadian sergeant who spoke German very well and served as interpreter with the Boches. There were also two Mexicans in the group; one insisted on trading a dollar for a cigarette. I gave him and his comrades all the tobacco I could lay my hands on. They were all optimistic and raised their thumbs as a sign of hope.

They would spend the night in the dormitory of the school. In small groups accompanied by guards, the soldiers went to the German depot of Champ de Foire to get straw. The meal we prepared in less than two hours consisted of beef soup (one hundred liters), cold meats, boiled potatoes, and cheese. I wanted to serve wine with dinner, but because the Germans objected, we had—with the consent of the American lieutenant—to employ a ruse. Many soldiers complained of dysentery, so I sent for Dr. Lévesque, who prescribed hot red wine. A few bottles distributed to the German guards suppressed their scruples, and almost all of the men had wine with their meal. During the dinner we received a visit from Monsieur Barbier of the prefecture, accompanied by Goupil, who had returned to help me. The straw was spread out, and by pretending that the guards' job would be made easier if they spent the night downstairs, I managed to let the Americans occupy the large dormitory upstairs, where a few beds were available, while the twenty German guards slept on straw in a small room downstairs.

While all this was taking place, I was able to speak freely with Lieutenant Fontaine. I informed him of the presence of four airmen in my home and asked if he wanted to escape. Clearly the temptation was great, but being the only officer in the group, he felt it would be an act of cowardice to abandon his men. I respected his decision and did not insist, but I did ask him to facilitate the escape of those soldiers who had already made up their minds to flee. I gave him all the necessary information regarding the area, including the location of shelters. The results were good; the next morning, sixteen soldiers escaped between Domfront and Juvigny-sous-Andaines and found refuge in friendly homes.

We agreed to comply with the instructions of the German sergeant to be at the school at 4 A.M. to prepare a meal before their departure; but I specifically asked him to calm the ardor of the machine gunners posted at the four corners of the school because, when I arrived at dawn, I did not feel like being shot full of holes like a colander. Early in the morning we arrived at the school to light the ovens and prepare a meal identical to the one served the previous evening. Before leaving, the Boches refused to give me any requisition vouchers, claiming that the city of Domfront was rich enough to pay the lodging costs. I argued that the city had been partially destroyed and was now practically deserted—and broke. This protest was in vain. Then the American lieutenant intervened through his interpreter: "If the Germans do not pay, the U.S. government will pay the expenses." He gave me a voucher stating that the city had served five hundred meals to his men and had provided one night's lodging. (This voucher would be found on my person at the time of my arrest and would greatly puzzle the Gestapo.) Then, by way of the abattoirs and the burg of Saint-Front, we reached the Couterne road. Walking in my stocking feet between the German sergeant major and the American lieutenant, I led the convoy. As we reached the main road, we passed the horse-drawn cart of Gontier, the butcher, who was on his way to the market in Saint-Front to sell his cold cuts. He stopped his horses, and realizing that he was in the presence of Allies, he distributed his sausages and pâtés to the soldiers—right under the noses of the flabbergasted Boches—until his cart was totally emptied. Then he declared, "Well now, the sale is over."

(Since then I have realized that I lacked audacity and missed a great opportunity. There were 240 American prisoners under the guard of 20 Boches. During the night we could have called on the help of Captain Lefèvre and his men from the maquis of Lonlay, taken the guards by surprise, and distributed the Americans in the homes of trusted friends in the area or, if need be, armed them and used their help. Because most communications had been cut off, including the telephone, the German services in Alençon, probably the only ones aware of the arrival of the prisoners—and even this was not certain—would not have been alerted.)

Around 10 A.M., after parting from the convoy on the Couterne road, I returned to Domfront. I learned, thanks to our radio, that things were going well: Grodno had been taken, and the Russians were seventy kilometers away from eastern Prussia. At the Châlet, Len and Tom were anxiously waiting for me. Hidden among the rocks, they had observed the arrival of their compatriots the previous evening, and they had many questions. Around 4 P.M. a violent air battle between a "Mustang" and two F.W. 190s took place east of Domfront. One of the latter was shot down. We heard later that it crashed near Perrou, and that the German pilot sustained a broken leg. In the evening we found out that the American fighter-bomber, also in trouble, had crashed to the right of the forest road from Champsecret to L'Étoile, five hundred meters from Gué-Vallier. The Resistance informed me that the pilot had parachuted and landed at L'Être-Guérin on the farm of Lafontaine, who took him in. Immediately I sent one of the maquis to bring him to me. He was Lieutenant Thomas Watkins Cannon, twenty-two years old, a student of medicine and pharmacy in Memphis, Tennessee. Once more we had a celebration at the Châlet to welcome a newcomer. He was likable and talkative; he related the air battle, told us about his parents, his four brothers and three sisters. It was very late by the time we retired.

On July 17 I stayed at the Châlet most of the morning. The number of my boarders had increased, and I had to look after them. I stressed to them that they had to exercise the utmost caution. In the evening, upon my return from patrol through the town, I found the three British airmen in a very perturbed state. While rummaging through some drawers, Len had found a set of dice (he had become more daring now that he had a countryman with him). Right away, a game of zanzi began between the two Americans and the three Englishmen. As I mentioned earlier, all the airmen had with them when they crashed in France was three thousand francs in hundred-franc notes. It did not take long for the two Americans to strip the Englishmen of their nine thousand francs. The winners were obviously boastful about their victory, and the whole episode nearly turned into a quarrel.

On July 18 Goupil decided to make two or three trips to move his furniture to Mayenne. He borrowed Monsieur Pottier's van—retrieved from the Boches—but the vehicle had been stripped, so we spent all of the next day trying to find replacement parts in ransacked service stations. Also on the nineteenth, we helped recover the bodies of two victims of the bombardments found by the first-aid team. We increased the patrols as looting and abusive demands increased. The S.S. of the Das Reich division had converted the military barracks into a large hospital for soldiers with minor injuries. The S.S. went out between 4 P.M. and 9 P.M. and systematically plundered houses. This forced us to portion out our work in order to patrol constantly and stop the ruffians from breaking down doors and windows. We strode up and down the streets every night, listening in front of each house for a "green rat" inside, ready to throw him out. While on patrol the firemen found a three-dimensional German survey map in the home of an attorney in La Croix-du-Faubourg, and they destroyed it.

Goupil, who was of such help to us, agreed to move some valuable items belonging to my aunt together with his own furnishings. The mayor, André Timothée, came to town daily from Saint-Bômer to take care of business. We were still subject to unfair demands and threats from the S.S. They came to city hall several times a day in search of furniture, radios, bedding, and food. They pulled out of gardens whatever vegetables were left.

On July 21, as was usual each Friday, there was great activity at the canteen. It was the day when the Domfront refugees came from the surrounding countryside to pick up their food supplies at the former rectory. The greengrocer, Monsieur Carré, had been willing to handle the allocation and had not missed the distribution once. At noon the regular customers gathered for lunch: Daligault, Cosson, Lafaye, Leclerc, Mustière . . . as well as those who had not totally abandoned their city. During the night a small truck loaded with tobacco from the warehouse in Le Mans arrived. We quickly unloaded the vehicle and hid its contents from the greedy S.S. The firemen handled the job efficiently.

Very early on July 22, Goupil returned to town and agreed to make one last trip to my friends' property in L'Épinay-le-Comte. We left with a truckload of valuables from city hall, some rare books belonging to Hubert, and many other things. In the evening the "brothers," Len and Cannon, listened to the radio. The news was very good: there had been an attempt upon Hitler's life, and there were signs of revolt in Germany.

On July 23 I heard from Goupil that young Lesellier, notary clerk in Lonlay-l'Abbaye, had been taken to the barracks following an argument with the S.S. We decided to go to the guardhouse and try to get him out. After a half-hour wait we were taken to an S.S. lieutenant; he was as cold and as unpleasant as could be. He told us the reason for the arrest was that the young clerk was at Martin's farm in Saint-Front, somewhat "warmed up" by several cups of coffee liberally spiked with liquor, when two S.S. men walked in to buy eggs and butter. The clerk said loudly to the farmer's wife, "Don't give anything to these bastards!" Unfortunately, one of the "bastards" understood French, and Lesellier was arrested at once. We pleaded in his favor, explaining that he had children and that he had been drinking too much. The lieutenant listened to us carefully and appeared to share our point of view, but in the end he brusquely refused to set Lesellier free. As we were standing near the door ready to leave, the lieutenant shook Goupil's hand, then extended his hand toward me. Pretending not to see his gesture, I kept my hands in my pockets. Obviously, this was an insult; the officer turned livid and said, "You are refusing to shake hands with a German officer?" I protested that I did not respond because I had not seen his gesture. He did not seem to believe me, and the consequences of this incident could have been serious; but after a moment of hesitation, he opened the door roughly. On our way back to Domfront, Goupil told me that he had thought for a moment that I was going to be arrested. He did not want me to accompany him to the barracks again. But I was pleased that I had not shaken hands with the Boche. And, finally, our intervention was not entirely useless; a very embarrassed Lesellier was set free the next morning. The evening was busy: setting of nails on the roads, patrols, then supper at the Châlet with the airmen. Later the two Americans went to Goupil's house to listen to the radio. Then they returned to the Châlet, where we spent more time around the dinner table; the night would be short.

Monday, July 24, was a rather calm day. We continued to chase the looters and recorded the license numbers of several German trucks loaded with stolen articles and furniture. In the afternoon two S.S. officers showed up at city hall and threatened to arrest André Timothée and me if the coal fire burning in the distillery since June 3 was not put out completely within twenty-four hours. It was no small job: there were tons and tons of coal. Besides, the flames served as a beacon to British and American aircraft, and I was aware of the danger the firemen would be exposed to. Gathered in haste, they left immediately for the distillery and spent all night and part of the next doing this perilous work.

In the evening André Geslin arrived on his bicycle and asked to see me in private. From his expression I could tell it was something important. He asked me, "Does your promise of last year still stand?" (When he had given shelter to the Americans, he had refused to accept money—I did not have much to offer—and instead had said, "All I am asking is that if I run into trouble, you take care of my wife and my two little ones.") Then he explained what had happened. He was hiding in his home a Madame L., supposedly secretary for the Resistance. A young woman from Giel denounced her to the Germans, and on July 21 the Gestapo (three Germans and a dozen militiamen) surrounded his farm. While Geslin and his wife were submitted to interrogation, Madame L. walked in. To make her confess, the Gestapo decided to put her through the "water test." They asked Geslin for a washtub and sent him to get water from the pasture. A German went with him on the first trip; the second time he went alone. The attention of the policemen being concentrated on Madame L., Geslin made signs to his wife to leave. Once she and the children were gone, he fetched his gun from the bakehouse and fired at the group before he fled. The young woman accompanying the Germans was injured as well as a militiaman. In revenge the policemen went to the farm a second time, set fire to the buildings, and took two pigs and a few chickens. I told Geslin, "Go get your wife and your oldest child"—the other was in Perrou. "You have been taking care of Americans in your home; now you will do the same thing here." So at nightfall, our new helper and his family moved into the Châlet. The house was really getting full.

On Tuesday, July 25, there was much aircraft activity late in the morning; bombs were dropped randomly over the countryside. The train station and the village of La Trappe were hit by machine-gun fire. At noon a furious Gabriel Hubert arrived at the canteen: one of his greatest pleasures was to cultivate his vineyard and make his own wine. He had stored in his home a number of small casks labeled with different colors, and he had just discovered one in the firemen's quarters. This discovery led to a bitter argument followed by the dispatching of a delegation—including the mayor, no less—to inspect said quarters. Finally the matter was resolved; it was of so little importance compared to the rest.

On July 26, around 6:00 A.M., an American reconnaissance plane was flying low over the town. Some action soon followed: at 8:45 A.M. bombers attacked the railroad bridge at the Varenne, facing Tertre-Chapon. One bomb hit the water; another fell behind the city hall of La Haute-Chapelle. We were all on the alert and wondered whether they were going to stop at that. A little later there was an attack on Torchamp, followed by another around Domfront. Toward the end of the afternoon, I received a surprising visit from a contractor from Flers, a longtime acquaintance (I had no idea he was active in the Resistance). He walked into my office at city hall and declared point-blank that he was aware I had been sheltering Allied airmen—how the devil did he know? Then, disregarding my vehement denials, he informed me that Mademoiselle Dubocq from Beauchêne had been hiding four aviators for some time, but was facing problems that intensified every day. Her property was near the road used by the convoys; isolated German soldiers were scouring the countryside, and her home had already been occupied several times. It was also impossible to obtain food supplies. He asked me first to procure some bread for her, and second, to give shelter to her protégés. I answered that I was at his disposal and gave him a note to take to Derouet, our flour supplier in Saint-Front. (I learned much later that he received a rather cool welcome from our baker, who complied nevertheless, ultimately realizing that my request had been made for an urgent reason.) I am sure he now doesn't regret that he gave the bread that day.

July 27 was rather calm. At home the atmosphere had remained a little tense between the three Englishmen and the two Americans since the zanzi game during which the Britishers lost all their money. The airmen argued frequently. American equipment, said the Americans, is better than British equipment. Not true, replied the Englishmen. One of the Britishers was a radio operator, another a navigator, and the third a mechanic; the Americans were fighter-bomber pilots. That rascal Len, putting on airs, often declared, "I would not want to be a passenger." I felt it would be wise to separate them and to transfer one "clan" to l'Ermitage. I informed Bourgoin, and it was decided that at noon I would accompany the three Englishmen to Tertre-Frileuse, where Roger Pépin would meet them with his horse-drawn carriage. So the three men and I went down the Cent-Marches, took the usual pathway of Château-Gohier, and reached Frileuse. Because we were very early, we stopped at La Noë-Blanche, where Girault, the owner, offered us a bottle of Anjou wine. At the agreed-upon time, the carriage appeared; the three men quickly climbed onto the seat next to the driver, and they were off. I never saw my English protégés again.

Since 1940 our friend Pépin had been scoffing at and harassing the Boches with mounting enthusiasm. He started modestly, as soon as they arrived, by stealing a chestnut horse from the German park in Briouze—even though the animal was carefully guarded by two armed sentries. He soon progressed to "borrowing" automobiles, trucks, even a mare tied up behind a forage wagon, cutting off the rope right under the nose of the dozing driver. Pépin was also a specialist in acts of war: the transfer of arms by light vehicle or cart in the midst of German convoys; the destruction by petards (small paper bombs), in less than a month, of about twenty German trucks; and the execution by machine gun, in the middle of the village and in broad daylight, of six Germans waiting in their parked truck. These, in short, were the accomplishments of this tall fellow known to the airmen as "Monsieur Parapluie" (Mr. Umbrella).

I returned quietly to the Châlet, where I found the Americans in very good spirits. They had done the housework and were lying out in the sun. Len, incorrigible, did not call me by my name, but always addressed me as "All is crushed." He gave me this nickname because every time I returned after a bombardment, I would say, "All is crushed" with a desolate expression on my face, and the angrier I was, the harder he would laugh. Whenever I was out, the Americans were guarded by one of the Passive Defense auxiliaries; Raymond Fouré, Leray, Gandon, Morin, and Nobis took turns watching over them. I had to let go of Urbansky, who had abandoned his post without notifying me.

By July 28 the looting was getting worse than ever; the number of Boches who had deserted increased every day. They hid everywhere, they were famished, and more and more were trying to get civilian clothes. The men from the Todt factory could not work anymore on

the railway; no longer being paid, or receiving food, they helped themselves. Despite our protests to their superiors, the patients treated at the
barracks hospital continued to break into private residences. I did not
know of one home in Domfront that hadn't been plundered. The closer
the battlefront approached, the more difficult the Germans were to deal
with, and the more tense our relations. We were exposed to threats of
all kinds. Their demands became unbearable; they wanted furniture,
radios, tobacco, everything. We had to resort to tricks to get rid of
them, and frequently I had to request the help of the Austrian, Medelkopf.

On July 29 and 30 there was increased air traffic, in imposing formations. Day and night, motorized troops, tanks, cannons, and hospital
convoys were constantly passing by. The night sky was lit up by flares
and fires; from time to time the countryside was illuminated as if it
were broad daylight. This brightness generally preceded the dropping
of bombs. We could clearly see the two battlefronts: the front of Caen
behind the town hall, and the front of Avranches on the Promenades.
Domfront, because of its location, was caught in a vise. Toward the end
of the morning, I received a visit from Mademoiselle Dubocq. It had
become impossible for her to keep her protégés any longer. Her house
was continually invaded by Germans in search of food and shelter for
the night. I told her that I would gladly take charge of her airmen
immediately.

On July 31 there was a new bombardment of the train station, the
distillery, and the nearby coal warehouse. Later that morning a man of
about twenty-five, with thick lips and a brutish face, asked for me. He
wore a fawn-colored leather coat and a cap, and he said he had been
sent by the gendarme Bruneau, whom he had met in Saint-Brice-en-
Passais. The man told me he was from Caen and had had to flee the
town before the battle; he added that he was a member of the Resistance group there, but said he had lost all communication with his comrades. He said he would like to join the group in Domfront. The gendarme had supposedly told him that I was the only one who could
direct him to the leader of the local Resistance. I was rather surprised
by his request (I could not figure out why Bruneau, who knew practically nothing of my involvement in the Resistance, would send me
this stranger). Without hesitation, I told the man that I had never done

any work for the Resistance and that I really did not know who could give him any information. I added that, as chief of the Passive Defense in a partially destroyed city, I had other things to worry about. As the man kept insisting, I became even more suspicious. To get rid of him, I told him I would make some inquiries and let him know if I found anything. Satisfied or not, he had no choice but to leave. That evening the coal was still burning in the distillery, and once more the exhausted firemen had to battle the flames all night, until 6 A.M.

Tuesday, August 1, was an eventful day. Around 9:30 A.M. there was heavy bombardment on the train station—about ten bombs—and American fighter planes harassed the convoys of armor and trucks on every road. Around 5:00 P.M. there were new attacks on the railroad tracks and the surrounding countryside. The action continued through the night, and there were rumors that the towns of Pontaubault, Ducey, and Bény-Bocage had been taken. Something was certainly going on; without respite, German convoys of all kinds—coming from the front—passed through the town in the midst of indescribable confusion, and there were numerous patrols by American fighters. Around 1:00 A.M. there was a bombardment on Bois-Halé. A piece of heavy artillery shipped from Mortain, where it had been stationed on the railways for a long time, arrived at the Domfront station during the night; no doubt the attacks would redouble.

On August 2 Mademoiselle Dubocq arrived in the afternoon. She told me her airmen were on their way from Beauchêne and asked that I send someone to meet them. Leray and Geslin left immediately while I headed back to the Châlet, where I waited for them, as planned, at the Cents-Marches. Len and Cannon danced with joy at the thought of the arrival of their compatriots. I had just reached the steps when I spotted, on the other side of the railroad tracks, the four men walking in single file, accompanied by Leray and Geslin. They were Captain Kenneth E. Hagan (pilot), Lieutenant Adolph Willmont Kalbfleisch (copilot), Sergeant Joseph Elmer Porter (machine gunner), and Sergeant Edward Nabozny (radio operator). I was able to obtain plenty of food, so that evening we had a feast at the Châlet. Len and Cannon were delighted to have new company, and they all related their stories. The new arrivals had attempted to cross the lines in the Caen region, but had had to retreat hastily after several failures. Undoubtedly these experiences had had a sobering effect on them; I noticed that they were much calmer than most of their comrades. Now the Châlet was "full," and setting up everyone for the night was no small job. Finally it was agreed that two of the Americans, Geslin, and his wife and child would sleep on the second floor; the others would sleep on mattresses in the drawing room. Before leaving, around midnight, I repeated to Geslin and the Americans, "Always be on your guard; one can never tell what will happen, and I could be arrested." I recall very well the reply of Captain Hagan: "Oh, but there is no reason why you would be arrested." Since then I have often thought about this conversation, which, alas, was a bad omen. After my usual nightly patrol, I returned about 2 A.M. to my room at my aunt's house. I thought about my new boarders and about their hostess, Mademoiselle Dubocq, who later told me her adventures (see Appendix).

16

THE ORDEAL

On the morning of August 3, 1944, I was up very early. Before washing up, I wanted to go to the canteen for breakfast. Usually I didn't leave without my Browning 7.65, which I had been carrying since mid-June, but that morning, by chance, I left it on my nightstand. At the canteen Mouzillat prepared my usual breakfast of two fried eggs, turned over. I had just sat down at my table when the man who had asked me several times before to introduce him to the Resistance group came in. Once more he asked if I could direct him to someone; once more I answered that I had no information, and further, that I was not aware of the existence of a Resistance group and did not know who its leader might be. The man insisted a little, drank his coffee, and left. Luckily for him I was not suspicious: it would have been easy for me to execute him right there in the canteen and dispose of him.

After breakfast, as I was walking to town hall, two young Parisian members of the Red Cross came up to me and said that they needed leather linings for their helmets. Soon we were joined by a refugee from Le Havre who had been working as a secretary at town hall since the bombardments. Our little group was conversing at the bottom of the steps when we noticed two tall men in beige trench coats coming from rue Saint-Julien. I learned later that the shorter one—blond, speaking French with a German accent—was Hans Roegler, assistant chief of the Gestapo of the Orne and by profession a trader at the stock exchange in Berlin. The other man—dark hair, height about five feet ten inches—was Bernard Jardin, militia chief of the Orne group called Action. They were walking toward us, and I assumed they were delegates from the prefecture, or with the supplies services, or perhaps just refugees from the evacuated region.

They came up to our group, and suddenly, from underneath their coats, they drew guns and aimed at us. Jardin shouted, "German police! Raise your hands!" Then he asked for our papers. As I handed over my identity card, he nodded to Roegler, and I realized it was me they were interested in. Immediately they handcuffed us and tied us two by two— the young men from the Red Cross together, the secretary with me. From his office Monsieur Marsollier heard our voices below the window. He came out and saw us. He asked me what was going on, and I replied, "They've asked me for my papers." Jardin turned around, and Monsieur Marsollier noticed his weapon and understood. The two men harshly ordered him to go away. At the same moment, I saw Emile Goupil coming toward us. He had noticed that something was going on as he opened the shutters of his bedroom window, and he was very puzzled. I wanted to keep him from coming any closer and being arrested, so when he was still at a certain distance I shouted, "Goupil, I have been arrested; please inform the mayor!" He turned back immediately toward the canteen, and I could hear him shouting, "Rougeyron has been arrested." But Goupil was followed by a third man (Pierrot Durut), whom I had not noticed earlier, and he was also put into handcuffs. I noticed that Jardin was holding a sheet of paper on which I could read Gilard's name underlined in red and, a few lines below, my own name, also underlined, with a notation, "Is often seen around city hall." Gilard and Goupil would also see this document.

Flanked by Roegler and Jardin, we left city hall, passed by rue du Docteur-Barrabé, and reached the Grande-Rue. We were followed at a short distance by Soureilhan, the tax comptroller; he wanted to find out where we were being taken. As we reached the Place du Tribunal, Jardin turned around brusquely, menacing Soureilhan with his revolver, and ordered him to go away. I pleaded with him, "Do not endanger yourself, Soureilhan, it's useless." Roughly pushed by the two men, we walked at a fast pace. At the bottom of the Grande-Rue, Goupil, held tightly by his captor, joined our group. A Simca was parked in front of the savings bank. Four of us were shoved into the back of the car, and our hands were tied to the back of the seat. The car took off so fast that our captors forgot to pick up Roegler's bulging briefcase, which they had just set against the wall before getting us into the car; I was glad of that.

The Simca headed toward Alençon. I tried to anticipate what was going to happen so that I would be ready to face any eventuality. Certainly the men of the S.D. had made a mistake by letting me have time to think instead of taking advantage of the shock of surprise. Shortly after passing the barracks, the car made a brief stop. Why? I never found out. Then, to my astonishment, the car got off the main road, turned right, sped through the village of Saint-Front, took the road to Mayenne for about three kilometers, and abruptly pulled into a little pasture opposite the Saint-Brice road.

The place was not deserted; there were already two Citroëns there, and I was perplexed because one of them had been camouflaged with a grayish paint and stripped of its four doors. A dozen or so men were hanging around the cars. They were tough-looking, unkempt, dirty, unshaven—all mercenaries for the Gestapo. Some were talking; some were eating canned foods and drinking from bottles; some were handling guns. Each of them carried a machine gun or a revolver. We were ordered to get out of the car and to lie down in the grass, two by two. I was still tied to the town hall secretary. Suddenly I noticed the gendarme, Bruneau, who had preceded us and was lying a few meters away. He was tied to Goupil. One of the "distinguished" policemen barked at Bruneau, "Bastard, you didn't have any problems being on Pétain's payroll . . . a gendarme and a notary, you two go well together!" (Later I would find out that this bandit's name was Haquin and that he had done just about everything: tire retreader in Falaise, policeman in Argentan, mercenary in Spain, leader in the P.P.F.) At that moment, American patrol planes fired at the area around the train station. Scared, Haquin ran to hide under a tree, saying, "Those swine are liable to get us." He forced us to remain face down in the grass and forbade us to raise our heads. Our captors were visibly worried and nervous. No doubt they would rather have been somewhere else. Jardin exclaimed, "Ah! It smells of the battle-front!"

One of the Citroëns left and returned a short while later. Out stepped Monsieur Barbier and his son (from Saint-Brice), handcuffed to each other. The torturers brought the son over and wanted him to confess that he knew us. He denied the charge energetically, and with

good reason: he worked as a fireman in Paris and seldom came to
Domfront, and he had never met us. Finally the father and son were
thrown onto the grass at the far left of our group. We were watched
by Haquin, very proud of the machine gun slung across his back. His
conversation consisted only of insults. I kept talking back to him and
raising my head, and he threatened to rub my nose in cow dung. The
secretary vainly asked me to be quiet; the poor man was absolutely
terrified. Our captor kept up his jawing without pause. He boasted that
he was with the international brigades during the war in Spain, saying,
"I've always lived by the war, for the war, in the war." I thought to
myself, "I hope he dies from it."

   In the meantime one of the Citroëns—the one without doors—
left, and then the Simca. Some of the militiamen were going back to
pick up the forgotten briefcase; they returned empty-handed and had
to endure the wrath of the Boche in charge. A short while later the
Citroën returned, and I was devastated to see Gilard, head of the Resistance of Saint-Mars. He was followed by young Chevalier from Bois-
de-Villaines. They were brutally thrown out of the vehicle and joined
us in the grass. They had also been handcuffed.

   It seemed that the "distinguished" policemen had decided to do me
the honor of having me go first. I was untied from the secretary, who
heaved, I imagine, a sigh of relief. My old trench coat was spread on
the ground to serve as a receptacle for the contents of my pockets: the
money—a little over eight thousand francs—which they divided
among themselves; my tie pin; a Dunhill lighter; two fountain pens.
They went through my wallet thoroughly. Each document they found
was accompanied by some sarcastic comment: "So, Monsieur is an engineer? So, Monsieur is in the gasogene business?" But Jardin made a
more important discovery: two authentic *Ausweise*—German permits—
to the forbidden zone. One was a pass to Cherbourg, from when I was
teaching a class at the Arsenal; the other was to Honfleur. They also
found the I.O.U. written in English by Lieutenant Fontaine certifying
that I had provided lodging in Domfront for the 240 Americans taken
prisoner in Saint-Lô. As anyone could see, there was nothing mysterious
about that, but the idiots were perplexed: "Ah, Monsieur speaks English. Monsieur will translate this for us later on." Then, paging through
my notebook, Jardin read the names of the three cities in the Manche

region taken by the Americans the previous night: "Well! Monsieur listens to the English radio station? Your goose is cooked!" The militia chief grabbed me by the collar, and with the help of two cronies dragged me, hitting and kicking me along the way, to the far end of the pasture, away from the road. The chief stopped to put another pair of handcuffs on me, tightening them until they dug into my flesh. He removed my watch, put it in his pocket, and said, "So that it doesn't hurt you with the handcuffs." My watch was not hurting me at all; and I never saw it again.

Seven or eight men were following us. They were lowlifes: Grivaux, Durut, Dangerville (secretary-general of the P.P.F. of the Orne), Kowisky (nicknamed "Little Hat"), Emil Moessner the killer, Vetter, Petrisieck, Ridel, Fernizon, all of them experienced assassins. One of them said, "It's too bad we have forgotten our tool to loosen tongues!" "Bah," answered Jardin, "a good strong stick will do." Then he ordered one of his aides to cut a branch off a tree. We reached the site they had selected, sufficiently far from the road and from my comrades still lying at the edge of the pasture. Suddenly, without warning, I was hit with a volley of slaps in the face, and they punched me with their fists—two or three of those bandits swinging at a time. My hands were cuffed behind my back, and I could not ward off the blows; the steel of the manacles dug into my flesh, and my wrists were swelling. The man with the stick returned and—to test it, probably—dealt me a terrific blow on my skull. The blood spurted, flooded my forehead, face, and shirt. Though staggered, I stayed on my feet. It was then that Hans Roegler, trusted assistant of the so-called "Colonel" Hildebrandt (later I would learn that he was only a sergeant, and chief of the Gestapo in the Orne region), put his face close to mine and, squeezing my arm as hard as he could while staring me in the eyes, said, "Now you're going to tell me, aren't you, where the chief is, where the maquis are, where the munitions are? You know it, don't you?" From these questions I realized instantly that he was ignorant of my exact activities. The information they had on me had to be rather vague, and Roegler hoped, through me, to get to Captain Lefèvre in Viel, and perhaps to Guesdon and other members of the maquis. As I had suspected, there had been no investigation in Domfront, and the Sicherheitsdienst—Security Service—was poorly informed.

This quasi certitude gave me courage. I thought of the terrible consequences that a moment of carelessness or weakness on my part could
have: investigations of my family; searches at the Châlet, where the six
American airmen and André Geslin might still be hiding (Geslin had
been on the wanted list for two weeks); arrest of my comrades in the
Passive Defense. Under the hail of blows, I tried to explain that I was
only chief of the Passive Defense in a city that had been bombed seventeen times, that I had too many other things to do to be involved in
the Resistance, and that I had absolutely nothing to do with anti-German activities. I repeated all this two or three times, in a firm tone of
voice, without hesitation and with the proper accent of sincerity, all the
while staring Roegler straight in the eyes. Unfortunately, my denials
did not stop the brutes from continuing to bludgeon me. A short,
heavyset man, built like an athlete and wearing a Basque beret, screamed
at me in bad French, "When I hit, I hit hard!" Then, while I was
turned around halfway, he gave me a formidable blow in the stomach
with his fist, a blow I would long remember. I rolled to the ground,
writhing from the pain, and started to vomit. And the beating went
on; there were half a dozen of them hitting me on the head, the body,
the legs, walloping me with sticks, kicking me in the ribs and chest.
During that time two of the bandits knelt and burned my arms with
matches and cigarettes. I kept on screaming, "I don't know anything, I
can't tell you anything, have pity, kill me, but please stop tormenting
me so!" At a time like that, death really seemed a small thing. The
brutes continued to torture me; I was almost unconscious and felt the
blows less and less.

Hans Roegler approached me again as I was crying out, "Please kill
me!" He told me, "No, not that, we don't want to kill you, but you
are going to tell us, aren't you, where 'he' is, the chief, where 'it' is,
the maquis. You do know, don't you? Are you going to talk? Or else
I'm not going to beat you myself, but I'm going to let the others beat
you some more." Then he asked if I was a Communist. I replied that
I had never been into politics, that I did not belong to any party and
knew nothing of the Resistance. He was enraged, but he tried to remain
calm. Approaching even closer, eye to eye, he threatened me again:
"Will you talk? Or I'll have them beat you more. I've known a few
tough ones like you who didn't want to talk, but you'll break down."

In spite of the zeal and obstinacy of Roegler and his torturers, I did not break down. It has been a great source of pride for me not to have talked. The Boches never did learn from me who the chief was or where the maquis was. The blows multiplied; I screamed more and more, which made one of the brutes—Jardin or Berthaut—say, "This bastard screams like a pig being slaughtered. He wants to attract people." Then an order was given—probably by Roegler—to put me on my knees. The restraints that kept my hands behind my back were removed, my arms were brought back in front, and then my hands were cuffed even tighter than before. They threw me down on my stomach, and the beating started again, this time on my back. More blows, kicks in the ribs, burning with cigarettes. It was horrible, but I was, fortunately, barely conscious and too weak to react. My cries were becoming weaker.

They definitely were not going to get anything out of me. Roegler ordered his mercenaries to stop, and they dragged me, half-conscious, to the entrance of the field. What a first-class drubbing! Goupil would later write that my ordeal lasted forty-five minutes. All I can say is that it felt like an eternity, and I will never forget it as long as I live. I had a gaping wound on the right side of my skull, four broken ribs, a long tear below my left breast, nine broken teeth; my whole body was black and blue, and I could not make a move without grimacing in agony. I had nearly passed out in the grass, and thinking of the violence I had just endured, I wondered what was in store for me next. Yet I was pleased to have given them a hard time, and I understood that despite the stool pigeons, they knew little of my activities. Resistant in 1941, member of the Defense of France since 1943, intelligence agent, agent for escape—undoubtedly I was a good catch.

I hoped that the effect of my silence would be that no one else would be interrogated. I tried to guess what had happened since my arrest. Alerted, my men must have taken the airmen to safety and gotten rid of the munitions, and my father had undoubtedly been informed. I tried to think of a way to warn my family. If I was going to be killed, there were certain affairs I wanted to settle. Goupil was lying not far from me, and I managed to give him some instructions, but our conversation attracted the attention of Haquin who approached us, uttering

insults and threats. I looked at him with contempt and then stretched
out on the grass.[3]

The torturers led to the far end of the pasture first Bruneau, then
René Barbier. Each was beaten for a quarter of an hour, but without
results because they did not know anything. Then Goupil was questioned about me; they wanted him to say that I was a Communist.
Finally it was Gilard's turn. Despite a number of kicks in the ribs, he
was tough, and they did not get anything out of him. At one point I
saw him making sudden, strange moves and scratching the ground. He
would tell me later that he was trying to bury the petards that had fallen
out of his jacket. The Barbier father and son were lying on an anthill
and asked to be moved; they were bluntly ordered to stay where they
were. Then a comical incident took place: the Gestapo brought to the
pasture a fellow named Prime (he was a mechanic in Saint-Hilaire).
Prime was accused of having thrown a cherry bomb into a German
truck, but he insisted that it was only an onion. Despite a hail of blows,
he took a huge white onion out of his pocket and declared, "I am
telling you guys, it was the same as this one here. As the truck was
passing me, I showed an onion to the driver and asked if he wanted it.
He nodded yes and I threw the onion!" One troublesome detail for
Prime was that his onion had exploded "a little." Despite the energetic
means used by the bastards, the fellow denied all the way. Vexed and
furious, they finally gave up on him and got back to me, the "star,"
determined this time to make me confess. I did not know how many
of them—four, five, or six—were hitting me, punching me, kicking
me. It was a repeat of the previous pounding, minus the burns. Goupil,
very pale, courageously tried to intervene, saying to Roegler, "It is a
human being you are beating." Amiably, Roegler answered that his turn
would come. They were bent on forcing me to admit that I was a
Communist; I called on Goupil to testify that I had never been in
politics and besides, for many different reasons, I could not be a Communist. I could easily guess the intentions of Roegler and his accom-
plices: he and Jardin had an inkling of my anti-German activity, but
they were unaware of its nature and importance. Unable to hold me
and justify their actions by establishing that I was a resistant or a Jew,
they wanted to nab me for being a Communist. Poupard, a good-for-
nothing and the disgusting Gestapo informant, must have been a laugh-

ingstock, and he must have been reprimanded by Jardin and Roegler because he approached me yelling, "Are you going to talk, bastard, you are making me look like a f—— ass!" At the same time, he was administering a savage volley of kicks in my ribs. It was certainly not the first, but one can judge the effect, considering that I had already suffered four detached ribs. I declared, between shrieks of pain, that I could not invent something just to please him and that I did not know anything.[4]

The only German in uniform, the driver of the Citroën, decided that he was going to give it a try and asked the scoundrel Haquin to cut a stick off the hedgerow. As soon as it was done, he rushed upon me—I was still lying on the ground—and beat me until the stick was in shreds. He was a strong one, and I think the tenth to beat me. So ended my ordeal. Bloody from head to toe, covered with wounds, ribs caved in, I passed out several times. Someone pulled me into a ditch against the hedgerow. An altercation occurred between Jardin and Gilard; the latter was going to be released, and he asked Roegler for restitution of the few thousand francs taken from his wallet. Roegler answered, "You people always say the same thing, but we are not a bunch of thieves!" He called Jardin, who got on his high horse and slapped Gilard a few times, saying, "This is nothing but sentimentality; in Russia you'd be shot for much less."

A heavy shower broke out, and my ditch was filling with water. The two young Red Cross men wanted to cover me with my coat, but the friction of the fabric on my skin was too painful. I asked them to let me die in peace. Someone insisted that I should be taken out of the water, but one of the bandits refused, saying, "It doesn't matter where he dies, here or somewhere else." I was very thirsty, and at Barbier's request a militiaman brought me two glasses of a foul-tasting cider. (In December of 1945, Jardin would confess: "We beat Rougeyron a lot because he would not talk and Poupard protested that he was sure.")

It was then 5 P.M. We had been in the pasture since 9 A.M. The policemen were facing a problem for the return: one of the Citroëns had broken down, and it had to be towed by the other. It was probably for this reason that they set free Gilard, Goupil, Chevallier, the Barbier father, the two Red Cross men, and the secretary from town hall. Later I learned that Barbier and Gilard had overheard the militiamen talking about me. One of them asked Jardin: "And this one, what do we do

with him?" Jardin replied, "Kill him, just like in Briouze," but Roegler
intervened and gave orders to drive me to Alençon. It is thanks to that
Boche that I am alive today.

Barbier and Bruneau lifted me into the backseat of the black Citroën
that was being towed. Poupard sat next to me. The car was driven by
the Boche in uniform; Haquin and Dangerville sat next to him (I would
learn later than Dangerville had become secretary-general of the P.P.F.
of the Orne after Lechat, his predecessor, was executed by the Resistance in April of 1944). In the other Citroën were the Barbier son,
Prime, and a militiaman. We left, headed toward Alençon. Ahead of us
in the Simca were Roegler, Jardin, the gendarme Bruneau, and two
militiamen. Lying across the backseat, I groaned with pain at each jerk
of the car. Poupard tried vainly to make me talk: "It's your fault we
have wasted the whole day; it's going to cost you." After we passed
Couterne, an American patrol plane flew over us. The cars stopped,
and these "gentlemen" ran to a ditch; Bruneau helped me out and took
me near the embankment for shelter. The alert over, it was back into
the car and on the road again. As we passed through La Lacelle, a second
stop was caused by the appearance of "Lightnings." This time, the Simca
having gone ahead, the driver of the first Citroën stopped the cars under
pine trees on the side of the road. Dangerville dragged me into a nearby
alley. Before getting back into the car, they tried for the umpteenth
time, to make me confess that I was a Communist; for the umpteenth
time, I repeated that I did not belong to any party. Furthermore, I
mentioned (now I don't know why) the name of a man in Domfront
well known for his pro-German feelings and for his activity as regional
chief of an anti-French movement:

"Ask X., if you know him."

One of the policemen answered with surprise: "You know X.?"

"Of course I know him; he is from Domfront, and I often had
business with him."

Another went on: "X., isn't he from our region?"

"No, he is 'Boucard.' "

"Well, that changes everything; we are going to have to redo the
investigation."

"Nonsense, we'll tell the boss [Hildebrandt or Roegler?] about it.
They know each other, and they'll do what they want with it."

(During my deportation I often wondered about that conversation. Incidentally, it was later confirmed by Dangerville during his trial on July 6, 1946, at the Court of Justice of Caen.)

We arrived at the mill of Condé-sur-Sarthe, the new haunt of the Gestapo since it had fled Alençon on the day of the landing. It was around 7 P.M. We were led to the vestibule of a lodge near the mill. I was unable to stand up, so Barbier laid me against a door. My clothes were in shreds, covered with blood and mud; I was in a pitiful state, but I tried to observe what was going on around me. I saw the riffraff militiamen entering, one at a time, a room where they set down their guns and ammunition. I had the distinct impression that the Boches did not trust the scoundrels working for them. Barbier was called into the adjoining room; then it was my turn. In a narrow office, I found myself in the presence of a man about forty to forty-five years old, brown hair, stout, dressed in dark gray clothing. He was Hildebrandt, chief of the Gestapo. Next to him was his secretary, Frau Müller—blond, classically German—who transcribed my answers. Among other questions, Hildebrandt asked me the name of my father, my mother, if there were Jews in my family, if I was a Communist or a Catholic. Then the secretary was instructed by her boss to write, on a file marked with a red line, a single word: *Feindsbegünstigung* (abetting the enemy). This was my indictment; Barbier's was the same. We were taken away in a front-wheel-drive car. A militiaman, a machine gun between his knees, sat between Barbier and me. He said, "Don't try to be clever, or else."

17

The Château des Ducs and Fresnes

We reached Alençon, crossed the center of town, and arrived at the Château des Ducs. The car stopped on a little bridge, and a German appeared; we had arrived at the old prison. We were led to an upper floor at gunpoint, and then there was a long wait, facing the wall. Barbier tried to hold me up, but the sentry separated us. One at a time we were called into a small room, where we were searched. I handed over my wallet and whatever papers I had left. We were given a bowl, a spoon, and a plate. A Wehrmacht soldier took us up another flight of stairs. Despite my condition, I tried to take it all in; prison was a novelty for me. This place was really sinister, and I was assailed by somber thoughts. The Boche opened a door, and we walked into a room located in one of the towers of the castle (I learned later that it was cell thirteen, which owed its ominous reputation to the fact that a number of men sentenced to death had stayed there). It was nightfall, and I could hardly see anything. Barbier, who was in better shape than I, undressed me and laboriously hoisted me to an upper bunk, the only one unoccupied. I was in such a condition that despite the uncertainty of the future, my multiple wounds, and the anxiety about the fate of my relatives and friends, I went to sleep. I did not wake until dawn, when the Boche on duty yelled, with the voice of a castrated rooster, "Aufstehen."

"Aufstehen"—I did not know what it meant, but everyone else was moving, so apparently it meant "Get up." A few minutes later a German came into our cell. Seeing that I was the only one not up, he approached and threatened me with "two days without soup." Once he noticed my condition, he left, only to return a few minutes later. With Barbier's help he took me to a lower floor, to the room we had first entered the night before. There a Boche medic, assisted by a male nurse, examined my wounds and asked me in French, "Who did that?" I answered, "German police." He shrugged his shoulders, exchanged some words with his nurse, then dressed the wounds with tincture of iodine, examined my mouth, felt my ribcage. Finally he tied together two large towels with safety pins and bound my torso tightly. I was taken back to cell thirteen, where I got acquainted with my comrades in misfortune: Boulanger, an engineer, director of the power plant of Rai-Aube; François Zoude, alias Raspail; Bétourné, from Sées; Laguesse, from Alençon; Léopold Duval, from Coudehard; Bidard, from the post office of Alençon; little Flouvat, assistant at the tax collector's office of Ecouché; Duzan, a young pilot from Dewoitine; and of course Prime, René Barbier, and myself.

Despite our misadventure, none of us was really despondent. Yet for many the future looked dark. Because of what had been found in his home, Bétourné knew that he faced a death sentence; every time the cell door opened, he thought it was for him. Nevertheless he remained imperturbable and calmly related to us the story of his arrest. One day the Germans burst into his home and questioned him: "Do you have a firearm?" "No," he answered. Bétourné added dispassionately, "I was not lying. I did not have *one* firearm, I had two tons!"

Zoude, a member of the maquis in Argentan, had been arrested at gunpoint by German soldiers on July 31. The Boches immediately shackled him with chains and locked him in a rabbit hutch for the night. The next morning he was questioned by Roegler and Moessner, assisted by Marinette, Roegler's sweetheart. Zoude did not answer, so Moessner—an expert at interrogation—dragged him into a barn and flogged him violently with a leather lash. Zoude stopped the brute by promising that he would disclose the location of the maquis headquarters. The Germans ran to the location and found nothing but a deserted house. In retaliation, they set fire to the house and gave Zoude a thorough beating. After another night in the rabbit hutch, Zoude was taken to the prison.

We all had similar stories to tell, but the funny thing was that because we feared the presence of an informant, we all swore our innocence and cursed the incomprehensible injustice that had brought us there. Despite the gloomy aspect of cell thirteen, our sojourn in the Château des Ducs was bearable: there were a few cots, a table, two benches, and a stinking latrine in one corner. Thanks to the Red Cross of Alençon we received, through the Boches, some supplies: cold cuts, a little pot of butter for each of us, and many other things. Every day I was taken to the lower floor, where the German medic changed my bandages and dressings. We prisoners passed the time in long conversations of all kinds and in endless card games (with a clandestine deck, of course). One unwavering hope sustained us: the ever-increasing rumble of cannons and the ceaseless marching of German troops driven back toward Paris. At night we took turns listening and looking out of the gun port. One morning that gun port provided us with an unexpected diversion: about 7 A.M. that day, poor Laguesse was on the lookout (it was forbidden) when we heard the footsteps of the German coming to yell his daily "Aufstehen." From our cots we warned Laguesse, "The Boche is coming; get down quick." But Laguesse, who was a little deaf (which we knew), did not hear a thing and kept peering through the bars of the gun port. The Boche opened the spy hole, saw our comrade engrossed in the view, walked into the cell, knocked down the surprised Laguesse, and took him away. The next morning our friend was back among us, after spending a frigid night in a damp and putrid cell.

One evening we were ordered to gather our tin cups and covers, and we spent the night in cell fourteen, a large and airy room. Compared to cell thirteen, it was a palace. In addition, the occupants of this cell regularly received foodstuffs and news from the outside thanks to an ingenious rope-hoist system concocted by the brave and worthy Madame Guillais.

Alas, the next day we were back in our tower. But that day I had the pleasure of seeing Bruneau arrive; I had been wondering where he could be. He had been kept in solitary confinement in the secret dungeon, of which he had kept the grimmest memories. On the morning of August 9 our cell was invaded by some new arrivals from cell seventeen. They were Moreau (from the Intelligence Service); Jean Mazeline; Bouillac; Daniel Desmeulles, chief of the Resistance of the Orne (I was to leave him just a few days before his death); Chasseguet from the Alençon post office; Frémiot, a farmer in Sées; and Henri Barbier, from Paris. All of them were fierce and dedicated members of the Resistance; although they knew what fate awaited them, none was sad or despondent. A little ray of sun was shining through the gun port, and there was a gay and noisy atmosphere during breakfast. Around 10 A.M. a Boche came in, accompanied by one of the Gestapo henchmen. They called some names: Moreau, Mazeline, Bouillac, Desmeulles, Chasseguet, and Frémiot. One of them asked, "Should we take our blankets and tins?" The militiaman answered, laughing, "It's not necessary." A few minutes later we heard the sound of a car engine in the courtyard; we rushed to the gun port and caught sight of the Citroën without doors. Jardin, standing on the sidewalk, ordered our comrades into the car, shouting, "The first one who makes a move, I'll shoot him." (This departure was a prelude to the mad flight of the Gestapo of the Orne and to the execution of five French patriots who, alas, were shot a few hours later—Daniel Desmeulles often reminded me of it—in L'Hôme-Chamondot.) In our cell all gaiety had ceased . . . we were worried about the fate of our comrades.

Toward the end of the morning we noticed a smell of acrid smoke permeating the air. We looked through the gun port and saw bits of burnt paper fluttering about. We were trying to figure out what was going on when a German came to get Prime, telling him he was needed to repair a Gestapo motorcycle. Prime returned two hours later and told us that Hildebrandt and his gang were burning the records of the S.D. in the castle. We were not surprised by this precaution; the roar of American cannons was getting closer and closer. On the other hand, we were surprised to hear a few hours later that Prime, who had been accused of blowing up a truck with a cherry bomb, had now been released. We came to the conclusion that Prime was probably a stool pigeon (this would be confirmed later when we learned about his shady past). Fortunately, thanks to our prudence, he had wasted his time in our group.

Bidard was also released. Before he left, I asked him—although without really counting on it—to inform his colleague Mademoiselle E. that I was alive and anticipated being transferred to Compiègne. The prison was emptying: many detainees had been released; two convoys had left for an unknown destination; cells fourteen and seventeen were no longer occupied. On the other hand, there was a lot of activity in the halls and in the street below. The roar of the cannons seemed considerably nearer and more frequent. All this made us nervous and edgy. We were a little suspicious of Henri Barbier, the Parisian who had arrived that morning. When our group was talking and Barbier approached, we stopped or changed the subject. In the end, infuriated by our attitude, he got very angry: "Who the hell do you think you are? I'm going to show you that I'm not a stool pigeon!" He pulled down his trousers, lifted his shirt. We all burst out laughing: his whole body was black and blue from a memorable thrashing. Henri Barbier and I became good friends, and he told me his odyssey. He was a wholesaler of champagne and owned a bar, which he was using as headquarters for the Resistance. Because his home had been searched on several occasions, he had left town and had decided to join the Allied troops. He arrived at Alençon on August 1. Not knowing anyone in town, he made the mistake of staying at a big hotel, the most pro-German in town. Thierry, the housemaid, searched his suitcase and denounced him. He was arrested on August 2, around 5 P.M., by Bertaud, Perrin, and associates. After a first beating, he had been taken to Condé-sur-Sarthe and stripped of all he had. Naturally, he had also appeared in front of Hildebrandt, in the infamous lodge near the mill. With the help of Frau Müller, he had been able to identify Barbier, and faced with the prisoner's vehement denials, Hildebrandt gave orders to put him to the "question." Barbier was laid on a table, feet and hands bound, and severely beaten for half an hour. Then Jardin led him to the pond and threatened to drown him. Seeing that their efforts were not bringing results, his torturers took him to the Château des Ducs, where he joined us.

The continuing agitation outside made us nervous. We feared an incursion of the S.S. into our cell and considered barricading the door, but we would not have the chance. Around 6 P.M. the door opened, and a Boche harshly ordered us to get ready. One by one we were led downstairs, where we were given back some of our belongings. The sound of cannons was closer, and we still nourished the mad hope of rescue. Suddenly, around 8 P.M., there was great commotion in the halls. The German sentries came and made us rush down the steps, pushing us with the butts of their guns. Near the entrance to the prison there was a T.C.R.P. bus driven by a civilian accompanied by an assistant. We were herded onto the bus, thirty-seven prisoners in all if I remember correctly, among whom were a woman (Flouvat told me that she was Madame L., arrested at Geslin's home in Sainte-Opportune) and half a dozen German deserters. The head of the convoy was an S.S. Feldwebel, tall, gaunt, typical looks for this kind of job. He stood on the running board, revolver in hand, waiting for the opportunity to butcher one of us.

The bus stayed in front of the prison for a long time. I was seated by an open window and took the time to talk with Guillais, the groundskeeper. Confirming a note that I had slipped him through the window of cell fourteen, I asked him to tell his friend from Alençon to notify my father that I was alive and on my way to an unknown destination. I also gave him messages from the other prisoners. At the time of departure, he gave me about thirty packs of cigarettes to be distributed among us. It was nighttime when we left Alençon. The woman prisoner, Madame L., had recognized me—how, I didn't know—and asked me about Geslin. I simply answered that he was all right, but later, how much I was to regret this reply! The trip was not without incident. The roads were crowded with all kinds of German convoys: ambulances, tanks, trucks, horse-drawn carts driven by Mongols—all this traffic flowing back to Paris in utter disorder, punctuated by yells and invective. There was a long wait a few kilometers from Alençon because a tank was obstructing the road. Later in the night, our bus got stuck in a ditch. The thought of taking this opportunity to escape crossed my mind, but René Barbier, who was sitting at my left, pointed out the consequences for my comrades—retaliation, perhaps even executions. Someone mentioned the presence of two militiamen in the bus, arrested for having robbed the Boches. Now we had to be more cautious than ever about mentioning our past activities. Finally we arrived near Trappes, in the midst of bombardments. Fires were raging; star shells incessantly streaked the sky. Our bus was driving through open country and made a perfect target. An order was given to stop. The Boches flung themselves into a ditch to take shelter for half an hour; we were forced to stay on the bus.

At dawn we entered Paris via Porte d'Orléans. The window near my seat was still open. My comrades hastily scribbled some notes, which I threw onto the road. I threw one I had addressed to my friend G. G.

(a year later I would learn that he did get it). Around 7 P.M. we reached the prison of Fresnes. The S.S. officer in charge of our convoy had a shouting match with the warden, and we were refused admission. The bus left, and the S.S. men were in a very foul mood, so they were meaner than ever. We asked if we could get out, and finally we were granted a stop near the Olida cannery on rue Olivier-de-Serres. Fearing for my comrades, I again passed up a chance to escape. The bus left again, then stopped at the barracks of the Pépinière. The Feldwebel went in, then came out furious—they didn't want us either. An order was given to the bus driver to take us to a street in the Madeleine district, near rue Suresne if I remember correctly. Taking Madame L. with him, our escort entered a hotel, where they stayed for about forty-five minutes. Meanwhile we were under the guard of a fat Boche, half-crazed from having lost his wife and daughter during a bombardment in Cologne. Finally the Feldwebel returned, followed by Madame L. She thought it necessary to tell us that he had been very pleasant and had let her use his dressing room. She must have seen certain documents because she mentioned to Barbier, "I know that a sum of fifteen thousand francs is following you." The bus then took us to the compulsory labor office, on avenue Kléber, where we stayed for two or three hours while a violent bombardment took place nearby. Another chance to escape missed. Early in the afternoon we were driven back to the prison in Fresnes, and this time we were admitted. To our great surprise, Madame L. left on the bus, accompanied by the leader of the convoy. (Later she would pretend that she escaped by jumping off the bus.) Wehrmacht soldiers took us to the first block of cells, and we were separated. My little group was placed in cell 793, on the first floor. It was supposed to hold only two prisoners, but there were seven of us: the two Barbiers, Léopold Duval, Flouvat, Zoude, Bruneau, and myself.

We were packed like sardines. The only furnishings consisted of a folding bed attached to the wall and a straw mattress. In a corner near the door was a stinking lavatory. The only way to get even a minimum of air was to break the window. During the first three hours Henri Barbier tried to carry out that mission while we watched apprehensively for the reaction of the S.S. sentry. When he opened the door, Barbier explained as best as he could that we were suffocating. The Boche inspected the broken window, shrugged his shoulders, and left. We tried to pass the time. To everyone's delight, I still had a bit of blue tobacco. Through the window we could glimpse some of the prisoners in the block opposite. If we shouted loudly, we could be heard in the cells above ours, particularly Boulanger's. We communicated in Morse code by tapping on the lavatory pipe. To do that one had to stick his nose into the commode, head covered with a blanket—the stench was dreadful and the transmission arduous. The incessant drone of planes above and the roar of cannons in the distance reawakened in us a long lost hope. There must have been a torture chamber in the nearby basement. Every day, especially in the morning, we could hear screams and calls: "Help!," "Mama, Mama!," "Have pity!," and, alas, much more.

René Barbier was suffering from a terrible case of scabies. All day he stayed wrapped in his coat, behind the door. No one dared go near him. His hands had become deformed and were extremely sore. We took turns urinating on them, which gave him some relief.

The best moment of the day was soup time. Apparently provided by the French Red Cross, the soup was brought every day by cart. During our stay in Fresnes—five days—the broth was fairly good, and abundant. Our little group had now gotten well acquainted, and we trusted each other. All of us were resistants, and we related our odysseys without reservation. Léopold Duval had been arrested in Coudehard for Resistance activity; poor Flouvat (who later died in Ellrich) was accused of participating in the robbery of the collector's office in Ecouché.

Early on August 15 there was a great commotion in the prison. After our 9 A.M. soup, the guards ordered us to get ready: "Raus! Raus! Schnell! Schnell!" We were taken downstairs to the large hall and put into two lines; then an endless roll call began (there were nearly four thousand of us). We saw some of our former comrades again, Daniel Desmeulles among others. He told us about the terrible tragedy that took place in L'Hôme-Chamondot. Our morale was still good despite the blows and the calls to order; we joined in singing a resounding "Marseillaise." Then we were led in groups of fifty to the entrance and loaded into trucks—one per fifty men. Our guards were S.S. specialists, true assassins looking for a chance to kill. There were three of them to each truck, two with machine guns trained on us, the third seated on the small cabin, facing the rear, watching us. We were ordered to remain seated or on our knees, without raising our heads. This was the way we crossed all of Paris until the Pantin train station. What a contrast: as we were going toward our deaths, thousands of people were enjoying the August sunshine and sitting idly at sidewalk cafés. A few noticed us, and I remember seeing, through the slats in the side of the truck, some horror-stricken Parisians watching our convoy pass by. A few women were weeping. At 11 A.M. we reached the Pantin station, where a long line of cattle cars was waiting. A few railway workers, kept at a distance by our guards, watched us go by with tears in their eyes. As soon as we got off the trucks, our torturers, lashing at us with whips and hitting us with the butts of their guns, prodded us into the cattle cars. We were crammed 80 to 120 prisoners per car, three times the capacity, and then the doors were immediately padlocked. The heat was suffocating, and we could neither sit down nor stoop; we would have to travel this way for five days and five nights. We threw messages onto the tracks through the windows, which were covered with barbed wire. Some of the railway workers made signs that they would pick them up after the train left. At the end of the afternoon we saw a pitiful group: 500 to 600 prisoners had arrived from the Fort of Romainville, on their way to Germany. They were also loaded into the cattle cars, the women in the five or six at the front of the train. At nightfall two "Posten"— Boche sentinels—came into our car and took their position in front of the door after having counted and recounted us.

The train started. It traveled one kilometer, then stopped on the Pantin bridge, where it would stay until midnight. At 11 P.M. we heard the sound of machine-gun fire, followed by yells from the guards running along the tracks: a dozen prisoners had torn off the barbed wire and escaped. Almost all of them made it, except one who was shot by an S.S. sentry as he was jumping onto the tracks. It was very late when the train started again and slowly crossed the suburbs of Paris. We were packed so tightly that we could not even move. There was no light. The hours seemed awfully long. Near me were René Barbier, Flouvat, and a very young Dutchman, arrested as he was trying to escape compulsory labor. A little farther from us were a dozen men from Brittany, members of the maquis in the Quimper region. These men gave us a lesson in courage: despite their tragic situation, they intermittently sang tunes from their native land during the trip. At dawn the train stopped in open country. The S.S. slightly opened the doors of some cars and ordered the first man they saw to get out; if he was too young or too old, they picked another one. The S.S. ordered these men to dig their own graves; then they hastily lined them up and executed them, assassinated them—horrible reprisals for the escapes of the previous night. Loud protests against these crimes rose from several cars; the Boches went into those cars, hitting the prisoners right and left with their sticks. Then they ordered them to undress and took away their clothes. Those poor victims would have to make the rest of the trip completely naked.

Finally the train started again, taking us toward the border, with lengthy stops at each station. The French Red Cross had brought many cartons of food to the Pantin station; there was more than enough to feed all of us, but we had nothing to drink, and besides, we could not even move. The heat was unbearable; our throats were parched and our thirst intense. The fetid smell coming from the toilet—actually a bucket in the middle of the floor—added to our discomfort. The night seemed endless. As we passed each station, we tried to see what time it was. It was only midnight when we thought it was 3 A.M. In the morning the train entered a long tunnel and stopped in it. The smoke from the locomotive was suffocating. False rumors were spreading among us: the front of the train had been attacked by the Resistance with a great number of well-armed maquis, and we were going to be rescued. Unfortunately, that was not the case. In reality this long stop was due to the bridge over the Marne, which had just been blown in half near Nanteuil-Saacy during a bombardment. The train had to back out of the tunnel. The destruction of the bridge forced a transfer; our guards ordered us to get out and to walk in single file along the tracks. The cars holding the women were also emptied, but a horrible stench came from one of them. A body was laid down alongside the tracks—a prisoner had died.

We were told to halt in a pasture, and some of us were assigned to fetch—under guard, of course—the S.S. men's luggage and supplies. There were about two thousand of us in this pasture bordering the Marne River: officers of all ranks and from all branches of the service, gendarmes, forest rangers, priests, professors, physicians, men of all ages and from all walks of life. The industry executive side by side with the common street tough or even the lowly pimp. After much effort I finally found Henri Barbier and Bruneau, who had been traveling in cars at the head of the train; we shared a few biscuits and some jam. One prisoner had obtained permission to draw water from the river, and each of us got half a quart. A young foreign doctor—Raphael— went from group to group offering his help. Alas, there was not much he could do.

After an hour's pause, the S.S. lined us in rows of five, shouting brutally, "Wieder," "Schnell," "Los," and led our pack in the direction of a village four kilometers away. Shortly before we arrived, some volunteer nurses from the Red Cross brought us bouillon, milk, and sodas, but the Boches were quick to chase them away. The inhabitants of this village made a great effort to help us, and I cannot stress their generosity enough. Our group was herded onto the platform of a small station on the other side of the destroyed bridge; another train would soon take us away. This time there were fewer cattle cars, and we were even more cramped than before. Any man who squatted or even bent over slightly was sure to be trampled immediately. We had to remain standing, always standing. Tempers flared, and arguments became frequent, often violent. We were crushing each other; our thirst was unbearable, and some prisoners licked the iron parts of the car to get a sensation of coolness. Despite all this, two or three of the Bretons persisted in singing tunes from their native province.

Our convoy passed Châlons-sur-Marne, Revigny, and Lérouville, and we arrived at Nancy, where a delegate from the Red Cross—Swiss, I think—produced documents stating that due to a recent agreement, our train was not to go any farther. But the Nazi in charge absolutely refused, and we were on our way again, sick at heart. We passed Saar-brücken, Mainz, Frankfurt. Finally, very late on the night of August 19, after five days and nights of sheer torment, our convoy arrived at the Weimar station, its final destination. The cars holding the women were separated from the rest of the train. There were several emotional moments as the women prisoners, whom we could hear but not see, began to sing the "Marseillaise" and the "Chant du Départ." The train stood still for several hours; then two new engines arrived. In our car four or five prisoners had died, and several had gone crazy. Our thirst was unbearable, yet we felt privileged compared to those who had had to make the trip completely naked.

18

BUCHENWALD

It was dawn; the train slowly set out toward Buchenwald, 16 kilometers from Weimar. The camp was situated at an altitude of seven hundred meters, and the two engines strained to pull our long convoy through this region of pine forests. Suddenly we made the last stop; we could hear the heavy footsteps of the sentinels. One after another, each car was opened. Surrounded by a pack of German shepherds, about fifty S.S. troops were waiting for us on the deserted and dismal platform. They got us out of the cars, lashing us with whips and hitting us with the butts of their guns and with bludgeons. We had to carry the dead and the dying. Then we were ordered to walk in lines of ten, surrounded by the dogs, who bit those who strayed involuntarily or did not have the strength to follow. Behind us, a group of prisoners carried the guards' luggage and supplies.

We crossed a square. On the left stood the legendary oak of Goethe, and in the middle was a sculpted wooden signpost painted in loud colors. I will never forget this caricature, which represented a potbellied and hook-nosed Jew in a suit and gray hat, a monocle on one eye, a cigar in his mouth. On the sign, behind the Jew, was a fat vicar carrying a red umbrella, followed by a corpulent missionary in a drugget robe. Trailing the group was an S.S. man carrying a weapon under his arm. Above the sign was an arrow with the inscription "Konzentrationslager" (concentration camp), and underneath it, the words "Those who have not understood." A second sign, perpendicular to the first, pointed in the direction of the S.S. barracks. It depicted three splendid soldiers exercising. We, of course, followed the arrow pointing to the camp. We crossed an industrial zone, a residential area with flower gardens, and a large parking lot. We skirted a second signpost depicting the same scene as the first, but this time the characters wore the striped uniforms of prisoners. Finally we entered the camp itself through a large portal, above which stood a terrace equipped with machine guns. This was the famous *Tor* (gate) that bore the inscriptions "Right or wrong, for my fatherland" and "To each his due." In front of us was a huge square, the too-renowned "roll call square" where some forty to fifty thousand emaciated and ragged prisoners were assembled every day. It was there that those sentenced to death were hanged, that the circus music blared when it was time to depart to work and also during the executions of *Häftlinge* (prisoners).

(As a matter of fact, the detainees were assembled in front of the gallows at carefully calculated intervals to view the bodies swinging from the ropes: Czechs, Poles, Russians, or Frenchmen guilty of minor infractions or just picked out by some bilious S.S. soldier. The bodies oscillated, writhing in last convulsions while the circus music—Arbeit in Freude—played louder than ever. We also were made to watch the frequent beatings: the victim, bent double, hands tied to a wooden post, received from a specially trained S.S. man the customary twenty-five blows, no matter the screams, the skin torn off, the blood spurting.)

Our group was led to the right of the square. We passed a cage full of monkeys. Next to it stood a sordid building; from its tall chimney came a thick black smoke smelling of burnt flesh—it was the crematorium. In the basement, cadavers were hung from hooks as in a slaughterhouse. A prisoner told us as we passed by, "Here one comes in by the door and goes out by the chimney."

Seated by groups on the rocky ground, we waited for three hours under a burning sun. Many among us were ill or dying; we suffered terribly from thirst, and some did not hesitate to drink urine. I observed the great variety of people who made up our convoy. There were many civilians, and some uniforms here and there reminded us of France: gendarmes, forest rangers, priests (among them the brave Father Hénocque, former chaplain of Saint-Cyr School, who despite his age walked briskly from group to group. He wore on his chest the Legion of Honor and the Croix de Guerre medals). The civilians were of all ages and came from all social classes. I was able to find my former cellmates.

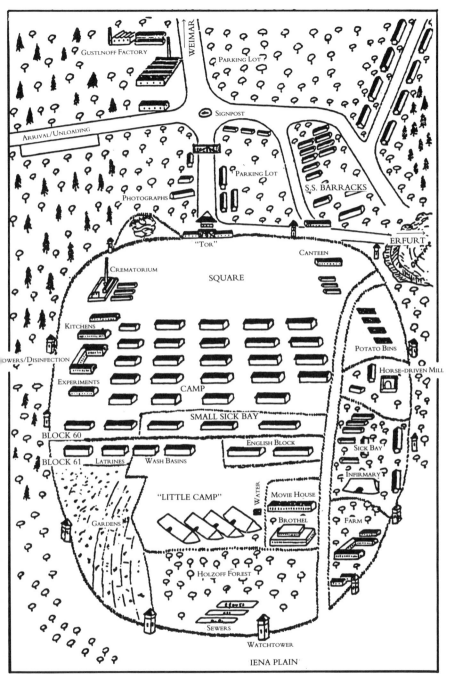

Map 2. The camp at Buchenwald.

We were taken in groups of thirty to a one-story building, the disinfection showers. Before going in, we had to undress completely and take our clothes with us. Inside, we went around a long table in the shape of a horseshoe. Polish or Russian prisoners took our clothes and placed them in a tagged bag along with our papers, wallets, etcetera. I protested when one of the Russians broke my pocket comb in half, but he pointed to the shaved heads around me; I saw that a comb was not necessary in Buchenwald. We were stripped of all our possessions. I saw them break an old man's wooden leg and crush the glasses of another unfortunate. Then we went into the next room. The Boches, being practical people with a fondness for jewelry, felt that the first search was not sufficient; one by one we were inspected by a "specialist" standing at the door. He pushed a finger deep into one's mouth and immediately stuck the same finger—just as deep—into the wretch's anus, then went on to the next man. There's no need to elaborate on the expression on the faces of the two thousand prisoners. In the next room, a dozen electric clippers hanging from the ceiling were operated by Poles. When it was my turn, I sat on a stool, and one of them started shaving me— with the requisite roughness—from head to toe. The clipper had lost most of its bite, and I spent a rather unpleasant fifteen minutes. Finally, it was the showers and disinfection. The water was alternately hot and cold, and after that it was a violent jet; then there was a spray of cresyl. We passed through this in groups of thirty, approximately one towel for four men. Then, arms stretched and legs splayed, we had to stand in front of a Pole who held an enormous paintbrush, with which he stroked us under each arm and between the legs, front and rear. The chemical stung horribly, and we went away skipping. I can still remember Father Hénocque, who was ahead of me, holding himself with both hands.

Then we were outside again, naked as worms. After a long wait in the yard we were led to the storeroom, where we were given some old clothes (I learned later that they had belonged to Jews who had been sent to the crematorium). This was how I inherited a pair of shapeless trousers and a jacket much too short for me with a label from a tailor in Belgrade. We were given one mess tin and one spoon to be shared among three men. Next came the identification process, which involved the distribution of a diamond-shaped red tag imprinted with a letter indicating nationality and serial number. Mine was 77.103; René Barbier's, 77.139; Henri Barbier's, 77.887; Desmeulles', 77.885. Last, we were led in groups of five—"Zu Fünf"—to the quarantine camp, known as the "Little Camp." As we walked between the cellblocks of the large camp, I called out to a prisoner who was watching us and asked if he knew Paul Alasseur. By a stroke of luck, he happened to be in the same cell as Paul's—block forty-eight—and he informed Paul that very evening of my arrival to Buchenwald.

Our feet bloodied from walking barefoot on the rocky ground, we entered the Little Camp, which consisted of only four wooden cellblocks, three circus-type tents, and an endless row of outhouses. The camp was located on the north flank of a hill facing the Jena plain. Originally it was built to house about one thousand to fifteen hundred prisoners, but on the day of our arrival, there were eight thousand of us from some twenty-three countries. It was a real jungle. This camp was an important provider for the crematorium. We walked barefoot on ground littered with human bones, spittle, shards of broken glass, sharp rocks; the least cut would certainly turn gangrenous. The ground exuded the characteristic odor of cadavers, and some prisoners could never get used to it. There was only one law there, the law of the strongest, and only one instinct, survival. Men killed each other for a hundred grams of bread, some tobacco, a blanket. Sometimes there were scores to be settled, for example when patriots found militiamen imprisoned by the Germans; the heads of these Vichy collaborators did not stay on their shoulders very long. Executions occurred nightly, and every day bodies were found in the large cesspools. By the way, the S.S. guards never intervened in these score-settlings; they just carted off the bodies to the crematorium.

We spent the first night in tent number one. We had to sleep sitting down in rows of thirty. I made the acquaintance of some of the men in my block: two professors, Maspéro and Mazeaud (who at the time of this writing is president of the F.N.D.I.R. [National Federation of Deportees and Internees of the Resistance]); Moussinet, former assistant prefect of Montargis (who was called out of the tent one night and mysteriously disappeared); an attaché to the Dutch Embassy in Paris; Commandant Henry; the secretary of the prefecture of the Rhône; Gasse, from the Hotchkiss Company; and others. Among us were also a substantial number of underworld figures of the same breed as the famous Spirito and Carbone from Marseille: these men were the wealthy owners of nightclubs in Marseille and Toulon, and they were always noisy and voluble. Some were tattooed from head to toe; I saw one who had "Neither God nor Master" tattooed on his forehead and "Alone in the World" on his chin. His closest companion was a priest, and as far as I could see, they got along pretty well.

The reasons for deportation were diverse. Some were there because of their political affiliations or their hostility toward totalitarian regimes—most of these were German Communists taken to Buchenwald as soon as the Führer came to power. There were the "racials": Israelites from many nations, but mainly from central Europe. These people were difficult to put up with; they were inveterate thieves endowed with a dexterity that confounded the imagination, filthy, always whining, liars and informers capable of the vilest servility toward the S.S. The common criminals, representing about twenty nations, were the most remarkable specimens. They were assassins, professional thieves, and pimps, and their presence among us was shrewdly calculated and exploited, giving our torturers reason to treat us all as if we were criminals. Last, but not least, were the resistants, whom the Boches called "terrorists." They were a minority whose attitude and principles stood out clearly from those of the other categories.

At sunset on August 21, the last convoy from France arrived at the Little Camp. The prisoners had left Compiègne on August 17; like ours, theirs had been a painful trip. Many among them had died: Brousse, Hamon, and many others. For the first time, I met Valentin Pons, director of the post office in the Orne region, who told me of his adventures. Daniel Desmeulles was there also, and he related his car trip with the Gestapo, Jardin, and his gang: the stop on the road, the announcement of his reprieve, the horrible slaughter in L'Hôme-Chamondot, his conversations with the killers.

Henri Barbier managed to slip everywhere, and he informed me that a comrade in the large camp was waiting near the barbed wire fence. It could only be Paul Alasseur, and indeed it was. With him were Onfray, Hébert, Gainche, Louvrier, Gobri, and Nicolas. I was to see them often, and their presence would be a great comfort to me. Unfortunately, Studer, who had been sent to Dora on June 6, was no

longer among them; Bernard Grisard had also been sent to a Kommando. We became acquainted with Lalouet, Phalandre, Renoult, Mar-
tain, Pitel, Trocherie, Denis, Brunet, Pierre Hamon, Boulerie, Fresnaie,
and all the others I mentioned earlier.

All day we wandered aimlessly about the camp, helpless. From time
to time there was a mad rush to the vats of soup (or I should say
dishwater) brought from the "Küchen" (kitchens). Since we had only
one mess tin and one spoon for three men, we only got to eat one
meal out of three. During the second night, the tents were so crowded
that we had to sleep outside, with four men sharing one blanket. At an
altitude of seven hundred meters, it was freezing cold. In the nights that
followed, two hundred of us stormed the latrines for shelter despite the
horrendous stench, the filth, the smell of chlorine and of the dysenteric
excrement. The next day I tried to find among the cellblocks my old
friend from the air club of Paris, Commandant Fremont, a pilot, dedicated resistant, and the associate of two great men now dead, Robert
Benoist and Williams. Fremont had been caught by the Gestapo with
a truck full of munitions; I was told he had already been sent to a
Kommando.

Rain or shine, we were submitted to endless roll calls, standing for
hours until the forty to forty-five thousand men of the *Lager* were
accounted for. Hundreds of little gypsies fell out of the lines, creating
much disorder. There were always errors, and the S.S. guards had to
recount four or five times. Some roll calls lasted seven or eight hours—
some prisoners died during them.

Four days after our arrival (Thursday, August 24, around noon), as
we were lying under the trees, several formations of "flying fortresses"
appeared in the sky. They circled the camp, and almost immediately the
bombs began to fall. The bombardment was intense; it destroyed the
munitions plant, the parking lot (including three thousand vehicles), and
the V-2 radio plant. A few shells fell on the camp, near the kitchens.
The S.S. barracks barely escaped the destruction, but many outbuildings
located at the entrance to the camp were destroyed, and the wife and
young daughter of the S.S. captain were killed. In just thirty minutes,
the Americans caused terrible damage: five hundred victims among the
prisoners and eight to nine hundred among the ranks of the S.S., who
for the first time appeared discouraged and scared. Some of them killed

the wounded prisoners in a frenzy of rage. Everywhere bodies were
carted away. Since the *Revier* (sick bay) and the infirmary could not
accommodate all the wounded, some were taken to the "special" house,
where they were tended to by the "ladies." It was said that Princess
Mafalda of Italy had been thrown into this brothel, where she was to
die in abject misery. Legend had it that on the day Goethe's oak was
destroyed, the German empire would collapse—indeed, the oak had
fallen during the attack.

When some semblance of calm had settled two or three days later,
five thousand of us were taken to the "Kino" room for anthropometry,
photographs, and indexing for the *Arbeits statistik* (job statistics). Not
wanting to be sent to a factory, I did not divulge that I was a mechanical
engineer. To the Boche who was questioning me, I said, "Expert." Not
understanding me very well, he asked, "Judge?" "Yes, yes, that's it," I
answered. They would never know my exact profession. Then came
the vaccination; we were inoculated against four or five diseases with
one shot. Bare to the waist, we lined up in rows of ten in front of
several doctors armed with large hypodermic syringes. They pricked us
haphazardly, often not even close to the area previously disinfected. No
other precautions were taken.

The sanitary accommodations were very bad. There were about a
dozen water faucets, which operated only one or two hours per day.
As soon as the water was turned on, eight to nine thousand men ran
to the washbasins, crowding and jostling each other to get a cupful of
water. As for washing, it was out of the question. We were filthy, covered with vermin and scabies. Like so many others, I suffered from
diarrhea. One morning I followed René Barbier to the medical clinic.
Each morning a prisoner, promoted to nurse, brought to the middle of
the yard an old wooden crate on which he placed three bottles. One
contained a white powder supposedly foolproof against dysentery and
all dyspepsia; the second was filled with the inevitable blue methylene
(fifty throats were painted with the same cotton wad); I never found
out the contents of the third. Once the crate was set up, five or six
hundred prisoners crowded around a so-called doctor (always a Hun-
garian, Pole, or Romanian) who had to be finished with his "consul-
tations" within an hour. That morning the practitioner gave me a little
bit of white powder. Soon afterwards, we heard an order: "All those

present because of dysentery must go to the side gate." Following this was a moment of great anxiety. What were they going to do with us? Were the Boches now considering us useless? Were they going to send us to the crematorium, or had they decided to give us treatment? We had heard so often in Buchenwald that "We want working men or dead ones!" But when we saw the large number of patients gathering by the gate, we felt a little more at ease. My comrades Daniel Desmeulles, René Barbier, Rouley (assistant to Mendès-France, mayor of Louviers), Father Hénocque, Sauter, and I decided to join the group. We were led to a cell in block sixty-one, the block for dysenterics. Next door was block sixty, for the infirm and the old, where I made the acquaintance of Monsieur Couraye du Parc, president of the tribunal of Le Mans, who despite his splendid courage and moral fortitude would never return home.

We stayed in block sixty-one for over fifteen days, five men crowded into each contamination ward, submitted to a regimen of white porridge-like substance and to the crazy rules of the celebrated attendant we had nicknamed V1. I shall mention only one of his ideas—he had forbidden us to go to the latrines from 7 to 10 A.M. because they were being cleaned, and also from noon to 2 P.M. because it was siesta time. Our needs did not adjust well to this schedule, and it is easy to guess the results.

I was reunited with some people I knew: Albert Picard, former adjudant to the air force in Africa; Commandant Berger, a dedicated resistant; Denis, inventor of the "V can"; Commandant Sautereau, the ace with the wooden leg; Valentin Pons, from the postal service; Réglain; François Zoude; Reverend Lecourt, a paralytic; David Highs, a young Canadian airman; and the American pilot Glenn Horwege. Finally our stay in block sixty-one came to an end, despite all the efforts of brave Dr. Boucher to keep us there. We were transferred to a departure block.

19

THE KOMMANDO OF HOLZEN

On September 14, 1944, about three hundred of us were assembled near the main gate. I found myself separated from all the comrades I knew, except Daniel Desmeulles. That evening we were loaded into cattle cars. At nightfall the next day, our convoy stopped in Eschershausen, a small town near Hanover. We were transferred into trucks; we traveled about ten kilometers through the country and forests and arrived at the top of a hill where some thirty "marabout" tents had been set up (five or six men to each). The next day at noon—the Boches did not waste any time—we heard the traditional "Arbeits kommando eintreten" (assembling of the work detail). We left for the valley. Our work consisted of digging trenches for the famous *Wasserleitung,* the water pipes. This project completed, we worked on the construction of a concrete road. It was there that I met a great man: Father Robert Beauvais, agent for the escape network "Comète." He was brutally arrested for his activity in the Resistance—along with his mother and sister, who would not return from Ravensbrück.

I was put in charge of operating the cement mixer for a few days. This sorry machine swallowed so much cement and gravel that we had a hard time keeping up with it. To get us some rest, I dropped a stone in the mixer to jam it. This ploy never failed—every time, we gained a half-hour respite, which was well worth risking the blows promised by our pugnacious *Meister.* Besides, we did not quite observe the proper proportions of sand and cement, and I have no doubt that "our" autobahn did not last very long.

Our next task was at the Debag quarry. Labasque (from Semur), an expert in this type of work, swore that fifty prisoners accomplished less than two of his experienced workers. We were now a close-knit little group: Desmeulles (from Alençon), Debenest (from Niort), Kergoustin (from Croix-de-Vie), Marie (an engineer with the department of bridges of La Roche-sur-Yon), Gianésini (with the postal service in Niort), Camille Délétang (from Le Mans), and Commandant Piketty. Unfortunately, we were soon to be separated: on the evening of Sunday, October 1, I came down with such a high fever that I had to go to the infirmary set up in one of the tents. My temperature was so high that Dr. Roux (a longtime prisoner in charge of the infirmary) decided to keep me there. I lay down on the straw-covered floor between Pierre Danic, a physician from Saint-Chamond suffering from sinusitis, and Jacqua, a young mechanic from Paris. Two days later I came down with phlebitis in my right leg. I remained there thirty days, lying on the straw with Danic and Jacqua, who every night was coughing out his lungs little by little. He was transferred in extremis to Holzminden, where he died on October 22 after a week of terrible agony. (Do you remember, Danic, our long conversations on the most various subjects, ranging from hunting antelopes in the Dauphiné to the minutest details of Lyonnaise gastronomy to the effects of the splitting of atoms—which you foresaw—to the jokes you used to hear when you were an intern at Lyon?)

Every day we eagerly looked forward to hearing news from the outside world—true or false—brought by Dr. Roux and our good friend Netter, the infirmary's interpreter.

On November 1, a month and a day after my admission to the infirmary, I was pronounced cured and immediately sent back to work. A new camp was under construction in the village of Holzen, just a few kilometers away. First I was sent to work on the ballasting of the roads, then to the rock quarry, and finally to an underground plant, the Franke Werke, where we pulled kilometers of enormous electric cables through tunnels. This went on until the end of December.

Christmas was one of the saddest I have ever spent. That morning the S.S. guards had spread news throughout the camp of the American defeat in Luxembourg. We were discouraged, and that evening we were all thinking about our families and homes. Desmeulles, Gianésini, Kergoustin, Debenest—all were morose. Despite my efforts to fight it off, sadness was beginning to get to me. Labasque was the only one trying to cheer us up, but without success. We French were a sorry bunch. What a contrast with the Russians, who all night long sang in chorus their beautiful national songs. All their cubicles were decorated with trees. For the past few weeks I had been bringing back the silvery ribbons dropped into the forest by "flying fortresses" to decorate our tree, but they had not been used.[5]

Some one thousand men had been added to the Kommando. We did not get any rest, and the food was terrible. The internal administration of the camp had been entrusted to the Poles, who naturally favored their countrymen. The rations distributed to the French got smaller and smaller. I cannot really describe the horror of departing for work at 5 A.M., in the pitch black, in all kinds of weather and all temperatures. The Kapos mercilessly hunted those prisoners who, to avoid the deadly Kommando work, hid under the straw pallets or in the *Abort* (latrine). I will not dwell either on the private habits of the "Polacks": each morning they would receive a visit from a young Russian boy, about twelve years old, and we would have to witness their frolics.

After Jacqua's death, many other comrades were to die within a few weeks: Massy, Le Limousin, Reboulat, Hirsch, Pincanon, Busset, Courdavault, Duvernet, Haynau, Herry, de Vichy, Thomas, Tournade, Schapira, Auvret, Pitel, Hamon, Trocherie, Pierre Lévry, Auger, and Rageau, among others. This was the inevitable and logical end for those who had managed to be admitted to the so-called infirmary of Holzen. The infirmary consisted of nothing more than a long room inside block one; the only opening was a tiny door. The false ceiling was very low, the daylight never came through, and the only lighting was provided by a few weak bulbs. At times there were as many as 130 patients crowded there pell-mell, no matter what diseases they suffered from. We witnessed some heart-rending scenes, the horror of which beggars the imagination. On February 4, during one of my stays in the infirmary, Pitel, from Tanville, was dying next to me. He was turned very gently on his side, and his breathing became irregular, then stopped altogether. Before I had a chance to intervene, his meager possessions were grabbed up by the Poles. A rope was tied around his ankles, and his body, still warm, was dragged through the infirmary and thrown on the heap of corpses.

Because Holzen was a small Kommando, there was no crematorium; we had to bury our dead once a week. In the meantime the naked corpses were piled near the entrance to the camp. A clamorous bunch of women from the village brought the children to view the spectacle. At the beginning, the dead were buried in the small Holzen cemetery, but soon there were too many. From then on they were buried in a nearby pasture, side by side with the remains of the free Italian workers. The same coffin was always used: it was very large, with room for two bodies, and we did not nail it shut. It was placed on a cart, which we pushed across the village—the only hearse I ever saw there. We buried the bodies, then returned with the empty coffin, ready to be used again.

Three days later, on February 7, Pierre Hamon died. His morale had been good, and he wanted to live, but Danic had warned me that he would not make it. That morning, lying in a dark nook, speaking loudly and volubly, he took his last breath. I also remember Henri Montant (a Martiniquan, installer of central heating in Orléans), who died from lung disease just after he received—by chance—news from his wife, a prisoner in Ravensbrück.

At my request I was sent, with Bellagué, Richard, and two other Frenchmen, to work in a garage in Eschershausen, eight kilometers from the camp. We went there on foot each morning, through snow and ice, but soon I had to stop because of the bad condition of my leg. Yet I did have time to repair the colonel's Volkswagen, for which he thanked me with threats and insults.

I returned to Holzen, very depressed, and spent a few days in the infirmary. I had just gotten out when a bout with pleurisy in my left lung sent me back. I was to stay nearly a month in this sad and miserable place. Jean Agliastro and I, huddled against each other, shared a bedstead seventy centimeters wide. Yet we spent a few good moments: do you remember, Danic, the guard nicknamed "Barnabé," a human wreck, a masterpiece of ugliness and stupidity, who had locked his jaw while yawning and came in woefully to get it "squared"?

Back again to the quarry. My God, it was cold at six in the morning. When discouragement overwhelmed my comrades, I tried to cheer them up by telling my adventures, my fantasies as a bachelor, endless jokes, happy memories of my youth. We formed an inseparable little group: Labasque, Marie (the expert on rocks), Debenest, Kergoustin. We would hear the sentinel bawling from the top of the hill: "Weg! Weg!" and every time Labasque would walk away saying, "This damn Rougeyron, what a phenomenon!" Among our group, Debenest and I were the only ones whose duty it was to break up two enormous rocks. Not wanting to expend much effort, we took advantage of the lessons of the *Meister;* we broke the rocks in the direction of the veins and got surprisingly good results. The old Boche who was supervising was quite impressed and showed a little leniency toward us.

Following an incident between Desmeulles and Klein, I was ousted from the Kommando and worked for a few days with a team in the forest (Eisenrich). We dug trenches in a mountain, about eight kilometers from Holzen. At the end of February, the weather was still very cold, and more and more men became ill. The infirmary was crowded: there were as many as 120 patients, and young Jean-Louis Netter (fifteen years old), the "cabin boy," could not keep up with the work. He was constantly mistreated by Stephane Homme, the appalling brute who ruled the infirmary.

On January 14 we heard about the Russian attack, and this good news gave us some courage. We also followed anxiously the progress of the Allies to our west.

One morning, thanks to Paul Gianésini, I was promoted to assistant electrician. My job consisted of repairing five thousand barbed-wire insulators. It's a beautiful story: for one month, followed by a Russian aide, I entertained the whole camp as I carried around a roll of wire (which I did not use) and an old bucket full of the most ridiculous tools. The S.S., who had no idea what this work entailed, left us alone. Soon we became famous throughout the camp. Incidentally, my job as Kommando electrician nearly did me in. One night in March there was a great tumult in the camp. Suddenly the Boches locked all our blocks, then made a roll call and second roll call. What was going on? In the morning we learned that six Russian officers and soldiers—determined men like so many among them—had escaped. Protecting their hands with discarded inner tubes, they had cut "my" electrified barbed wire. The S.S. officers were raving mad. Their colonel—a young brute, fat as a barrel, violent, rude, and obstreperous—had been wakened in haste in the guard forester's house. He sent his German shepherd (a dog we hated because it would find everything when sniffing our straw mattresses) on the tracks of the runaways. The voltage was not cut off, and my installation functioned perfectly—that I was sure of. The dog was electrocuted. To avenge himself, the colonel pumped a bullet into the head of a poor Russian devil peacefully coming out of the latrine. I was rather concerned: was I going to be blamed in some way? The following morning I rechecked my wiring. I had noticed before that one wire near an escape hole was broken—but only one was not significant, and I had not reported it. But I could still be in trouble. Fortunately, all went well; the Germans went around the camp several times without noticing anything, and I was not summoned by the terrible *Lagerführer.*

As the situation in Germany worsened, our guards became more unbearable. Their greatest fun was to make us stand at attention and slap our faces to see us react. They shot those who resisted. Each time I turned pale and looked the S.S. straight in the eyes, but I managed to contain myself. One Sunday they threw me into the snow and beat me up in front of two hundred comrades for being unable to finish my work (cutting wood) because of my bad leg. The evening was the only time we got some peace, from soup time (the vile rutabaga juice) to "Licht aus" (lights out). Around the tables or on the straw pallets, we talked or organized lectures. The survivors among us remember well the clear and detailed reports given by Daniel Desmeulles on Canada and on the formation of the United States. He had a regular audience presided over by Dr. Roux and Netter; his stories puzzled the Poles, Czechs, and other foreigners. For a long time Desmeulles and I shared the same pallet; at night we were always the last ones still talking. This was how I learned in detail about the history of the Resistance in the Orne region, the many exploits of the maquis, the executions (among them that of Morineau), the acts of the "Mataf," the dismal affair of Lignières-la-Doucelle. Daniel also told me about his arrest, carried out June 13, 1944, by Duru and Lotti. For Daniel there were many unanswered questions. He often talked to me about Terrier, a brave man who despite his advanced age had participated actively in the Resistance, transported munitions, and hidden Daniel. I came to have much esteem for this courageous old man.

I wrote a lot, despite the distrustful looks of the Russians and the Poles, who did not seem fond of intellectuals. The only paper we had was pieces of cement bags. Debenest, Desmeulles, and I had given each other our last wills, written on the paper sacks. I was to be lucky enough, at the time of my escape, to salvage Daniel's will as well as my notes.

Our life was far from monotonous; there were many unexpected happenings, even comical moments. One morning while walking in the camp I was apprehended by a Kapo who took me to the latrines, where I joined a half-dozen other prisoners equipped with old buckets and ropes. Unmistakably, it was the shit duty, the *Scheisskommando*. But my lucky star did not fail me: an S.S. passed by and did not agree with the Kapo on the dumping site. The two of them decided to ask the advice of the *Lagerführer*. When they returned, we had all disappeared into thin air.

Each evening Altmann, the German tailor who, as a privilege, worked in the village, brought back comforting news that helped our morale.

One day a convoy of Jews from central Europe arrived. They were terribly emaciated and in rags. The whole afternoon long, they were beaten into the dirt by the Poles. What an ignoble spectacle. One night at the end of March, a "herd" of women arrived from Auschwitz. When they left, there were twenty-eight hundred of them. Traveling in coal cars, they reached our camp after a seventy-three-day trip, their group reduced to six hundred; the dead had been thrown off the cars. Some of them carried babies in their arms. Several of those children died during the night. In the morning I had the opportunity to speak with the wife of a Dutch diplomat and with a working girl from Armentières; their odyssey was heartbreaking.

Suddenly the S.S. received orders to evacuate the camp because of the Allies' advance. On March 29 a first transfer to Buchenwald took place. Marie (the engineer) and Guilloteau (from Niort) left. This convoy was destroyed, and we were never to see our comrades again: Bellagué, Billon, Mugnier, Carrey, Bizouerne, Bouron, Claude, Devault, Picard, Christol, Guilloteau, Mathieu, Obry, Pourtalet, Richard, Delaboge, Prat, Rousseau, Troupénat, Rouley, Zara, Gosse, Hulback, Lorée, Meslay, Meunier, Monod, and the rest. Our turn came on April 5. We had been on the alert for two days. Finally, after many orders and counterorders, we were loaded into coal cars in Eschershausen. There had been no food distributed. On April 6, after numerous detours along secondary tracks, the train arrived in Immendorf. From there we walked to the Hermann Goering factory, in Drutte. This huge factory had just been bombed, and a large number of the outbuildings had been destroyed. We were taken to the cellars. Some three to four thousand deportees were already there; they were in a frightful physical condition. In the evening, when food was distributed, the Kapos and Vorarbeit intentionally started a disturbance. It gave them an excuse to appropriate our rations, and we did not get any food. The next day we heard of a new evacuation order.

20

THE ESCAPE

The evacuation began on the morning of April 7, 1945. It was a warm and sunny day. We were loaded into metal coal cars, and soon we were covered with black dust. With no regard for the condition of the sick and dying, they were put into an open railcar. The preparations continued until late in the evening. The convoy consisted of about three thousand prisoners and five to six hundred women detainees brought there at the last minute. Their heads had been shaved entirely. We were guarded by 130 S.S. soldiers. The train finally started in the direction of Hamburg. Again, no food rations had been distributed; we had not had anything to eat in more than thirty hours.

The train traveled all night and all morning on secondary tracks. On Sunday, April 8, a little before 2 P.M., the train stopped at the Celle station. The weather was beautiful—a clear and sunny sky. We were impatiently waiting for the allocation of bread and margarine announced that morning. Suddenly, around 4 P.M., a dozen twin-engine planes appeared, shining in the sunlight. They were approaching from the west at a fairly low altitude—one thousand to fifteen hundred meters, and I recognized them as "Mosquitoes." In combat formation, they flew southeast over the station and came back northwest. The prisoners, their noses in the air, were in awe. I must confess that I was not too thrilled; I had gone through several bombardments and knew both the way the R.A.F. operated and the results of their projectiles. A Belgian man said to me, "I wish I were somewhere else!" "So do I!" Alas, our fears were justified. The maneuver by the English was a warning to evacuate the station, but the Boches disregarded it. It was to result in twenty-five hundred deaths.

What took place was devastating: the formation of "Mosquitoes" returned like a whirlwind, diving on the antiaircraft battery, the fuel trains, and our convoy. I can still hear the piercing hiss of the diving planes, followed by the crushing explosions of the first bombs. It was a hell of fire, flames, and iron. The explosions succeeded each other within seconds, in a shower of twisted metal. A fuel tanker car of the nearby train caught fire—200,000 liters of gasoline were burning. The antiaircraft battery stationed on the third track was pulverized (I clearly remember seeing a heavy cannon catapulted into the air). A bomb crushed the women's railcar, which was hitched not far from ours. We were surrounded by thick black smoke; the acrid smell of phosphorus burned our throats. Lying on my stomach along the left rear wall of the car, I protected my head in the corner, mentally thanking the Boches for having put us in metal cars. What had become of my comrades Desmeulles, Pons, Gianésini, and Kergoustin?

I remained in this position through the first two waves of the attack. Then, when I could stand it no longer, I leaped over the side of the car, four meters down to the track, landing awkwardly on the shriveled, half-burned body of a prisoner. I crawled under one of the rear wheels of the car until the next wave of planes passed. Then I dashed across the tracks littered with dead and wounded: deportees, civilians from another destroyed convoy, soldiers (White Russians from a hospital train). They all fled, screaming. I had to cross about ten tracks under a shower of shrapnel.

Finally I reached the end of the railroad ballast; I passed the body of a German solider lying there, his head crushed. I ran across a garden in which a young, blond S.S. man, his back broken, held out his arms, begging me to help him up. I did not stop. Waves of planes were following each other incessantly. I had to take shelter for a few minutes in the basement of a destroyed house, and I didn't even think to explore it. I couldn't stay there; because of their proximity to the Allies' target, all the surrounding buildings were in flames. Besides, I risked being discovered. I ran up the street and heard my name; it was Delphin Debenest, calling me as he fled. He had been wounded in the forehead by a shell splinter, but it was only superficial. What a relief: at least the two of us would be together. We did not have a chance to reach one another before the new wave arrived. Again, I rushed into the basement; I saw Debenest throw himself on the ground between two walls.

The alert over, we ran like mad and reached a field, then a nearby forest. Within minutes our minds were made up. We were certainly not prepared to make a successful escape: we had no money to speak of (6.5 marks between us); we were wearing the blue striped pajamas of prisoners; our heads were shaved; we had little knowledge of the German language; and we were ignorant of the topography of the region. Yet without hesitation we decided to escape. We hid in a deep furrow between two pine trees and formulated our plan of action. Debenest had lost his cap, so I gave him a strip of green sock I had wrapped around my neck. He made some kind of turban out of it. He was incredibly thin, and he had a large wound on his right temple and a beard like a hobo. With his new headgear, my friend the public prosecutor had a sinister appearance, worthy of an inhabitant of "Zone" (the miserable hutments of the military zone outside the fortifications of Paris). The next task was to hide the visible parts of our uniforms: we could, of course, turn our collars inside and button our raggedy overcoats; but it was impossible to hide the legs of our trousers. We scraped off as best we could the brightly colored crosses from the backs of our coats, and we managed to make them a little less conspicuous.

At nightfall, violent gunfire could be heard throughout the forest. Those S.S. who had survived the bombardment were searching the area with the help of the garrison of Celle. Any fleeing prisoners they found were gunned down on the spot. For several long hours we crouched at the bottom of the furrow; then, in the middle of the night, we started walking toward the east, using the polestar as our guide. We reached the edge of the wood, crossed a forest road, and immediately went into a second wood. The night was pitch black, and we advanced with difficulty, falling into holes, bumping into downed tree trunks, branches whipping our faces. Debenest walked in front, and he hurried me up and encouraged me constantly. We continued our slow and dangerous trek through the wood. In the dark our steps were hesitant, and branches cracked underfoot.

After a while we reached a main road, oriented east-west (like many German roads). We followed that road, going west, walking on the lowest part of the shoulder, throwing ourselves into ditches at the least sound. At first all went well: the walk was much easier than through the wood. Suddenly we heard voices and footsteps about one hundred

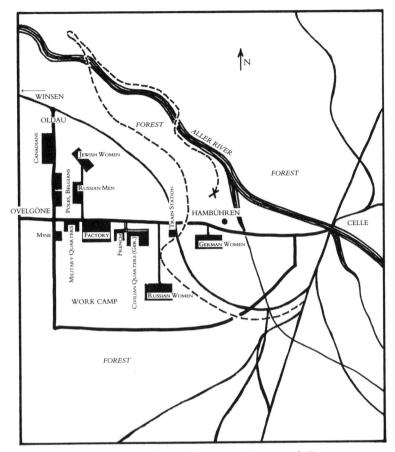

MAP 3. The dotted line indicates the approximate path Rougeyron traveled between the train station at Celle and Hambühren upon his escape.

meters ahead. Always fearful of German sentinels, we left the road for
the underbrush, but soon we came to a barbed wire fence. In the dark,
we perceived the outline of barracks—we were near a work camp. To
avoid it we were forced to make a long detour before we could reach
the road. We seemed to be having a run of bad luck; a short while later
we came across another *Lager.* We went around it. A few kilometers
farther, we wandered into the deserted streets of a hamlet. It was late,
we were exhausted and starving, and the only thing that sustained us
was the comforting thought that we were *free!*

We made our tour of the village and of the nearby construction
yards and tried to force the doors of several tool sheds where we might
sleep, but our strength failed us, and our efforts were in vain. As a last
resort we lay down on a board, huddled against each other, at the
entrance of an underground shelter. But it was very cold. I told Debenest, "Let's go, otherwise we'll die here." Shivering, we were on our
way again, through dirt roads and pastures. We made numerous stops
to rest or to listen. Suddenly we heard footsteps: a sentinel was walking
not far from us, making his rounds. We jumped into a ditch. Another
man passed by and stopped to chat with the sentinel. One of them told
his *Kamerad* that it was four in the morning. We could hear their steps
on the boards. No doubt this was a guard post: field police, Wehrmacht,
or Volkssturm? We did not know, but we had to avoid it at all costs.
On our right and left were barbed wire fences; behind us, fifty meters
away, was a dirt path leading deep into the wood, the only way out of
that dangerous site. We tiptoed as lightly as we could—it was easy
because the two of us together weighed less than eighty kilos—but our
wooden clogs betrayed us. At once the sound of hobnailed boots re-
sounded on the asphalt. Fortunately the footpath was close by, and we
ran to it. Already a flashlight was aimed in our direction. We squatted
in a thick bush. The alert over, we continued on the path. New alert:
ahead of us we saw the lights of barracks. This time it was a military
cantonment, and again we had to go deeper into the forest. Because of
these endless detours, we were not making much progress. We had only
one thought: to get as far as possible from Celle. When the coast was
clear, we went through another small wood and got back on the road.
There we could walk much faster. Suddenly the situation worsened as

cyclists passed by constantly. We jumped into the ditch at each alert, sometimes in extremis, because the bicycles had no lights.

After three or four difficult kilometers, we swerved left to follow a towpath along the Aller River. Daylight was beginning to break through a dense fog, and the air was extremely cold. We found some empty cement sacks near an abandoned construction site. We carefully cut them and wrapped them around our legs with strings, to hide our striped trousers. To go west we were going to have to cross the Aller, but the bridges were guarded. We looked in vain for a fishing boat. Swimming across was out of the question; it was wider than the Seine. Besides, without a change of clothes we would risk catching pneumonia. Sick at heart, we walked away from the river. It was now broad daylight. Three schoolchildren sighted us. Quickly we crossed the main road and sought refuge in the nearby woods. (We found out later that we were, on that morning of April 9, on the outskirts of the town of Oldau.) We lay among the ferns for several hours, near a bridge guarded by Wehrmacht and Landsturm soldiers who came and went just a few meters away from us.

Huddled against each other, we talked in whispers. I had frequent fits of coughing and feared that I would be heard by the sentinels. Finally, after a long wait, we took our chance. When the guards strayed a little farther away (though we could still hear their voices and footsteps), we dashed across the Aller bridge, clogs in hand, and immediately rushed back into the woods. After these perilous minutes, we deserved some rest. We crouched under a dense thicket. Sweating and shaking, we were elated to have escaped, once more, a return to prison or a hail of bullets. (After my return to France, I found out that we were tremendously lucky: just a few hours earlier, four of our comrades—the unfortunate Daniel Desmeulles, Netter and his son Jean-Louis, and Lieutenant Sarrasin were caught by Landsturm soldiers on that very bridge.)

The pine forest where we were hiding was deserted. There were no German depots or units. The forest was surrounded by farmland. From the edge of the wood we could see a few peasants planting potatoes. This was a godsend for us: at nightfall we would pull some plants so that we wouldn't starve to death.

We walked to the middle of the wood, where we found an old

wooden structure that appeared to have been deserted for years. After circling it, we looked inside. It had once been a shed for bees. Inside, the shelters were set up in a horseshoe; all that was left were some termite-eaten shelves and an old beehive, from which we tried to retrieve a little wax. After scraping hard and long, a few grams of a gray and dirty paste fell off—it was edible, and better than nothing. After looking over the premises, we decided to set up our "headquarters" there. We lay down on the moss in the middle of the apiary, under the sun's warm rays. A few minutes later, we were fast asleep.

Late in the afternoon Debenest, the first to wake, heard footsteps. He called me. We caught sight of a prisoner (wearing the striped uniform) walking toward the shed. It was a Russian who, like us, had escaped from the Celle station. He gave each of us a spoonful of soup from a tin can. He was holding a lighted, grease-covered wick (which seemed odd to us). Gesturing that he would be back, he left mysteriously. Puzzled by this apparition, we deliberated anxiously: Could we trust this Russian? Where did he get the soup? Where did he go?

At nightfall we went to the edge of the forest to dig up a few potatoes and to collect some dandelions. Our harvest was fruitful, and we also found a few onions, some garlic, and to our great delight, two year-old heads of cabbage. I will always remember the sight of the prosecutor Debenest meticulously washing these vegetables in the brook. While crossing the pasture we caught sight, in a nearby bush, of a beautiful, fat chicken apparently brooding her eggs. Without a word, the same thought crossed our minds, and Debenest said, "Yes, but if we catch it, we'll have to eat it uncooked." Then he crawled very slowly and carefully under a bush behind the fowl. I foresaw what was next: the chicken took off, and our hopes of eating meat flew away with it. Since this incident I have often threatened to reveal to the prosecutor's colleagues his attempt to steal other people's property; in the justice system, the intent is as good as the deed.

Just as we were getting ready for a second try, Debenest spotted, at a distance, a farm woman coming toward us. She was probably looking for her chicken. As soon as she saw us, she turned back, frightened, and started running to the village. Because of our strange appearance, we were clearly not a very reassuring sight. The smart move for us was to run as fast as we could; surely this woman was going to alert the townspeople, who were already aware that a train of "terrorists" was bombed at the Celle station and that some had escaped. We returned to our shed empty-handed. It was almost dark, and we had to prepare for the night. We set up a few boards to form the sides of a "bed" and spread some branches, which we covered with moss and leaves. We lay down side by side. Though we had slept during the afternoon, we were still very tired and soon went to sleep. In the middle of the night I woke up, freezing. Debenest, who had been awake for a long time, was shivering, but he hadn't made a move for fear of disturbing my sleep. It was too cold to remain motionless; we got up and started pacing around the shed. It seemed that the night would never end. Sometimes we lay down; sometimes we stood and stomped our feet. We had no respite from cold, fatigue, or hunger. Finally the sun came up, and we were able to get a few hours' sleep.

It was now April 10. We absolutely had to find a way to get some food. We could not keep subsisting on raw potatoes and dandelions. We were becoming weaker and weaker: I suffered almost constantly from headaches and dysentery, and our morale was pitifully low. We discussed our predicament at length. We had only 6.5 marks between us. It was imperative to go to a farm to buy cooked potatoes or matches. (We could not ask anyone to cook the potatoes we had, because we would surely be accused of stealing them.) Our undertaking was not without risks. We were in a deplorable condition, thin, dirty, unshaven, with torn overcoats, leggings made of paper sacks, and prisoners' clogs. I wore a shapeless cap and Debenest his ridiculous turban. Yet it was a matter of life and death; we had to make a bold decision. In the afternoon we started walking through the woods toward the village at the edge of the forest, about one kilometer away (we learned later that it was called Oldau).

With great hesitation and looking attentively all around, we approached the houses bordering the forest. Two children were playing in front of a cottage; seeing us, the younger ran away. He returned a minute later with a blond, heavyset woman, about thirty-five years old. I told her several times in German, as well as I could, that we were not bad people and that we had some money and wanted to buy a few cooked potatoes. I also asked her for something to drink. She looked us over, then went to get some water and told us that we should ask for potatoes at a farm a little farther away. It was not prudent, but now that we had gone this far, we could not turn back. The street was deserted, and we went to the farm she indicated. There were so many people in the courtyard that we did not want to get too close. We approached a woman standing near the door. We told her we wanted to buy something, but at that moment we caught sight of a German soldier walking out of a nearby house. We preferred not to wait for the woman's reply.

It would have been unwise to go farther, so we decided to turn back. As we passed the farm again, a child ran to Debenest and gave him, without saying a word, a large turnip; then the child ran back into the house. A little later we saw a farmer unharnessing his horses. He looked at us but did not seem particularly surprised. We asked him to sell us a few potatoes. He gestured for us to wait and went to speak to his farmhand. We were worried—was he going to have us arrested? But it was nothing of the sort: the farmhand returned with a basket full of rather bad-looking potatoes. The farmer refused our offer of money.

Before reentering "our" woods, we passed the small house we had stopped at first. The blond woman was standing by the garden fence, and we asked her for a few matches. She answered that she did not have any. We knew that matches were scarce in Germany, but most likely she feared we would make bad use of them. To our great surprise, she handed us a small paper bag containing a dozen cooked potatoes. This was a real windfall for us. Smiles on our faces, we quickly returned to our shed. Our morale was up. These three hundred grams of potatoes would temporarily ward off the specter of hunger—another twenty-four hours to stay alive. On the way we stopped at a brook to fill a tin can with water. It was no easy feat to traverse the forest with this open can full of the precious liquid. Cooked potatoes and a few slices of turnip would make an exceptional dinner menu that night.

With our two or three kilos of tubers and the possibility of getting more from the fields, we were now rich, but we still faced a problem: How to cook them? How could we make a fire without matches? We would have to find some embers and also a container. At the edge of the woods, we noticed a heap of scrap iron; there we found two buckets. One had no bottom and the other no handle, but after searching more, we found what was needed to make them usable. We used one bucket to carry our potatoes and filled the other with pieces of wood and twigs to preserve the embers we hoped to locate. Suddenly, in the middle of the wood, we heard branches crack. It was the mysterious Russian, walking toward us: this time he was barefoot, and he wasn't wearing his cap or jacket. With a series of gestures, he tried to tell us something we could not understand, and then he was gone again. We called him back to ask for a match; incredibly, he had some. We were able to cook the potatoes and other vegetables, and we tried to keep the embers glowing. Alas, the next morning the fire was out.

We could not return to the village, where our presence had surely been reported. We decided to go to the two farms at the edge of the forest to ask for fire. From there we could see endless lines of vehicles and pedestrians heading east. That was a promising sign, and it gave us more confidence to take the paths. Peasants were working in the fields. Buckets in hand, we continued walking, staying as close as possible to the edge of the woods. In the middle of a field, a group of people were gathered around a soldier holding a bicycle. Hoping to go unnoticed, we were passing about a hundred meters away when a tall fellow called out to us, "Kommt! Kommt!" Should we flee or obey the injunction? The forest was very close, but still they would catch up to us before we reached it. After all, it was better to give the impression that we were not afraid, so we walked toward the group. The soldier accused us right away of having stolen the potatoes. We protested and explained that a peasant had given them to us. He looked into our bucket, and seeing the poor quality of the potatoes, he believed us. But then he suddenly opened the flaps of our overcoats and noticed our prisoners' stripes. He exclaimed: "Celle, Celle!" "Ja, Celle," we answered. He ordered us to take a footpath leading to the road, then to turn left and go east. We obeyed unhesitatingly. A peasant shouted, "Schnell! Schnell!" We acted like we were hurrying, but soon slowed our pace.

The soldier caught up with us on his bicycle and called out, "Schnell! Schnell!" We accelerated our pace. To our stupefaction, he did not stop but passed us at a fairly good clip, signaling us to follow the directions he had given earlier. Soon he was about one hundred meters ahead of us. From time to time he looked back to check on us.

We took advantage of a slight curve in the road and a few trees to leave the path and slip back into the woods. Oh, what a close call.

We decided not to go to any farms. Yet we were hungry: in the last six days we had eaten nothing but two to three hundred grams of potatoes and one turnip. We could not keep eating raw vegetables; that would certainly lead to dysentery and to death. Come what might, we had to brave the village. In the evening we stopped at a couple of houses: no matches, no fire. Desperate, we turned back. On the way a man about thirty years old, accompanied by a small child, noticed our discouragement. We asked him for some hot embers, but he was a refugee himself and did not have any. He called out to an old man, who after some hesitation gave him two or three matches. But we needed something to strike them against. The old man reluctantly gave us a matchbox, enjoining us not to build a fire in the forest, especially at night because of aircraft; we promised we would not and went away happy. The old man was watching us from his doorstep, so to put him at ease we picked up some twigs and made a pile at the edge of the underbrush. Debenest said, "You go ahead; I'll join you as soon as the old man goes inside." He caught up with me a few minutes later.

We were thrilled at the thought of eating cooked vegetables. Debenest began to prepare a hearth in a corner of the shed. It was important to hide the flames and the smoke as well as possible. A square of stones, a clever scaffolding of branches, and the potatoes were cooking. We ate this hot meal with great delight. At nightfall we prepared our "bed" in anticipation of the intense cold of the previous nights. As we had every night since our escape, we lay down side by side. Debenest fell asleep right away; as for me, the hot meal seemed to have restored my strength somewhat and stimulated my mental faculties, and I lay awake for a long time, assailed by a multitude of thoughts.

The night was beautiful; the sky was clear. At a distance—about fifty kilometers—I could hear the sound of cannons. All of a sudden, a series of terrific explosions broke the stillness of the night. The din was coming from not very far away. The northeast sky was aglow, and we jumped to our feet. The explosions intensified. What was happening? It was not an air raid; we had not heard any planes. It could not be Allied cannons: they were still too far away, and besides, the spectacle we were witnessing did not look at all like artillery fire. The fact that the explosions continued with increased intensity and at regular intervals led us to believe that the Germans were destroying war factories or military installations. We attempted to determine how far away the detonations were taking place. Fires must have already started, because a wall of flame was illuminating the sky; it looked like it was daylight. Debenest and I, standing in the middle of the apiary shed, were very worried. The cold was getting to us, so we decided to take a walk. It was around midnight, and we paced through the woods, talking. Our precarious situation added to the nervous tension, the fatigue, and the hunger made us—I must confess—quite irascible, and at times we exchanged sharp words. On several occasions since our escape, we had almost parted, but each time common sense told us to stay together.

We continued our walk and suddenly noticed the glow of fire a few hundred meters away near the edge of the forest. Approaching cautiously, we were surprised to see our Russian sitting next to a fire in the middle of a clearing. A few minutes later he pulled out of a cooking pot a whole rabbit, which he started to devour heartily. The site was so bright that we immediately noticed a bucket full of cooking utensils, among which was a clock. We left quickly, convinced that the Russian's imprudence could have disastrous consequences for us. His fire would certainly be noticed by the villagers. Besides, the Russian had not been content with taking food; obviously he had also stolen the bucket, the pans, and the clock from some house. Under the circumstances we had everything to fear, especially if the Boches decided to conduct a search. The more agile Russian would disappear; we would be accused in his place and shot forthwith. It did not take us long to reach a decision: we had to leave our refuge, cross the main highway, and take the towpath along the Aller. Soon it would be daylight. We returned hastily to our apiary shed, shared what was left of the potatoes, picked up our buckets, and we were on our way. We were uneasy about leaving the ruined hut that had sheltered us so well from the unknown. It was, I think, Thursday, April 12. I will always remember Debenest's comment as we were leaving: "I have the feeling this is going to be a good day." Little did he know!

We had just come out of the woods when we heard a voice shouting in German. The fog was very dense, and we could barely discern a battery of artillery about a hundred meters to our right. We swerved to

the left and rushed among a file of trucks. We were going to have
to cross the lines and reach the road, then the river. It was not going
to be easy. At every moment we came across artillery positions, trucks
camouflaged in the fields, soldiers coming and going in all directions
from post to post. Come what might, we had to pass. Before attempting
to cross the road, we made a stop in a dense and high thicket.

Not only our appearance was striking, but also our equipment. We
each carried a battered bucket and a wooden stick. As we were attempting to cross the road, a patrol of cyclists passed without seeing us,
but their leader, following a few meters behind, noticed us and got off
his bicycle. We did not make a move. Apparently he was concerned
about getting too far behind his men, and he hopped on his bicycle
again. Another close call. Although our strength was failing us more
and more, we darted across the open road as fast as we could. We
absolutely had to find something to eat and devise a plan—no matter
what—to carry out during the night. By following the river, we hoped
to get closer to the lines. Near a small train station, we saw two field
policemen heading our way. It was wise not to stay too long around
those parts.

We had been walking alongside the Aller for a while when I noticed
some rags in a nearby coppice. We found two tattered pairs of trousers—one had only one leg, the other no seat—and a couple of old,
torn sweaters. It was a stroke of luck. Letters written in French were
scattered across the ground; apparently some compatriots, free workers,
had undressed there. We took the old clothes into a grove of pines, and
Debenest began to mend them as best he could. He had a needle, but
very little thread. The lining we ripped from one of our overcoats made
a perfect seat for one pair of trousers. The leg of the other was sewn
with great difficulty, but the seam held, and that was what mattered. At
long last we were going to be able to "disguise" ourselves as civilians.
Debenest made himself a cap out of a rag. Dressed in trousers and
pullovers, overcoats on our arms, we were on our way again.

A few hundred meters farther, we passed two young men speaking
French. Twice we called out to them, "Êtes-vous français?" We got no
answer. We climbed over the embankment and saw a group of "civilians" gathered around a mass of suitcases and packages. A little farther
down, a man was drawing water from the river. We approached him.

He was French—an S.T.O. (compulsory labor worker). He took us to the group, and we introduced ourselves. They gave each of us a Basque beret, and a tall fellow, resourceful and good-natured, told us we could easily get civilian clothes from some deserted barracks not far away. But soon our conversation was interrupted by gunfire. An S.S. patrol was making the *Kontroll* and shooting fugitives. Quickly we hid. We went deep into the woods, but an antiaircraft cannon barely a hundred meters away prevented us from going farther. We had no choice but to hide where we were, under a small pine, perilously close to the path. The gunfire had stopped, and we could hear loud shouts coming from the area where we had met the group of S.T.O. workers. Soon three S.S. soldiers, machine guns in hand, appeared on the path. We played dead. If they found us, our goose was cooked. Fortunately, they walked away, talking. Soon afterward, the gunfire started again.

When the alert was over, we went back to the French group. Now there were no more than six or seven ready to leave. Debenest and I picked up suitcases—so as not to be noticed—and walked in the middle of the group across the plain, in the direction of the supposedly abandoned barracks. Debenest had kept his striped "pajamas" under his civilian togs; as for me, I carried my prison jacket, rolled up in a rag, under my arm. I got rid of it in a furrow near the railroad track, and the comrades behind me kicked dirt over it.

A short while later, we reached the barracks. We cleaned up a little and hid our old clothes, which we would burn as soon as we had a chance. The S.T.O.s had already lit the stove and begun to cook the potatoes. Debenest and I noticed on the table three mess tins filled with a rather unappetizing mixture. We gulped it voraciously despite the protests of our hosts, who told us it was several days old. This didn't matter to us: the mélange tasted delicious, and it would not prevent us from eating potatoes when they were cooked.

Debenest's clothes went into the fire, piece after piece. Now that we were freshly shaven and decently dressed, nothing would differentiate us from the others except our haircuts and our extreme thinness. They reassured us by telling us that there was no *Kontroll*. Also, if it became necessary, we had a carefully prepared story. We had both been hired as S.T.O.s by a firm in Hanover. We had gone through the bombardments and lost our papers. As for our hair, we had to cut it short because of lice. In these panicky and disorganized times, this story would surely be believed by the Boches—they were not particularly perspicacious.

We were given some blankets and spent the night in a room with three nice fellows, among whom were two of those who had led us to this hospitable spot: Hippolyte Facon, from Juigné-sur-Sarthe, and his friend Gabriel Fredou. For the first time since our arrest, we were able to appease our hunger. Only someone who had suffered as much as we had can truly understand the sheer joy we took in eating potatoes cooked in the hot ashes. We did not care that they tasted of coal. What a relief it was not to say any longer, "I'm hungry," or "I could eat another helping or two."

The next day we helped out by going to fetch water, but we did not dare to go farther. It would be a shame to take risks now that we were so close to our goal. At soup time that evening, a civilian told us he had heard that a jeep and a motorcycle, driven by Englishmen, had been sighted on the road. We were skeptical: there were still many German troops in the area. The comrades who had gone to the silo to get potatoes advised us to stay put because the Germans were firing on civilians. The explosions of munitions stored in the bunkers were increasing, the cannons sounded nearer, and everything raised our hopes for a better tomorrow. In the morning our first and only thought was, Are we liberated at last?

Friday the thirteenth, around 8 or 9 A.M., we heard the good news: British vehicles had been spotted on the road, speeding to the east. As I stepped out of the barracks, I could hardly believe what I saw. A British captain from a unit of parachutists was standing in front of me. He had just climbed out of a jeep and was surrounded by four or five men in red berets. I wondered if I was dreaming! The officer realized immediately that Debenest and I could not stay; we needed medical attention. Furthermore, because the Allied advance was just beginning (a retreat was still possible), he felt it would be wiser for us to join a group of twenty-five French prisoners of war, survivors of a Kommando in Hambühren. The British captain told us to join this group immediately, to dress in military uniforms, and to mingle with the others so that we would pass for prisoners of war in case the Germans came back.

Sergeant Major Bockler, from Lorient, was in charge of this small group. Without hesitation he agreed to take us in. We were welcomed with enthusiasm by all the prisoners, who tried as hard as they could to make us feel comfortable. They brought us the best food they could find from their reserves. We will never be able to thank these good men enough: Petiteau, Rumpala, Brugnon, Aumont, Hubert, Lassus, Cayrousse, and the others. They were horrified at our emaciation. In the afternoon the British officers returned to examine us: they were appalled at Debenest's skeletonlike appearance. Captain Jacob, of Langston, immediately took a photograph of him, completely naked. The British of the Royal Army Service Corps were very considerate toward us, and I am forever grateful to Captain Jacob Meerman and Lieutenant Bradbrook Spearing for all they did for us.

Late in the afternoon a very sad ceremony took place that proved once more the savagery of the Germans. The previous evening a Boche plane, skimming the ground, had dropped a load of air grenades on the prison camp. Two prisoners had been wounded and a third (Sergeant Gérardin, from Nancy) had been killed. There was no reason whatsoever for this unforgivable attack. That afternoon Debenest and I insisted on following the sad procession to the cemetery of Hambühren. A hand-pulled cart carried the coffin draped with a blue, white, and red flag made of paper. Walking in single file under the trees on each side of the road, we accompanied this comrade, a family man, killed on the very day of his liberation. The burial in the cemetery of this small village at the edge of the forest was most touching. Gérardin now rests over there, in the sand, side by side with six Canadian airmen killed a year before in Rixfords, all of them sacrifices, like so many others, of the gigantic fight of humanity against barbarism.

Later that evening, feeling good and proud—liberty was giving me strength—I walked to the main square of Hambühren, where a convoy of Canadians (the technical and mechanical units of the 144th Tank Force) was stationed. I met the driver of a huge workshop truck. He proudly declared in an unexpected suburban accent, "What do you think? I am as French as you are. My name is Lagassé, and I am from Sainte-Hyacinthe, Quebec. I have traveled seven thousand kilometers to get my ass shot at! You know, when we landed in Bayeux, the Boches called us 'the demons'—they don't like us!" He gave me the latest issue of the *Canadian News;* it was the first newspaper I had seen in a year.

Lagassé also informed me of the death of President Roosevelt the day before, and I was overcome by a great sadness. What a loss for Europe! What a disaster for France! It is true indeed that there is no joy without pain.

The following morning, the English doctor—who came almost daily—brought us two hundred kilos of powdered sugar, as well as milk, boxes of cookies, and meat. I accompanied him to the farms in Wietze, Ovelgöne, and Oldau. The Germans were forced to give us canned fruits and meats, eggs, and poultry. We thoroughly ransacked a grocery, and we returned with a fully loaded jeep every time. The sugar, milk, and cookies saved our lives. From then on, the mayor of the town was ordered to put at our disposal all the meat we needed. Every morning he designated a farmer to surrender a cow, and we always picked the best one. If we did not take these animals, they would be taken by the Poles and Ukrainians from nearby camps who were now roaming the countryside, terrorizing and pillaging the Boches.

Our war prisoner friends took good care of us. Now that we were rid of the filth and vermin that had covered us, we looked much better. I spent a lot of time in the nearby Mouna factory and brought back spark plugs, rolls of film, and an electric motor. This made my comrades laugh. But after a few days of waiting, we were haunted by the idea of returning to France.

The British captain in command of the new unit stationed in Hambühren, who had extended us the warmest welcome, advised us to wait for faster and less tiring means of evacuation than those presently available. He told us that there was a huge repatriation camp some one hundred kilometers away, but that there would probably be a long wait. The doctor also felt that in our condition we should not attempt the trip at that time. One day Debenest and Sergeant Major Bockler walked to Celle (seven or eight kilometers away), where they met a noncommissioned officer who told them it would be wiser to wait and who promised he would notify them as soon as the means for a quick repatriation was organized.

Yet the days went by, and we were getting impatient. All of us got along very well. Debenest and I had become good friends with our comrade prisoners, and we will never forget their welcome and their kind attentions. On April 24, Omont and another soldier went to Celle.

When they returned, around 7 P.M., they called their comrades together and gave them the long-awaited news—the British had agreed to fly us to Brussels in two days. We were deliriously happy. In the morning we slaughtered a cow and quickly carved it, then cooked the roasts to take with us on the trip. Everyone was busy packing.

At five the next morning a cart sent by the Bürgermeister, at our demand, arrived at the camp. The luggage was loaded, and we were on our way to Celle. There the British verified our identities and sprayed us with disinfectant. Next we were taken by trucks to the airfield, where "Dakotas" were landing and taking off without interruption. They unloaded food, ammunition, and arms and almost immediately departed with a load of twenty-five repatriated men. Around 4 P.M. it was our turn. We left aboard a "Douglas" piloted by Americans. Right after takeoff a soldier came out of the cockpit and distributed cigarettes—life was great! The weather was beautiful during the 450-kilometer trip. We could clearly see the German countryside below, from the smallest village to the largest city. There was much destruction. Around 6 P.M. the plane landed at the Nivelles airfield thirty kilometers from Brussels. British soldiers and noncommissioned officers took our baggage and led us to a hangar where we were offered biscuits and hot tea (as only the English know how to make it). After these refreshments we were driven by truck to Brussels.

It is impossible to describe the enthusiasm of the Belgian people all along the way: words fail me. The sight of the blue, white, and red flag unfurled at the rear of the truck unleashed a frenzy of joy. Those moments are forever etched in our memories. We were so proud to be French. Our Belgian friends were even closer to us than we had ever thought. We spent a restful night in the Ucclestadt reception center (very comfortably set up in a former factory). Early the next morning I made a telephone call to Roger Pichio, a comrade of mine from the other war. Shortly thereafter, he came to pick me up; we took Bockler and Debenest along. We were served an excellent breakfast by Madame Pichio, and then we toured Brussels. The crowds, the stores, the English military music playing on Place Royale: all these made our heads spin. It seemed like a dream, this unforgettable, wonderful day that marked the beginning of our newly recovered freedom. We returned to the reception center in the evening, and the following morning we left for Hazebrouck.

I had expected to feel intense excitement as I set foot on French soil, but the outpouring of welcome from the Belgian people had been so overwhelming that I did not experience the same height of emotion. Besides, though the people of Hazebrouck showed us much kindness, their small city had been terribly battered by the war, and they could not emulate Brussels. Our convoy numbered four to five thousand repatriated men. First we underwent a medical checkup, then debriefing by military intelligence. We turned over our German marks, and each of us received one thousand francs; we had never thought we would see French money again. The following day, April 28, we left for Paris amid shouts of joy. Debenest was going to Niort, and he joined another convoy. We had to part, not without much regret. We promised each other that in Paris we would celebrate our return to France.

As the train left, I thought about all those who had helped us: Facon (of the S.T.O. group), who had sheltered us until the arrival of the British troops; our war prisoner comrades from the Kommando of Hambühren, who had welcomed us so warmly; our friends the British doctors, who had given us such good care. The train stopped at all the main stations, where we were welcomed warmly and offered broth, sandwiches, and hot wine. We reached the Gare du Nord in Paris around five in the morning. As we made our way across the platform, through the dense crowd, one of my comrades pointed to a cardboard sign waved not far from us. I was stupefied to read my name on it, and I saw the old friend I had telegraphed from Hazebrouck firmly holding his sign at the end of a broomstick.

I spent two days in Paris, where I learned, with great relief, that all the members of my family were well. Then it was time to board the train from Paris to Granville. As I was walking along the platform looking for a car with a vacant seat, a good Norman woman, surprised to see me alive, stuck her head out of a window and shouted, provoking the laughter of my companions, "What do you know! Here is M'sieur Rougeyron! They got the fat, but they didn't get the skin!"

Appendix
Mademoiselle Dubocq's Story

The adventures of Mademoiselle Dubocq are related below, exactly as she wrote them.

On the evening of April 5, 1944, the "Liberator B 24-870" was on a mission. After two years of fighting, its crew of volunteers was a very close-knit group. The cockpit carried the Cross of Lorraine, an honor awarded for services to the French cause, and a mark of recognition for five official victories in air combat.

The heavily loaded four-engine aircraft advanced into the night at low altitude to elude enemy pursuit. At 11:15 P.M. the plane was flying over Bernières-le-Patry. Suddenly there was a terrible explosion from an antiaircraft battery: the big bird had been sighted and was right in the line of fire. It could not escape this hell. Hit broadside, it caught fire. Its cargo was dangerous. The alarm rang, and one of the pilots jumped out of the side door, his clothing partially aflame. The tail gunner reached the parachuting door at the center; the soles of his shoes were burning. The Germans were firing at these defenseless soldiers!

The plane was in distress and faltered in the illuminated sky, shaking from the shell bursts. It crashed to the ground and exploded. The drama, which lasted just a few seconds, took the lives of six young sons of the United States of America.

Protected by the darkness, as the enemy was hurrying toward the plane, the copilot, Adolph Willmont Kalbfleisch (from Jeannette, Pennsylvania), who had parachuted into a field, started walking south. He came across a little brook and headed upstream, walking in the water. In his haste, he twisted his ankle, but despite the pain, he kept walking. He had only one thought: to escape from the enemy. Where could he go for help before daylight? A dog approached and sniffed him, yelped softly, and guided him to the door of a house. Kalbfleisch knocked. He did not speak our language, and he uttered just two words: "American, parachute." Thus he was received into the home of Monsieur Henri Leprince in Ménil-Ciboult.

Sergeant Joseph Elmer Porter (from Carthage, Indiana), a gunner, had touched ground hard. With great fright he saw, very close by, artillery and men in uniforms. Also taking advantage of the darkness, he crawled to the right, crossing fields, warily changing directions several times. For hours he kept walking, until it would soon be daylight. He hid in a haystack and went to sleep.

On April 6, in the county seat of Tinchebray, it was dawn. A man frantically rang the doorbell at Dr. Albert Ledos' house. Everyone in the area knew well the doctor's pro-Allied sentiments. Monsieur Leprince informed Ledos of the presence of the American pilot in his home and asked him to find another shelter for the airman; Monsieur Leprince did not want to keep him because of the danger to himself and his family. The doctor immediately began searching for a safe shelter. He inquired all day long, but in vain. The task was bound to be difficult. Everyone was well aware of the official notice of the "Militärbefehlshaber in Frankreich": "It is forbidden to hide, lodge, or help in any manner any member of enemy armed forces (specifically air crew members or enemy parachutists). Noncompliance is punishable by DEATH."

On the morning of April 7, the doctor had just finished seeing his patients and was ready to leave his home when Monsieur Félix Angot (from the village of La Madeleine in Tinchebray) arrived. He was accompanied by a young stranger who was visibly ill at ease in clothes too small for him. The young man was Joseph Porter. During the night he had left his hiding place and walked south until he reached the gates of the town. He found shelter in another hay barn. At dawn he saw a resident of the farm passing by and introduced himself with one word: "American." The farmer took him inside the house, but it was impossible for them to communicate, and because Dr. Ledos spoke English, the farmer immediately led the airman to the doctor's house. The doctor intensified his search for possible places of shelter, but without success. The situation was further complicated by the fact that the farm where Joseph Porter was hiding was a very busy place, and the least indiscretion could be fatal. Caution demanded that Porter be taken away from this too convenient site.

On April 8 the doctor expanded his search to Flers. Still no luck. He stopped in Chanu to see Father Jamet. The priest did not know of any haven, but he told the doctor to contact me. Around noon Dr. Ledos arrived at my home. He looked pale and worried. Immediately I agreed to take the airmen under my roof. The doctor then left, visibly relieved. In the afternoon a car stopped in front of my home, and out stepped two tall young fellows. They were very likable, but anxious, fearful, and tired. I assured them of my solicitude and devotion, and we sealed our friendship with a glass of old French wine.

For the preceding three weeks, Robert Thomas, assistant to the chief of the Resistance in the Caen region, had resided in my home. Robert and I were affiliated with the same Resistance group, the O.C.M., and had been militants since 1940. We had worked for the Intelligence Service and the network Hector, and also for the network Centurie of France Combattante. Thomas, whom we had nicknamed "Bobby," came from the maquis of the Ain region, where he participated in a variety of operations under the command of Colonel Romans-Petit. He had been given orders to return to Normandy, but he could not stay in Calvados, where his activity in the Resistance was too well known. The Gestapo was looking for him. His father, an engineer for the highways and bridges department, had been arrested and then freed, but three of his sisters were incarcerated in the German prisons of Caen and Lisieux: a family of true patriots. Bobby was full of initiative. He, my friend Jeanne Cochin, and I formed a trio determined to stand up to the enemy and follow the example of our leader, General de Gaulle.

It didn't take us long to arrange our house for the new arrivals. We wanted our protégés to feel at home; we wanted them to get their strength and their smiles back—and we figured that a comfortable bed, good food, and our friendship should help. Like their mothers back home, we called them by their nicknames, "Duffy" and "Joe." First of all we had to find them decent clothes, so Jeanne went to Flers to see Monsieur Victor Lajoye (nicknamed "Totor"). (Our friendship goes back more than twenty-five years; he was my faithful liaison with the Resistance center in Caen.) Jeanne explained our need for clothes, and it did not take him long to find the necessary items, thanks mostly to the generosity of Monsieur Pierre Leportier, a manufacturer in Flers.

We did the necessary alterations, and our airmen were quite nicely outfitted.

Our days were well organized. Jeanne mostly took care of the housework while assisting us with surveillance. During the daytime no outings were permitted; we had to avoid unhealthy curiosity and compromising chatter. Wasn't it rumored that our next-door neighbor lodged a military member of the German air protection service? No one could tell the reasons behind this gossip. Was it foolishness? Malice? The road bordered my house; we were constantly on watch and felt relatively secure. In the evenings our boarders took walks in the adjoining orchard they called the "park." Then, inside the warm kitchen, we had long talks: the airmen spoke of their families, of the people dear to them, of the bombardments, of their faraway homeland, of their anguish and of their hopes. We spoke of France, of the sufferings of our country, of the executions and tortures inflicted by the occupiers, of our profound humiliation but also of our clandestine struggle and our immense hope. The Germans had confiscated most of the radios, but I still had one, and we could listen to the news. We did a lot of drawing to clarify our explanations. I used the little English I knew, and we tried to teach our protégés a few French words. They thought our language was very difficult.

We were able to meet their needs despite the rationing and coupons. French cuisine, especially the food of Normandy, stirred up their admiration as well as their appetite. To obtain the basic supplies, it was sometimes necessary to go out of the way. A good man, a baker in La Graverie, north of Vire, supplied bread, often even white bread. On Sundays the menu was more elaborate, and we regularly had an extra guest: Robert Dédeystère, nicknamed "Little Bobby," who spoke English very well. I had found a farm where he was lodged for fifty francs per day; I had also given shelter to his father when he was in danger of being caught by the Gestapo, just after the arrest of his Resistance chief (Loiselet, from Condé-sur-Noireau, who was deported and died in Germany) following their receipt of parachuted arms. For disrespectful language toward the Führer, Little Bobby had spent two years in German prisons in the Calvados region, but he had returned unconverted.

Bobby (Robert Thomas) had made a trip to Paris to contact the center for repatriation of airmen, which had already been notified by Monsieur Léonard Gille, from Caen. We had informed Gille that we had "two barrels of oil at his disposal." Also, the foreign currency carried by our protégés—about five hundred Belgian francs and Dutch guilders—had been transferred to the center. I insisted that they keep with them about one thousand French francs. We were waiting for orders to transfer the aviators to a location beyond Saint-Brieuc from where they could embark for England. They had been given identity cards, employment certificates, and bilingual census cards (which we had made ourselves). I attempted to cut their hair "in the French manner." It was not without apprehension that they entrusted their heads to my scissors, clipper, and razor; they thought these were dangerous tools in the hands of an inexperienced barber. When I finished, they pronounced themselves pleasantly surprised by my talents, adding that they did not get such a good cut in the American army.

Having recovered their strength and courage, they were impatient to return to combat and had not forgiven the enemy's cowardly actions on April 5. I had related to them, as kindly as I could and with a heavy heart, the tragic fate of their "Liberator": the discovery of four burned bodies in the cockpit, the poignant agony of one of their comrades who had either jumped at too low an altitude or had been hit by machine-gun fire—we did not know exactly. He had fallen into a tree and then had been caught by the Germans, who left him lying on the ground for forty-eight hours, surrounded by guards who did not allow anyone to help him. Finally he had been killed in cold blood by an enemy commandant. A sixth body had been found under the wreckage of the plane. Despite the opposition of the Germans, the French people had built caskets as a final sign of affection for the unfortunate young men. The burial was conducted under the watch of German soldiers. The enemy had not allowed a procession, had opposed a religious ceremony, and had refused military honors because the "Liberator" had been carrying a load of provisions and munitions undoubtedly intended to be parachuted to "terrorists" of the French maquis! I learned most of these details from Father Jamet (who was to be killed on August 15, during the bombardment of Caen). Bobby had taken a photograph of the airmen's grave in the cemetery of Truttemer-le-Grand. Under a broad, anonymous tumulus, in the shadow of a simple white cross engraved only with the letters *R.A.F.,* rest the bodies of those who forever closed their eyes on our French soil: Lieutenant William W. Nicoll, pilot, age twenty-four, from Lakeland, Florida; Lieutenant William G. Harris, navigator, twenty-eight, from Memphis, Tennessee; Lieutenant Thomas F. Davis, bombardier, twenty-three, from Brooklyn, New York; Sergeant Warren A. Brewer, radio operator, twenty-four, from Greenville, South Carolina; Sergeant Richard C. Bindel, mechanic, twenty-five, from Sabetha, Kansas; and Sergeant Ralph L. Kittrell, machine gunner, twenty, from Los Angeles, California.[6]

In early May of 1944, a "Lancaster" crashed near Tinchebray. When the enemy arrived at the site, they found no one in the aircraft. Three airmen were recovered near Ger by Monsieur André Rougeyron of Domfront, assisted by Monsieur Guesdon of La Baroche-sous-Lucé. Inside the plane a few bloodstains on the abandoned overalls led the suspicions of the occupiers to physicians in the area. German investigators questioned Dr. Ledos, but he had been warned beforehand by his daughter Françoise and did not run into problems.

Once more the game was won, but the Germans were enraged at seeing their prey escape. Systematic searches by the Gestapo began. Each night from 10 P.M. to 5 A.M., enemy trucks filled with armed soldiers patrolled the roads, stopping here and there, inspecting, searching under various pretexts. The danger was increasing, and the vise was tightening!

Once before, in 1942, I (along with my friend Koebel, from Caligny) had barely escaped the Gestapo during an "intelligence and radio communications" undercover operation. Many of my comrades were caught in their deadly net, and few of those ever saw the French sky again after the Liberation. Fresnes (the anteroom of death), the German jails, or the extermination camps of Natzweiler, Stutthof, Mauthausen, and Dachau had devoured almost all of them: Darchy, Lacombe, Lethiec (from Laigle), Menut, Dr. Planchais, Ganivet (from Mortagne), Bernadette and Jean Mars (from Alençon), Vattier (from Evreux), and so many others. In October of 1943, another close call resulted from the discovery of false identity cards by the enemy: the Thomas family was hit hard, and Bobby had to flee to the maquis with the help of my friend Totor, who on that particular day was carrying my "papers" to the Resistance center of Caen.

Now we had to evade capture once more, and at the same time

protect our protégés, whose fate would be no better than ours. We set up a nocturnal "residence" and planned an escape route. Everything was painstakingly prepared, including warning devices: each evening we went outdoors to spend the night, fully equipped for a potential getaway. Ordinarily, Bobby accompanied the airmen and stayed with them through the night, but when he had to be away (intelligence, transport of arms, missions, etcetera), I took his place. The nights in May were cold. We took turns keeping watch; when I was on duty, I spent the hours listening for the slightest sounds (I knew how to distinguish the cries of nocturnal birds) and counting aircraft: "Liberators," "Halifaxes," and "Lancasters" on parachute-drop missions somewhere in France. Sometimes my heart beat faster at the sound of enemy soldiers' voices on the road, of cars passing by, of a vehicle that broke down nearby. We had no firearms. I had gathered all the axes I could find; perhaps we could use them if we were desperate. At 5:30 A.M. we would go back inside, where a cup of hot sugared wine warmed us from the penetrating night chill. Jeanne, who stayed inside in charge of the house, was ready to face any "undesirables," and she kept watch while we got some sleep during the morning.

Generally the days went by calmly, interrupted from time to time by a German truck stopping in front of the door, its occupants in search of butter or eggs. I got rid of the intruders. One day their untimely visit caused the sudden flight of my protégés, who hid in the attic under a pile of branches. One afternoon we set up a shelter in the back of the "park," in expectation of the coming invasion. We had just been informed that the Allies, concentrating all their efforts in preparation for the landing, were no longer carrying out the repatriation of airmen. We had a hard time explaining this to our two Americans, but discipline had to prevail.

By May 15 the Gestapo was intensifying its investigations of Resistance activities. Monsieur Léonard Gille had just arrived from Lisieux by bicycle, and we had a long conversation. He gave me details about the government in Algiers and the outlook for the future. We made a survey of the situation in our region: important forces of G.M.R. had arrived at Argentan (that was not encouraging, because a general and several high-ranking officers of the Secret Army were stationed there). Gille also told me that he had learned from Durmeyer that an armaments depot near Ecouché was no longer safe, so it was necessary to transfer several tons of equipment to the Calvados area and find a reliable means of transport. We also talked of the necessity of setting up an intelligence liaison network between Vire and Argentan in anticipation of the time when all normal communications would be cut off. I had notified Totor; he arrived on the morning of May 16. He was very concerned because he had been stopped three times on the way and asked for his papers. Totor also told me that two hundred militiamen were combing the forest of Saint-Clair. Troops were now being deployed very close to my home, and the situation was getting serious. But it was Bobby's birthday, and we would celebrate (four days earlier, we had celebrated Duffy's twenty-fifth birthday).

It became common knowledge that all these searches were aimed at finding the airmen. At Carrefour-Blondel, Dr. Ledos' car was stopped and searched. The enemy was getting warmer, but they were still empty-handed. In the afternoon, when the coast was clear, Gille and Bobby left for Vire to contact the Resistance and the command post of Le Tourneur (Calvados).

May 19 was my saint's day. Monsieur and Madame Koebel and their daughter Micheline arrived just in time for dessert. Joe gave me a bouquet of flowers and started a congratulation in French (Bobby had given him lesson after lesson), but the poor fellow got all mixed up, forgot the words, and in desperation plopped the flowers into my arms. I was very touched by his gesture, and we all had a good time.

Though Totor had been unable to find a reliable carrier in Flers, the transfer of arms was nevertheless under way. The load would cross the Calvados in German trucks "borrowed" during the night by some of our fearless men. We could see signs of the impending invasion: air traffic increased; fighter planes attacked German trucks on the roads; and there was another bombardment of the Domfront train station on Pentecost morning. I had the very definite idea that the invasion was going to take place in Normandy and that the Cotentin peninsula would provide an excellent departure point for the Allies' offensive. On June 3 an air attack took place right above my house. A plane strafed the road, and a civilian car was hit. I went out to tend to the injured.

On the morning of June 6 I could hear an uninterrupted muffled rumbling, which seemed to come from navy cannons. Bobby was in

Vire. I turned on the radio, but the power was out. I woke my protégés to tell them the invasion had probably begun. At 4 P.M. Bobby returned and confirmed the facts. I had just bought a crystal set, so now we could hear the news reports. We could see a red glow in the sky in the direction of Flers, Condé-sur-Noireau, Vire, and Domfront. The bombs of the Allied forces were spreading total destruction. I thought mainly of the civilians. We had not heard from Totor. He finally arrived, unshaven and black from the smoke. He told us feverishly of the tragedy that had taken place in Flers, my hometown. It was hard for us to comprehend, and we grieved the deaths and the ruin. I translated the conversation to the airmen; they both looked horror-stricken and worried. We reassured them at once that our feelings toward them would not change in any way: they were not responsible for these events, which we did not understand but yet which had to be of the utmost importance in the eyes of those who had ordered them.

With some delay, German reinforcements were heading north. The one-way road was covered with convoys harassed by Allied planes. We were deafened by the sounds of engines, planes, and machine-gun fire. Jeanne went to Flers and invited Monsieur and Madame Totor to take shelter in my home. They accepted and arrived in the afternoon.

On June 10 we dug holes in the "park" to hide various objects. Several German trucks passed by, and three of them stopped in front of my property. About one hundred S.S. troops stepped out. Duffy and Joe were inside with me, and I quickly sent them out into the fields. The group was made up of injured men returning from the front, and they had stopped here purely by chance, for a three-hour rest. Only one of them, a lieutenant, could speak French, so we felt a certain measure of safety. Bobby thought it was a good opportunity for our protégés to see at close range some pure specimens of the Germanic race. He went to get Duffy and Joe. A few minutes later, a half-dozen Germans were mingling with two Americans in the kitchen while the lieutenant showed us on a map the positions of the combating armies on the Saint-Lô front. He gave us his opinion—a rather unflattering one—of the Allied forces, and added with cynicism that his trucks "were leaving the front with wounded, but when they returned, they'd still be carrying munitions . . . under the Cross of Geneva." The conversation was pretty animated. Before leaving, the German officer pock-

eted my map, a soldier swiped the leather leash of Totor's dog, and all
gave warm handshakes to the two likable strangers who had just realized
a few minutes before that they were having their first real contact with
Boches.

That night we heard more convoys, machine-gun fire, and the distant rumble of cannons. Bombs and flares illuminated the skies.

On June 17 a motorcycle stopped at my door. It was Dr. Ledos,
who announced, "An Allied fighter plane has crashed into a wheat field.
The pilot has escaped unharmed and has found temporary shelter on a
farm. We must get him out." I replied, "Of course." We opened the
survey map and located the site. It was the James farm at La Grande-
Corbière in Tinchebray. We planned our strategy: we would take the
direct route there, then return with a detour through Yvrandes to avoid
the Germans, who were everywhere. The doctor left to notify Madame
James. Bobby jumped on Totor's bicycle. I told Duffy and Joe that a
third American was coming, and they were very pleased. At last we
would know exactly what was going on on the other side of the lines.
Two hours passed by, three, then relief: here they were. My new guest
was all smiles, sitting on the frame of the bicycle, carrying under his
arm a little khaki bundle . . . his military clothing. He came in. Joe and
Duffy rushed toward him, and they engaged in an excited conversation
whose flow could not be checked. I brought out a bottle of wine to
celebrate.

Our new boarder was Captain Kenneth E. Hagan from Lincoln,
Illinois. He was pilot of a "Mustang." After an engine failure four miles
away, his aircraft had hit the ground violently, turned over, and split in
half. Kenneth escaped with nothing more serious than a scrape on his
forehead. He set fire to his plane and took off. Bobby told us he had
gone to the site to take a photograph of the "Mustang." This explained
the delay in their arrival. On the way, they had passed German soldiers;
the aviator had never seen any before.

The captain's uniform was hidden away in a safe place where we
had already stored many compromising items: maps of parachute-drop
sites; photographs; coded messages; the cipher I used when I was a
transmitter; a series of articles written in 1943 in cooperation with a
Paris attorney, Maître M. Philonenko, for the underground press; liaison
signals; and so on.

I took care of completing Kenneth's outfit. He had been given some good clothes at the James farm, but we had a fit of laughter at the large **V** shaved right in the middle of his brown hair during a recent haircut. This mark had to be kept hidden at all costs, and I gave him formal orders never to remove his Basque beret.

Finally, we made his identity card and other required papers. Duffy had become Adolphe Vilmont, adjuster; Joe was Joseph Portier, mechanic; and Kenneth would become Max Haigan, carpenter. All three were residents of Caen. Since Kenneth's arrival, we had details on the scope of the invasion and on the awesome weaponry of the Allied forces. We were more confident than ever in the rapid conclusion of the operations. The Allied front slowly developed, with the American and British troops progressing toward the east.

On June 20 Bobby received orders to return to Caen with the airmen if they wanted to attempt to rejoin the Allied front. The airmen agreed, and their departure was imminent. A photograph was taken of all of us, and we spent the evening preparing the supplies for their trip. Despite their protests, Jeanne and I insisted that they take along certain provisions.

On June 21, at dawn, Jeanne and I watched the road as four shadows faded out of sight, headed toward their destiny. The house seemed strangely empty, and the dinner table too large. I wondered, "Will they get through? Will they make it?"

To guard against any eventuality, Jeanne and I installed a bed in the former "night residence" of our airmen. The inhabitants of the areas close to the battles were leaving and going south; this was the beginning of a lamentable exodus that would increase each day. At night the convoys rolled incessantly, and there was much aircraft activity; we were getting used to all the uproar and the machine-gun fire, which was more and more frequent. Little Bobby visited us often to hear the news.

We were served with a German summons to lodge officers. A captain stayed at my house for a while. Jeanne and I managed to avoid him, but I found among his papers some notes in French concerning his unit. The unit commandant was some Austrian brute; the general was billeted in a nearby château. I asked Totor to relay all this information to the Resistance network of Vassy. We had not heard from the Resistance group of Flers since the arrest of its chief, Jacques Durmeyer (who had been deported to the Neuengamme camp and was missing). These Germans left and were replaced by more Germans; my house was constantly occupied. The troops and their vehicles (most bearing the Red Cross) made stopovers in the orchards during the day to hide from Allied aircraft. We learned that Cherbourg had been taken, and of the battle of Caen. Had our friends made it?

July 14 was the last day we spent under the enemy boot, and Caen had just been liberated. Outside a second-story window, I displayed an arrangement of blue, white, and red flowers. The German columns going to the front marched past our three colors. The flowers of our soil welcomed a group of American prisoners passing on their way to Lonlay (they had been taken into custody near Saint-Lô). They came from Tinchebray, where they had received an enthusiastic welcome from the French people. They were the first part of an Allied convoy, and half of them were evacuated from there by truck. For them we made a collection throughout the city, killed a fatted ox, and prepared a salad. There was plenty of wine to accompany this feast. While Madame Ledos and her assistants were taking good care of the American prisoners, sheets from Dr. Ledos' notebook were being passed from hand to hand, and that evening Father Leblanc, vicar of Beauchêne, brought me numerous sheets of paper with 501 names, addresses, and serial numbers. (I communicated the lists to the headquarters of the 28th Division of Patton's army.)

On July 15 I took advantage of a providential absence of the occupiers to bury a trunk full of articles with the help of my employee, Claudius Gascon (who was later killed during the bombardment of August 15). A familiar silhouette appeared near the little entrance gate to the orchard. Was I having hallucinations? No . . . it was Duffy! A thousand thoughts crossed my mind. He was overjoyed to find me. His comrades were waiting in a field, and I rushed to get them. I found Joe and Kenneth, then a third American, the radio operator of a "flying fortress," Sergeant Edward Nabozny from New York, whom they had found in Caen (he would be given the name Jacques). Our "big children" were in a pitiful state: pale, unshaven, dirty, exhausted, and starving. Their feet were scratched and blistered. On top of that, they had scabies. Jeanne and I cleansed and dressed the wounds and gave them a light meal. Most of all, they needed rest.

The battle-front approached, and there was a fierce battle in Mortain (fourteen kilometers away). We could expect to be infested with German soldiers like a plague of stinking bugs. We were going to have to play a dicey game, because it was out of the question to abandon our Americans. We hoped luck would be with us. We got the large bedroom ready. Monsieur and Madame Totor had been occupying it, and now they would stay at the "little residence." Opposite my house, the field police had set up their offices in a building I had been renting, and they were using two of my beds. I had to get one back for my protégés. I waited for the gendarmes to leave, and then, helped by Joe, I quickly removed the bed I needed. Now we were all set.

We inspected the airmen's clothing. All their spare clothes had been lost in Caen. We raided Little Bobby's wardrobe, and a friend, Bernard, brought some socks and a few canned goods. I went to Tinchebray to see Dr. Ledos, and he gave me a pair of shoes and said he would have more repaired promptly.

The airmen related their extraordinary odyssey since June 21. They had encountered their first difficulties on the way to Caen. The Germans had asked for their papers. These were in perfect order, and the place of residence justified the trip: home, family, alibis Bobby presented with flair. Kenneth (alias Max) was taken for a German boxer, and the likeness brought him demonstrations of friendship. The food supplies they had brought also proved very useful. In Caen they had made contact with the Resistance command post, rue de Bayeux. They were told that the front line was impenetrable; therefore they would have to hold on until the liberation of the town, and get by until then.

Bobby then took the airmen to his parents' home (they had evacuated) in rue Montaigu. The premises had been partially damaged by air raids. Everyone settled in. Besides the continuous bombardments, they were faced with many problems: the scarcity of food, lack of water, and plain day-to-day living in the midst of the enemy. These were dark days of deprivation and anguish. The British had reached the Orne, but the Germans were holding the southern bank, and they defended the passage furiously. The "flying fortresses" released their bombs unrelentingly on the Teutonic positions. It was a hell in which the enemy, panicked and exasperated, pursued the lowliest civilian, robbed and pillaged at whim. Taking advantage of a short lull, our friends retreated to Ifs, but as they reached the road to Falaise, Bobby decided to return to Caen and pick up his bicycle. He told the Americans he would be back the next morning at the latest. None of them had had anything to eat for almost five days. The bombardments resumed, accompanied by artillery fire. And Bobby did not return.

On July 14, at 8 A.M.: no Bobby. Noon, 2 P.M.: still nothing. In Ifs, the Germans became aggressive: no civilians! The airmen had no support and felt hopeless without Bobby. They were certain that he must have been killed or captured, so they decided to return to my house in Beauchêne. It was the only haven they knew in France. They took the southern route, carrying little bundles as if they were evacuees. To guide them, they only had a miniature map of the region; to sustain them, they had the hope of finding help, protection, and comfort in my home. They avoided the enemy formations and the main highways as much as possible, which made their journey longer. Twice their identity cards were checked. The road was long, and their stomachs were empty, but they kept going. A German patrol requested their papers—this time it wouldn't be easy. The four of them were taken to a nearby headquarters where, fortunately, a certain amount of confusion prevailed and the man who questioned them did not speak French. The airmen glibly recited all the French words they had learned, and their loquacious chorus left the German dumbfounded and embarrassed. Suddenly he offered them cigarettes, and with an imperative "Raus" he let them, miraculously, out of this wasps' nest.

On July 15 they reached Flers and crossed the destroyed town. The next fifteen kilometers would be the hardest. They had to push and drag Edward, whose strength was failing. They had nothing to eat, their shoes were falling apart, and the heat was intense. Finally they reached the familiar fields and saw the roof of my house. They had reached their goal.

From this odyssey there remained a kind of bewilderment in their eyes and great pity in their hearts. They had suffered our sufferings and seen the gaping wounds of our cities. They understood what we had endured, our sorrows, how dearly we had paid for the Liberation. Their resolve was unanimous: if they rejoined the Allied forces and resumed combat, they would bomb the daylights out of Germany, but not France.

We were all worried about Bobby. The airmen told me about his courageous and often daring conduct, and about his solicitude toward them.

Aware that danger was all around us, we organized our way of living with the utmost caution. Once again the Germans invaded my house, searched the grounds, requisitioned some of the rooms, and installed themselves. This did not happen without occasional flare-ups of emotion, but our reflexes were good. The occupiers slept in the room next to the Americans, and during the night their snoring mingled. Jeanne and I kept watch on the staircase landing. During the day, because of the constant comings and goings of soldiers and ordnance, we had to be ever vigilant. Sometimes we had to clear out our protégés in a hurry: a gesture or an eye movement was enough. We were playing a cat-and-mouse game, and the mice did not intend to be eaten.

My airmen had one obsession: to reach the lines as soon as possible. I think they were so insistent on leaving because they saw the danger increasing every day. The battle-front was approaching. The fighting lost some of its intensity—like a lull before the storm. Map in hand, I explained to my friends that in my opinion the Allied forces would pass to the south. I believed the American push would start from the Contentin peninsula, cutting off Brittany at the Loire River, with one flank using the plains of Alençon and the Beauce to reach Paris. Such a maneuver would disorganize and stretch the German front.

On a slack day—one without too many Germans around—Totor and I made a trip to Domfront to visit André Rougeyron. In case of extreme emergency, I wanted to have a retreat ready for my "birds." We found Rougeyron at city hall, faithful to his post as chief of the "Passive Defense"—kind of an ironic title for him. We informed him of the latest developments: no possibility for the airmen to reach the Allied lines. He assured me that he would take my boarders in at the first sign of danger. I knew I could count on him. This settled, we went to Saint-Front in search of bread, which had been sorely lacking since my protégés' return. Then we hastily returned home, where Jeanne had been looking after everybody.

Our daily life went on—amidst the comings and goings of the enemy. It was a very anxious, very exhilarating period.

At 10 A.M. on August 2, two tall S.S. men stopped at my door. They spoke French impeccably. I barely had the time to hide three of my boarders. Unflappable, Joe remained in the dining room the S.S. men had commandeered to set up an office for their unit. Now the danger was compounded by the presence in my home of these two devils who spoke our language so well. We were heading toward a catastrophe. The Americans were well aware of the anguish of the moment, and they relied on my solution. Though it was very painful, I decided to send them to Domfront. Hurriedly we ate lunch, and then, once again, we prepared their bags. After giving them meticulous instructions on the route to follow, I sent the Americans out of the house two by two, each time taking advantage of a moment of inattention by the enemy; and as I saw them go, I wondered anxiously if I had made the right decision.

I jumped on my bicycle and joined them at the agreed-upon location. The road was covered with German trucks. These vehicles were unremittingly harassed, pursued, and fired on by "Mustangs," "Lightnings," and "Thunderbolts," which were controlling the skies and having a field day. Duffy was frightened by the danger I was exposed to, and they all strongly opposed my going ahead to Domfront. I did not pay attention, for I had to act quickly—no time to wait until the air raid was over. I kept going amid the deafening roar, the clouds of acrid dust, the bursts of firing. The road seemed endless; I passed nothing but Germans cowering in ditches. At last I reached the train station and some respite, then city hall, where Rougeyron greeted me. He called two young men, René Leray and Geslin, and told them to accompany me. We turned back, this time in an almost complete calm, and rejoined our four Americans, who were very relieved to see me; they hadn't thought I would get out of that alive. I entrusted them to my two escorts, and we parted at the edge of the fields—it was a sad moment. I returned home.

Now that my protégés were in Domfront, I expected that the vicissitudes that had marked our lives these past few months were over. The Liberation seemed imminent. Just as I was entertaining these thoughts, a young Frenchman from Vassy, Henri Vivien, arrived on his motorbike. He informed me that a "mission" was going to set up a center of operations in my home: in all there would be six people. A convoy was stationed in my yard, there were swarms of Germans all around, and the S.S. office was operating. We parked Henri's motorbike in the kitchen. Minutes later, two determined-looking young men arrived, Jean Dissler and Eugène Hergault, from Condé-sur-Noireau. They handed me a paper. I recognized the handwriting of Monsieur O. Dédeystère—these two were fine. Their bicycles joined the motorbike in the kitchen. We prepared lodgings for the group. Finally the others arrived: Emile Bâtard (notary), Roger Amaury (from Vassy), and a Monsieur "Charles" (in the Underground, we did not know each other's names and had to use pseudonyms only). Now there were three more bicycles to stow away. Extra leaves were added to the table to accommodate ten persons—there wasn't much room left in the kitchen.

"Charles" informed me that he had crossed the German lines with the intention of reaching the enemy communications lines and gathering intelligence to facilitate and hasten the Allied advance. He had been entrusted with this mission by the G.Q.G. (main headquarters) of the F.F.I. (Forces Françaises de l'Interieur) of Caen under the orders of General Koenig. My house had been designated as a center of operations and command post. Charles had contacted the Resistance groups in the area, and those of Condé-sur-Noireau and Vassy had assembled the young men: Dissler, Hergault, Amaury, and Vivien, all volunteers whose duties were to slip through the enemy lines and transmit military information to the nearest headquarters. Emile Bâtard was to help Charles in that task.

Since Charles had just come from Caen, I questioned him about my other comrades: Thomas and Gille were in good health. This was a great relief. He also told me that Bobby had been arrested upon his return to Caen July 13. Accused of being an English spy, he was kept under constant guard while the Germans decided his fate. Knowing too well what was to become of him, Bobby took advantage of a providential and intense bombardment, during which his guards took shelter in trenches, to take his last chance for freedom, barely escaping the fusillades of enemy machine guns. He made it and finally joined the Canadians.

On August 3 the Resistance operations center was set up on the second floor, in the room previously occupied by the Americans, just above the S.S. office. Everyone got to work. I had all the Lower Normandy ordnance survey maps of the Army Geographical Services. A general of a panzer division was quartered with some officers in the farm of La Cour five hundred meters away, and Germans came and went incessantly. Bâtard and Charles went to a rendezvous in quest of information. A German officer demanded that I hand over the motorbike "that was brought here yesterday." I called Henri Vivien, who vainly tried to prevent the seizure of his vehicle. We watched the new "owners" test the bike on the road, then park it against the wall of my garage where their ammunition was stored. The Allied planes were patrolling—I wished they were somewhere else.

Amaury, Vivien, and I consulted together. How could we put the motorbike out of order? I crushed a few sugar cubes and poured the powder into a little paper cone. We went into the yard, walking around, chatting, pretending to be interested in the doings of the occupiers, all the while getting closer to the motorbike until Amaury stood right in front of it. He poured the sugar into the gas tank, and then we innocently strolled a little longer. The unit that had stopped for a rest in my yard was due to decamp at midnight. I was waiting for their departure. On three different occasions, I had to retrieve from their vehicles various parts they had stripped from my car. After I protested vehemently, they finally stopped their pilfering. They loaded Vivien's motorbike, and the trucks left at 6 p.m. I felt pretty good: the sugar would work just fine.

August 4 was occupied with intelligence work. On the ground floor we noticed a certain nervousness in the S.S. office. Straggling German soldiers were looking for any means of transportation, including bicycles (mine had already been taken). Amaury, Vivien, and I took the ones we still had and hid them in my farmhand's house.

On August 5 Henri Vivien was leaving on a mission. He would cross the lines to the south and join the American headquarters. Inside his belt buckle I slipped reduced maps drawn on cigarette paper together with a message asking the Allies to avoid bombing the La Cour farm, where many French civilian evacuees were staying. As an extra precaution, I asked Father Leblanc to go to the farm and warn my fellow citizens.

The S.S. men were particularly agitated on August 6, and they came and went constantly. German troops were still flowing in. The big "Tiger" tanks were passing on their way north. We listened to the radio to try to hear a message expected to be sent by the B.B.C. in London.

Dissler and Hergault were leaving on a mission. They would have to break through the lines between Mortain and Sourdeval, reach the Allied headquarters, then continue to Caen as quickly as possible. I gave them all the necessary details regarding the itinerary to follow. They left confident (and they did succeed). At long last, the S.S. packed up and left, taking my typewriter.

We spent the night of August 7 without a single German on the premises. Back from his mission, Henri Vivien was staying with us. Outside, the agitation continued. The right flank of the German army was seriously threatened. Charles and Bâtard informed me that they were going to attempt to reach Sées, a predetermined point where they would be joining a group headed by Parléani, chief of the F.F.I. of the Calvados, to carry out a mission.

At 11 A.M. a young Frenchman, Gabriel Desdoits, asked for me. He explained that seven weeks before he had taken in a British lieutenant, pilot of a "Mustang" hit by an antiaircraft battery. Gabriel was forced to evacuate and could no longer keep his boarder. He had heard about me through Bouchereau and Voisvenel, members of the Resistance of Vassy. Bâtard knew the young man, and I immediately agreed to take in the pilot. Monsieur and Madame Totor decided to leave Beauchêne and go to Saint Bômer. At 1 P.M., under circling planes above, Jeanne and Henri Vivien went to meet the British airman. Some time later, George F. Pyle, from Westoe (South Shields), arrived at my house. At 4 P.M. it was time for Charles, Bâtard, Amaury, and Vivien to leave. We promised to meet each other again after the Victory, and I watched them leave, so calmly, on their perilous adventure. (In 1943 Bâtard had escorted Allied airmen in distress. Charles—real name Jean Huard— was an officer in the valiant Scamaroni unit, which crossed a minefield and cleaned out the barracks of the château in Caen, before the arrival of the Allies. Amaury would die of a war injury at the age of nineteen.) All brave young men!

The "mission" fulfilled its task beautifully. The enemy was never able to discern by what means the Allies knew so well the sites of their tanks, fuel reserves, munitions depots, and troops. This obscure and dangerous work accomplished by our young men prevented many Allied losses and much destruction on French soil.

While Jeanne was out on an errand, George and I were chatting when two Germans burst into the kitchen and ordered me to show them the premises. One of them bore on his sleeve the large, gray-green stripe of the Das Reich division. To stall them for a few seconds, I told them to wait for me. Coughing loudly, I rushed upstairs (followed by George), slammed a couple of doors, and rushed back downstairs, ostentatiously unfolding a handkerchief. My stratagem gave me the few seconds I needed to hide the crystal set I had imprudently left out, tuned to the London channel.

At night the traffic was heavy. It was impossible to sleep amid the roar of tanks and trucks, the loud yells. Allied planes patrolled without cease, shooting star shells. We gave a tall devil of an officer and several soldiers the run of the house and decided to camp in the orchard. George stayed in the "little residence," and Jeanne and I settled close by in our shelter.

On August 8, no change. More stragglers—it seemed that the Wehrmacht was no longer cohesive and that its ranks were beginning to disband. Totor came for a visit and decided we were going to drink a bottle of Moët in anticipation of the Victory. The sun was shining in the clear sky, and the Germans were conversing by the open door. I set out four glasses, and we raised them in front of the perplexed occupiers, savoring to the last drop the golden wine of the Champagne region. Totor left us. The roar of the cannons was getting closer, and the Germans came and went nervously. George and I went for a walk in the orchard. Jeanne joined us a moment later. The ordnance officer had asked her in a peremptory tone of voice for two geese in exchange for twelve packs of cigarettes and two of tobacco. My first thought was a flat refusal, but the result would have been pure and simple abduction of my fowls without compensation: better to go along and accept the trade—besides, there was such a shortage of tobacco. So I agreed to this first deal with the Germans. The officer returned with two cronies, and one of them approached George and tapped him familiarly on the shoulder to make him understand his help was wanted. My geese were roaming free in the orchard, and they would have to be caught by hand. What ensued was the most hilarious chase I have ever seen. It was a crazy race through the orchard, an Anglo-Franco-German pursuit that included exclamations, misses, collisions, falls that provoked guttural curses, intentional clumsiness on our part, the shouting of incomprehensible orders. George and I kept our composure, but we could not help being overcome with an irresistible gaiety at the sight of this inconceivable gathering that lasted more than twenty minutes; and the Germans, seeing us laugh so heartily without understanding why, joined us with loud hilarity.

The geese were finally caught, and we went back into the house. The ordnance officer reappeared, affable and smiling, carrying the packs of cigarettes, which he dumped into the hands of our petrified George with a friendly "Pour vous, Monsieur," to which I hastily replied, "Merci!" We refused to cook the geese, so the Germans had to take them to a nearby restaurant. George and I were smoking their cigarettes, and we were still laughing about the unforgettable comedy of the afternoon when the Germans returned precipitously. They had not been able to finish their meal—what was going on? They rushed to their car and took off at top speed. We heard the American tanks were in Lonlay-l'Abbaye, four kilometers away. All evening long, we watched for their arrival.

On August 9, more Germans. Always more Germans. Several F.F.I. members from Flers who had retreated to Lonlay came to see me. They told me that the Allied tanks of yesterday had stopped only for a moment in Lonlay and that the inhabitants, thinking they were liberated, had welcomed them with great joy. This show of friendship had been seen by some Germans hiding in basements. In retaliation, the enemy had ordered the total evacuation of the town, then had ransacked it and set it on fire. Some American airmen sheltered in Lonlay were said to have left with the tanks. Could they be my former protégés? But what would they be doing in Lonlay? George was anxious to rejoin his comrades.

On August 10 waves of Allied planes succeeded one another. The German artillery thundered, but its positions had changed and stretched toward the east. A "Thunderbolt" swooped down on a mobile battery, which prudently backed away. A fighter-bomber, heavily protected, was repeatedly circling over a precise area. Its persistence intrigued us, and we timed the explosions at every three minutes. Apparently the aircraft had spotted something. There was a German munitions depot within the sphere of action. There was a lull toward evening. An F.F.I. member came to inform me that there were not as many troops in Lonlay: perhaps George could attempt to cross the lines the next afternoon.

We returned to our outdoor shelters for the night. Suddenly we were violently shaken by a percussion fuse exploding ten meters from our shed; bombs and star shells were streaking the sky. It was three in the morning, and a few trucks had just stopped in the orchard. We heard footsteps: the Germans. We decided to fetch George. In the "little residence" the bed was empty, and I found my pilot crouching in the back. I got him out of his hole and took him to our shelter. The Germans had visited and had swept their flashlights over him from head to toe. Though George was feeling pretty nervous during their inspection, he had strictly followed my recommendations and had not flinched. I went back to check what the Germans were doing. They were S.S. troops of the Adolf Hitler division, and they had parked three trucks. We stayed up for the rest of the night.

On August 11 the order was given to evacuate the township by noon. We packed our belongings, and George and Jeanne transported them to the center of town in a wheelbarrow. They made it in two trips, amongst swarms of Germans. In the course of the afternoon, I realized that I had forgotten to hide the car tires: now it was impossible to do so. Take the tires with us? I could, but I wanted to lead George to the Allied lines, and there was no time to waste. I slipped the last cookies I had into my pocket. We left our home with a heavy heart. Would we ever see it again?

George and I took the road going south. As we passed the cemetery I thought of my loved ones who were resting there. We reached the village at the bottom of the hill, then took a left across fields to avoid the compact group of Germans massed along the riverbank. The heat was oppressive, and the walk through the fields was arduous. George carried only a cookie tin filled with a few kilos of millet to feed his bird in England, which did not have any seed. For the moment, that millet was his most precious possession—along with an empty tobacco pouch, a gift from a German. As for me, I carried nothing but my wallet, which had become very light after four years in the Resistance. We took turns carrying the tin. I was determined to reach the main road; because it was under surveillance by Allied aircraft, we should not encounter any Boches. We reached the road near Lonlay. On our left, light armored cars were camouflaged at the side of the road; then we passed a tank, and farther down, on our right, I saw a group of Germans behind a hedgerow, with machine guns in position. I didn't think George saw them, and we kept going. I felt indescribable anguish as I wondered if, at any moment, those machine guns aimed right at our backs were going to fire. Finally we reached Lonlay—no man's land. The city seemed dead; the fire set by the Germans had ravaged the town. Near the church, the flames were still raging. An acrid smoke rose from the ruins, the stench of gunpowder was everywhere, the heat was intense, and the air was full of a gray dust stirred up by bombs and shells. Our throats were parched. We met a young man who confirmed that the Americans were very near the Grille-Souris road and that he had not seen any Germans in the center of town. I hesitated to go on: I was not familiar with the road ahead, and I did not want to risk meeting a German patrol on the way. I decided instead to locate the F.F.I. member who had stopped at my house the previous evening. He should be able to guide my airman. We turned back and quenched our thirst with cool water from a pump in a pasture. A German whose motorcycle had broken down appeared rather uneasy to find himself exposed on the road. We felt just about the same. I found the young man I was looking for and entrusted George to him after sharing the few cookies we had left. It was almost 5 P.M.; we had not eaten anything in nine hours, and we were exhausted. No longer fearing for his safety, I said good-bye to my British lieutenant and wished him luck.

I took a shortcut to the evacuation site where Jeanne and I had agreed to meet. On the way I passed German soldiers and armor, but it seemed easy now that I was alone.

May, 1945—we were liberated on August 15, 1944. We returned to our house, but it had been terribly ransacked. This was the month that marked the Victory of Right over Oppression. It was spring, and the birds were singing. Jeanne and I received two letters, which we opened eagerly. One came from America, the other from England.

Kenneth (Max) wrote:

Lincoln (Illinois)

. . . you have surely been told what happened to us and how we were liberated. I'll briefly narrate the details:

On August 2 you left us in the care of two men who led us
to the home of a Frenchman in Domfront. His name was André
Rougeyron. We spent the night in his château built on the side
of a bluff overlooking part of the city. Early the next morning,
André was arrested by the Gestapo. The four of us fled his home.
One of the men who was left, René Leray, led us to a little village
a few kilometers southeast, where we were met by Raymond
Alexandre Guesdon. From there we immediately went back to
Domfront, crossed the city, and headed toward Granville. Shortly
afterward, we turned toward the hills southeast of Lonlay l'Abbaye. At this point Raymond Guesdon left us (Joe, Duffy,
Jacques/Edward, and me) in the care of René Leray to look for
a route that would allow us to cross the lines and rejoin the
Americans. We stayed in a little hut (for bread-baking) near a
village and enjoyed some tranquillity and sun for three days. The
sounds of the battle were getting closer. On the third day, August
7, Raymond Guesdon came back after having spent a night with
the Americans. He said he was going to take us across the lines,
but first he wanted me to go with him to Lonlay l'Abbaye to
survey the situation and obtain information likely to interest the
Americans. When we arrived in Lonlay, we heard that six Germans were holding the city and that ten hostages were going to
be shot because someone had killed two soldiers during the night.
They were also going to set fire to the town. We decided to join
the Americans immediately to see if they could take Lonlay right
away, before a tragedy took place. We returned to the place where
Joe, Duffy, and Jacques were hiding; then we walked the twelve
kilometers to the American lines. I gave all the information to
the American commander, who told me he would try to save
the people of Lonlay. Then we were evacuated to a safe location,
so we never found out what happened. Do you know if the
people of Lonlay were spared? We spent the night of August 7
at the air force general headquarters. On August 8 we went by
jeep—via Saint-Lô—to an air force camp off the coast of Brittany, from where we flew to England by transport plane. Joe,
Duffy, and Jacques flew to the United States on August 20; I
stayed with my squadron until the end of the month. I didn't

leave London until September 1, flying from London to Prestwick, then from Scotland to Newfoundland via Iceland. I landed in New York on September 2.

George wrote:

> Westoe (South Shields)
>
> . . . I was wondering if you knew that I returned safely last August—all the while being worried about you on the roads, which I knew to be very dangerous. It was such a relief to be back home and to let my family know that I was safe. They knew I had not been killed, but after nine weeks without news, they were very worried. They were overcome with joy when I came back. When they saw all the birdseed, they told me I was crazy to worry about a bird at such a time. Yet they were very happy, and the bird was thrilled! There is still some left!

Mademoiselle Dubocq's journal, written in Beauchêne (Orne), was dated March 1, 1947.

NOTES

1. After a number of daring operations, Paysant was sent to the northern region, then put in charge of the B.O.A. in Brittany. He mysteriously disappeared from the Pontivy prison where he, together with Madame Croisé, had been thrown by the Gestapo. They were carrying a transmitter radio and a large sum of money when arrested by Ukrainian soldiers in the German army, and they barely escaped the firing squad.

2. Claude Monod's actions as a member of the Resistance can be divided into three stages: sabotage (in four months: 280 train derailments in his sector, Burgundy and France-Comté); guerrilla warfare; joint actions: his men (the Forces Françaises de l'Intérieur, or F.F.I.) assured the liaison between Delattre's and Lecler's troops, at the same time isolating twenty thousand German troops in the Morvan, where they were forced to surrender.

Following a number of stints at various officer training schools, Colonel Claude was posted to the 4th Moroccan Artillery Regiment, the first to cross the Rhine. After the crossing of the Rhine at Germersheim, Monod was killed April 2, 1945, while leading his men to Graben. His citations are eloquent testament to his activities:

"Officer of great initiative and courage. Joined the Resistance in December, 1940. In early 1942, he was responsible for setting up the information service Liberation. Director of Defense of France by the end of 1943. Inspector of the Forces Françaises de l'Intérieur in March, 1944. Chief of the D. region on May 8, 1944. Showed at all times untiring enthusiasm and dedication in instructing his men, organizing guerrilla warfare, and sabotaging communications and railroad lines. Having mustered twenty-two thousand volunteers, in August, 1944, he led the attack in the Dijon region against the retreating German troops, inflicting heavy losses on the enemy and capturing eight thousand prisoners and a significant amount of materiel."

"Claude Monod, Lieutenant Colonel, 4th Moroccan Artillery Regiment. A Resistance leader from the beginning, he never stopped believing in victory and in the recovery of France. Volunteered to join a Moroccan artillery regiment. Requested to participate actively, on April 2, in the capture of Graben and led the attack with utmost bravery and scorn of danger. Standing on the front line, he led the sharpshooters to the attack while guiding the light infantry through the forest of Graben, target of the battalion. He was counterattacked by a murderous enemy strongly supported by tanks. Rallying his men around him, he became the designated target of enemy snipers and fell gloriously, facing the enemy. Before dying, he voluntarily used his body as a shield for a sharpshooter continuing the fight. Up to the last breath of a life dedicated to his country, he was an example of abnegation, duty, and honor, to the supreme sacrifice."

3. I learned later what took place in Domfront after my arrest: Leray was taking a

stroll in the garden of the rectory. Informed of my arrest, he rushed to the center of town at the very moment when Goupil, the notary, was being handcuffed by Durut. Accompanied by two firemen, Leray went to Goupil's house to get rid of the crystal set. Then he rushed to the Châlet to evacuate the four Americans. At the bottom of the Cents-Marches he met Geslin and his family, who had already been alerted. All of them—Leray, Geslin and his family, and the four Americans—left immediately. They went across Madame Brault's farm (which had been visited an instant before by a German armed with a machine gun); then, taking a shortcut across fields, they reached the Alençon railroad tracks, which they followed up to the side road of Mayenne. Their aim was to reach La Baroche road. Because of Germans working on the telephone lines, they had to make a detour through Bois-Hallé; from there they followed the railroad tracks in the direction of Saint-Front in order to get back to the road. Near the village, Leray told the four Americans and Geslin to wait in a field (Madame Geslin had gone ahead by bicycle with her granddaughter). Then he headed for La Baroche. There he met Guesdon and informed him of the events that had taken place earlier in the day. Guesdon told him he could not take charge of my airmen because the area was swarming with deserting Germans.

Fortunately, Raymond Guesdon (same last name as Roger) had just arrived in town. He was on a mission for his maquis, and he agreed to take charge of the airmen. Accompanied by Madame Geslin, they headed back to Domfront. One of the Americans, his feet bleeding, took Raymond Guesdon's bicycle and followed Madame Geslin to Saint-Front. They crossed Domfront rapidly. Finally Madame Geslin left the Americans with Leray and Guesdon. Again the group left, but the Yankees were showing signs of fatigue. They crossed the train station district without problem. A little farther, at a site called the Red House, there was a roadblock set up by the field police. The airmen were stopped by the Germans, who even offered them cigarettes. At last they arrived at the crossroads of Rouellé in Lonlay, where Raymond Guesdon was waiting for them. They stayed five days at Marie's farm; then Raymond led them to the other side of the lines, where they were reunited with their compatriots.

At the time of my arrest, Len and Cannon were sheltered in the home of our brave Louise, above the café. Hiding behind the curtains, they had witnessed my arrest. Immediately, they fled through the gardens. In his haste Len bashed in the roof of a hen house. Then they got out of town with the intention of getting to La Baroche by crossing fields. On the way they found themselves in front of a camouflaged German antiaircraft battery. They took shelter in the house of a railroad signalman in La Métairie. His wife, Madame Chevalier, was very surprised to see these two men, who spoke neither French nor German and who kept asking her, in a comical gibberish, directions to Monsieur Rougeyron's house in La Baroche. Two days later, Roger Guesdon and Fouré came to pick them up and took them to the maquis of La Sermonnière, where they finally experienced the joy of liberation. For the three Englishmen hiding at l'Ermitage, it had been very simple: Bourgoin handed them over to the first Allied troops that arrived.

4. As to Poupard's activities and the role he played preceding my arrest, the follow-

ing information was furnished to me later during various investigations and confrontations, which resulted in the scoundrel's being condemned to death. Poupard had come to the Domfront area around the end of July, 1944. Before that he had visited, among others, the regions of Silly-en-Gouffern and La Ferté-Macé, for the purpose of obtaining information about the Resistance. One morning in a Domfront café, he met two firemen and asked them if they knew where he could find a man from Exmes he used to know. It was established later that Poupard did in fact eat with this man in the only restaurant still open at the time, and that after this meeting he circulated in the Saint-Front and Saint-Brice areas in quest of information, all the while pretending he was a member of the Caen Resistance trying to join another group. It was about that time that he made the acquaintance of Gendarme Bruneau, who, as I related earlier, sent him to me. Some other matters also came to light later: On August 1, 1944, between noon and 2 P.M., Poupard and Haquin, on orders from Hildebrandt, came to the C.O.S.I. in Domfront to seek information. The C.O.S.I. was an organization subsidized by both Vichy and Berlin. Under the cover of an assistance organization for refugees, it was in fact a vast enemy espionage network. The C.O.S.I. of Domfront distributed its subsidies the first of each month. It was set up in a room at city hall. According to his own statements, Poupard went to this room on August 1. There he met a man about thirty years old and a woman—brown hair, pudgy, very ugly. The man gave Poupard a list of suspects, which he took to his superiors. Two days later we were arrested. No doubt this list was the one Jardin had in his hands when he arrested me. That was the same list Gilard saw in the pasture of Saint-Brice, and again the same one mentioned in the report Goupil wrote on August 6, 1944. After the Liberation, this report was turned over to the Court. Goupil had written, "The Gestapo chief had a list written on C.O.S.I. letterhead. The handwriting was well-formed, and in red pencil. It read: 'Resistance group of Saint-Mars-d'Egrenne, chief of group: Gilard.' "

5. The Allies had found that dropping strips of metal or foil would deceive or jam the enemy radar [translator's note].

6. The French citizens who buried the American airmen apparently believed that "R.A.F." applied to the air forces of both Britain and the United States [translator's note].